COMPARING LIBERAL DEMOCRACIES

COMPARING LIBERAL DEMOCRACIES

  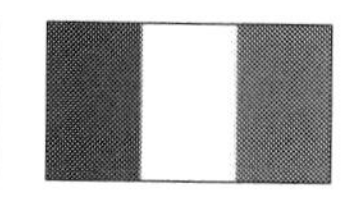  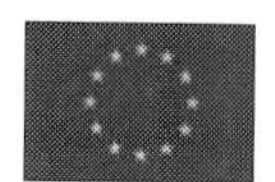

THE UNITED STATES, UNITED KINGDOM, FRANCE, GERMANY, AND THE EUROPEAN UNION

ARTHUR B. GUNLICKS

iUniverse, Inc.
Bloomington

Comparing Liberal Democracies
The United States, United Kingdom, France, Germany, and the European Union

iUniverse books may be ordered through booksellers or by contacting:

iUniverse
1663 Liberty Drive
Bloomington, IN 47403
www.iuniverse.com
1-800-Authors (1-800-288-4677)

ISBN: 978-1-4620-5724-5 (sc)
ISBN: 978-1-4620-5725-2 (e)

Printed in the United States of America

iUniverse rev. date: 1/16/2012

Contents

List of Figures and Tables

Figures

Tables

Preface

Before retiring from the University of Richmond in 2005 as professor of political science, I taught a variety of courses in the field of comparative politics, including introductory courses in comparative politics, courses on the politics and governments of the major European states, and courses on European politics with emphasis on the European Union.

For each of these courses I usually assigned a core text—for example, in the introductory course a paperback text dealing with the general subject of comparative politics and one or two supplementary books on other subjects such as selected democracies, less developed countries, or politics in certain regions. For my course on Great Britain, France, and Germany, I selected separate paperbacks for each country; however, I was always on the lookout for a book that would cover these democracies as well as the United States and the European Union, so that there would be time also to assign supplementary books on other topics, such as a brief history of twentieth century Europe. And for my course on European politics, I assigned one book on the EU and one or more books on other subjects dealing with European politics or current history. In each case I was usually unsuccessful in finding a book that I could use in any of the three courses that would introduce students to the institutional frameworks of the countries I wanted to cover, compare these in a systematic way with the United States—the country most students knew best (if not as well as they thought)—and include the EU as the most state-like international organization, with twenty-seven member states, which exercises a strong and growing influence not only in Europe but also worldwide. Indeed, I was not able to find such a book that was also relatively brief and relatively inexpensive and yet offered the instructor great flexibility in adding supplementary reading for a variety of comparative politics courses. A main purpose of this book is to fill that void.

In addition to searching without success for a relatively inexpensive paperback that covered the major European democracies as well as the United States and the EU, I was also looking for a text with a thematic approach rather than the more common country-by-country approach. That is, I wanted a book that would compare the countries in a systematic manner, in this case organized around concepts generally familiar to American students such as separation of powers, checks and balances, and terms of office as well as the different political systems such as presidential and semipresidential democracies versus parliamentary democracies; unitary states versus federal states; very different electoral systems; states with the British and American common law traditions versus the continental civil or Roman law traditions; and, finally, the more individualistic free enterprise-oriented United States versus the more collectivist social welfare states of continental Europe, with Britain somewhere in between.

The major purpose of this book, then, is to provide the reader with the background knowledge necessary to be better able to make comparisons among the major Western or "liberal" democracies on the basis of a number of common concepts and variables and also to see the major similarities and differences among four democratic states and the EU, which is not a state but is the most state-like international organization today and a model in many ways for similar organizations in other regions of the world.

As a final note, I wish to thank my wife, Regine, who has been patient beyond reason in tolerating my spending so much time on this book ever since I was supposed to be retired. It turned out to be a lengthier project than I had anticipated because of so many interruptions, caused primarily by voluntary activities and performing with my wife the happy but time-consuming role of engaged grandparents.

Arthur B. Gunlicks
Professor of Political Science, Emeritus
University of Richmond, Virginia

A Note on Terminology

The title of this book contains the term "liberal democracies." Given the ideological polarization in the United States today and the contention of those on the right of the political spectrum that "liberal" means far left or even socialist, some American readers may think that the subject matter of the book is biased toward the American left's perspective on government institutions and policies. This, of course, is not the case. Indeed, as will be noted throughout the book, from an historical and international perspective "liberal" refers to the beliefs and practices of philosophers and writers in the eighteenth and nineteenth century who challenged the political, economic, social, and religious conservative traditions associated with the prevailing monarchies, whose roots could be found in the feudalism of the Middle Ages.

These original European "classical Liberals," to whom I refer with a capital "L" to distinguish them from current small "l" American "liberals," believed above all in individual freedom. Individual freedom was seen as the classical freedoms of speech, press, and assembly, and as freedom of religion. It was also seen as individual freedom in the economic sphere, and thus Liberalism is very much associated originally and still in Europe today as the philosophical underpinning of capitalism and free enterprise. Liberalism is also identified with political and legal equality, that is, the extension of the right to vote to all males with property, then to all males, and finally, after World War I, to females; legal equality meant, above all, equal justice under the rule of law.

As Liberalism gained adherents, it challenged the old conservative order by promoting various reforms in parliament, as in England, or by revolution, as in the United States and France. Liberal revolutions also took place in Europe in the middle of the nineteenth century, and, even though they were only partially successful, they did result in more pressure being placed on the traditional elites for significant changes. Some of these changes were also brought about by the rise of political parties and unions before and after the turn of the nineteenth to the twentieth century. By the early twentieth century, and especially after World War II, growing numbers of states became democratic republics or constitutional monarchies with only elected decision makers in a developing system of parliamentary democracy that guaranteed individual freedoms in the political and economic realms, provided religious freedom, and promoted legal equality for their citizens. They were all characterized by free, fair, and regular elections. Today these democratic states are referred to in the comparative politics and international relations literature as "liberal democracies." "Western democracies" is also a term that is used frequently, but there are a number of states today, for example, India, South Korea, or Japan, that are not "Western," even though they have been strongly influenced by the Western—especially American and British—democracies.

As noted in chapter 5, European Liberalism is the main philosophical tradition in the United States. As in Europe today, there are two basic components in this tradition: on the one hand a focus on individualism in the sense of basic freedoms, such as freedom of speech, press, assembly, and religion (the first amendment rights of the American constitution), and political and legal equality; and on the other hand a focus on individualism in the sense of free enterprise and individual effort in the economic realm. Whereas in Europe both components are usually found more or less united in an uneasy alliance that constitutes two wings of Liberal political parties, they represent the major values of two separate and competing parties in the United States, the "liberal" Democrats and the "conservative" Republicans. Thus "left" and "right" in the United States represent the two basic components of classical Liberalism, whereas Liberalism in Europe has been, since the last half of the nineteenth century, an important part of the ideological center, between traditional European conservatism on the right and European socialism on the left.

Chapter 1

Foundations of Comparing Liberal Democracies

States and Nations

The world today is divided into 192 states, often referred to as "nations" or, in the United States, as "countries." The classical definition of the "state" is an entity that has a defined territory, a population, a government, and sovereignty, which means it can act without the interference of other states in its internal affairs and enjoys international recognition.

This definition is, however, somewhat problematic for at least three reasons. First, there are some governments, especially in Africa but also in Haiti, for example, that are so weak and ineffective that they have little, if any, control over the population and developments within the territory of the state. A famous German sociologist in the early twentieth century, Max Weber, defined the state as the institution with a monopoly of legitimate force in the society. In so-called "failed states," the government is challenged by military personnel or rebel groups that defy or fight to replace the government for reasons of religion, ethnicity, economic deprivation, or even for self-enrichment through "criminal exploitation" of natural resources, e.g., of diamonds or other mineral resources.[1] As a result, the state may have military and police units, but these have no recognized monopoly of legitimate force and may be internally divided in their loyalty. Indeed, a key problem in failed states is that no group, party, or individual enjoys widespread legitimacy in the population, that is, the recognized right to make authoritative decisions. This lack of a generally recognized "right to rule" that elicits obedience is usually associated with a nondemocratic or antidemocratic process by which the would-be rulers come to power; however, a lack of legitimacy can also be the result of widespread corruption that benefits a very few leaders at the expense of the impoverished population. In the cases of Iraq and Afghanistan, the governments, though elected, were or are not perceived as legitimate by many of the population for reasons of religion or ethnic and tribal ties, but also because of their origins in the governing arrangements that resulted from the American-led invasion and occupation.

A second, related, reason why some states lack full sovereignty is because they are "challenged states." That is, they have not "failed" as states, but they are being challenged—unsuccessfully in the case of Chechnya in Russia, successfully in the case of Kosovo in Serbia—by separatist ethnic or religious groups seeking more autonomy or even independence, or by revolutionaries of various kinds that want to take over the government in order to pursue different policies and goals. Examples of the latter would be Columbia, Peru, Nepal, and India, where governments are or until recently were being challenged by Maoist-Communist revolutionary forces. In still other cases, for example, Pakistan, it is one or more extremist religious groups, such as the Taliban, that are challenging the state with a radical program.

A third and increasingly important reason why the classical definition of the state is problematic is because the degree of sovereignty in international relations that most states enjoy is in fact constrained by a number of factors. Sovereignty refers to the location of final decision-making authority, and, according to the definition above, it is located in each state; however, dependency for security on other states, trade relations, the international banking system, multinational business corporations, economic dependency, the Internet, and even international organizations place direct or indirect constraints on state sovereignty. Even the United States, as the world's only superpower, must take into consideration the concerns of its allies and friends and its various international obligations under certain treaties, alliances, or diplomatic practices in pursuing its interests abroad, although it is often accused of acting "unilaterally."

Limitations on sovereignty are not, of course, equally distributed among states; indeed, in our highly interactive and globalized world relatively few states, especially the United States but also Japan, the European Union as a collective organization of member states, and, more recently, China, exercise a dominant economic influence and, in the case of the United States, dominant military power that makes them in fact "more sovereign" or independent in their decision making than others.

As noted above, another term often used as a synonym for "state" is "nation." The problem with using these two terms interchangeably is that "nation" refers more accurately to a "people" who usually are identified by some combination of a shared language, history, culture, and/or religion and who perceive themselves as belonging together. States that contain only one or one predominant "nation" are "nation-states," good examples of which would be Japan and the Scandinavian states.

Most states contain several "nations" and are therefore known as multinational states. Good examples would be Russia, China, Nigeria, India, Switzerland, and the former Yugoslavia. Canada is also a multinational state with a predominant English-speaking population and an important French-speaking population that lives mostly in Quebec. Whether the United States is a multinational state or a different kind of nation-state is subject to debate. One can, of course, point to the many nationalities, ethnic, racial, and religious groups in the United States and conclude that this is a multinational state. But after the second generation most members of the many groups that comprise society speak English as their first or only language, adopt American cultural attributes, and generally consider themselves to be "American." Also in contrast to most multinational states, the different groups in the United States are not located in a particular territory that is identified with them and in which most of them live. As a result some scholars have referred to the United States as the first "new nation," that is, a state composed of many groups, most of whose first generation immigrated voluntarily—with the obvious exceptions of the slave and native Indian populations—and accepted and adopted the common language, culture, and political identification (in the United States, often associated with the "American creed") that are usually associated with a "people."[2] On the other hand, there is controversy today about the degree to which some groups are, in fact, being assimilated or integrated into American society and identifying themselves as "American."[3]

In spite of the conceptual differences between "state," "nation," "nation-state," and "multinational state," Americans often refer to states in general as "nation-states" or "countries." One reason for this imprecision is undoubtedly the fact that there are fifty sub-national territorial units in the United States that we call "states" (but which are called "provinces" in the Canadian, cantons in the Swiss, and "*Länder*" in the German federal systems). To prevent confusion with the concept of "state" used by most of the rest of the world, Americans often avoid that term when talking about international actors. (One can make a good case that the United Nations is a misnomer, because it is in fact an organization of almost two hundred "states," not the thousands of "nations" that exist in the world.)

Classifying States and Political Systems

The "state" as defined above is a legal concept. It is therefore of limited application in reference to nonstate entities. "Politics," however, in the sense of "who gets what, when, and how," can be found in many nonstate organizations ranging from an Indian tribe to the unique international organization that is the United Nations or the European Union; it even applies to many nongovernmental organizations such as Amnesty International, Oxfam, or the Red Cross. "Political systems" is a broader concept that includes the decision-making structures, processes, and influences of both states and social-economic arrangements that we would not call states. But normally we apply the term to states.

The world is divided into a wide variety of states that differ significantly in terms of origins, ethnic and racial composition, religion, economic conditions, territorial organization, recruitment of leaders, governmental processes, public policies, popular participation, civil liberties, and stability. In looking at the political dimension, they are most simply distinguished by a simple dichotomy, democratic and nondemocratic. This distinction is, of course, too simple to be very meaningful, so more refined distinctions are often made in an attempt to arrive at a more useful categorization.[4]

Nondemocratic political systems. Most modern states, that is, political systems that emerged from the seventeenth century and after, were at first monarchies and/or parts of empires. In part as a reaction to the power of local and regional rulers and the fragmentation of territory and instability their many conflicts brought with them, monarchies arose that engaged in state-building actions that incorporated the territories of the lesser rulers, centralized government institutions through the development of efficient bureaucracies and military organizations, and grew increasingly powerful with fewer constraints on their authority. These regimes became "absolute" monarchies, in which legitimacy was usually derived from a so-called "divine right," with internal sovereignty—the source of final authority concentrated in the "sovereign," or monarch. Absolute monarchs did differ, however, in the degree to which they accepted competing authority, such as relatively independent courts that represented the rule of law. Thus while Frederick the Great of Prussia, for example, was very powerful in his realm, he accepted the rule of law, while his Russian counterpart, the czar, remained above the law. For historical reasons, including the Magna Charta of 1215 and the conflict between the monarch and parliament in the seventeenth century, the English monarch never became as powerful as the monarchs on the European continent. This was especially evident in the seventeenth and eighteenth centuries, when the English Parliament developed a countervailing power unmatched by any other state in Europe, a power that, in effect, made Parliament rather than the monarch "sovereign." However, it was especially the French Revolution of 1789, which not only deposed the French monarchy but also led to the long process of weakening the other European monarchies and their aristocracies, resulting in the rise of parliaments that insisted on their right to raise revenues and pass laws binding on society. Thus "constitutional monarchies," political systems with a constitutional order that limited the power of the monarch and established the organization of the state, emerged in some states, such as Great Britain, the Netherlands, Belgium, Norway, Sweden, and Denmark (while Great Britain does not have a written constitution, it does have a series of laws, traditions, and customs that are functionally equivalent to a written constitution). In most other states, either in the nineteenth or twentieth centuries, monarchies were replaced by "republics," that is, political systems with no monarch, governed by representative institutions.

Today the remaining monarchies of Europe are "constitutional" monarchies in which the monarch serves as the ceremonial head of state. Other constitutional monarchies exist in Asia (Japan, Brunei, and Thailand). There are relatively few "ruling" monarchies in the world, and those that exist are in the Middle East (Morocco, Jordan, Saudi Arabia, Oman, Bahrain, Qatar) or sub-Saharan Africa (Swaziland).

In the modern world, "absolute," or ruling, monarchies have been largely replaced as a type of political system by various forms of authoritarian regimes. These vary rather significantly in type, but in general they are characterized by a leader or group that exercises power with few or no constraints. Recruitment of elites takes place via the military, membership in a particular group or political party, loyalty to the leader, or personal contacts and relationships.

The more rigid authoritarian regimes are often called dictatorships, the most extreme of which are totalitarian dictatorships. Totalitarian regimes not only exercise political power with few or no constraints; they also attempt to control and manipulate all aspects of society, not only educational institutions, the mass media, the military, and bureaucracy, but also religious groups. The regime is usually based on the rule of a single party that represents an all-encompassing ideology that purports to have a monopoly of truth. To oppose the regime is, therefore, especially dangerous because it reflects opposition to or denial of the truth and the "good" society advocated by the regime. On the extreme left, the most obvious example of such a regime is that of Josef Stalin, especially from the mid-1930s to his death in 1953. Other examples would be Communist states in eastern Europe in the 1950s and Communist China under Mao. North Korea and, to a lesser extent, Cuba, would be the best examples today. On the extreme right, the best example would be Hitler's Third Reich. An example of a totalitarian religious regime would be Afghanistan under the Taliban until its removal at the end of 2001 by American and other NATO invasion forces and their Afghan allies. Iran is also a theocracy that denies many basic rights, but it does allow carefully controlled elections, the results of which may still not always please the supreme leaders.

Some observers use the term "autocratic" to describe dictatorial regimes. This term, like "authoritarian," is very imprecise; however, it usually refers to more personalized rule, where a leader is supported by the military and police forces and possibly by other groups, such as certain ethnic groups or large landowners, with whom he is allied. Examples can be found in recent history in Africa (Nigeria in the 1990s) and Latin America, where the military dictator, Fulgencio Batista, was overthrown by Fidel Castro in 1959 and where the Somoza family was overthrown in Nicaragua by the Sandinista movement in 1979. Some observers would argue that a number of states that emerged from the old Soviet Union have autocratic leaders today. In 2011 various uprisings have replaced autocratic regimes in Tunisia, Egypt, and Libya and threatened the longtime unelected leaders of Syria and Yemen. For our purposes, the term "autocratic" will be included in the concept of "authoritarian."

In somewhat less "dictatorial" regimes, elections may be held but are manipulated in such a way and/or opposition groups are repressed just enough that they represent little or no threat to the ruling elite. Zimbabwe, Egypt under Mubarak, a number of states that emerged from the old Soviet Union, including Tajikistan, Belarus, and perhaps even Russia, would be good examples. As a result, rulers are largely unaccountable to the public. Some authoritarian regimes allow the existence of opposition groups, such as the Catholic Church in former communist countries and in some former Latin American military dictatorships, but the opposition of such groups must not involve any attempt to threaten or overthrow the regime.

Many authoritarian regimes are military dictatorships—which vary in their degree of repressiveness—while others are theocracies (Iran) or systems based largely on personalities (Syria and some Latin American states in the recent past) or group membership. Military dictatorships were common in Latin America until the 1980s (e.g., Chile, Argentina, and Brazil), and they are still common in many African and some Asian states (e.g., Burma or Myanmar).

While there are certain basic similarities among nondemocratic states, as suggested above, we have seen that there are also significant differences among these systems in the extent to which they deny human rights, including free speech, free elections, and rule of law. As a result it is best to think of nondemocratic states as falling along a continuum that reflects the fact that they are not all alike in every respect and that some regimes are far more rigid and nasty than others. The continuum below represents a somewhat arbitrary attempt to demonstrate the diversity of authoritarian states; other scholars or the reader might prefer other examples and/or might place the examples provided below in different positions along the continuum, depending on his or her assessment of the regime.

Figure 1.1

A Continuum of Nondemocratic Political Systems

Soviet Union (1933-53)	Nazi Germany (1933-45)	Taliban Afghanistan	Czarist Russia	Absolute Monarchs in Europe	Franco's Spain (1939-1975)
Totalitarian					Authoritarian
North Korea (1946-?)	Mao's China	Military Rule in Myranmar	China after Mao	Military Rule in Chile and Brazil (1970s)	Egypt under Mubarak

Democratic political systems. Democracy as a concept emerged first in ancient Greece, where it meant "rule by the people." For Plato, it amounted to mob rule, that is, rule by the masses in their own selfish interest. For Aristotle, democracy would be mob rule if for selfish interests, but if a majority of the people were middle class and therefore interested in the broader common good that would include the protection of property rights, then such a system would be more acceptable (that is, better than the negative alternatives of rule by one [tyrant], by a few [oligarchy], or by many [the mob] in their selfish interest but not as good as the positive alternatives of rule by one [king] or by the few [aristocracy] in the interest of the common good).

The democracy of the ancient Greeks and of the Roman Republic was direct democracy, where citizens would assemble and make decisions binding on all. There was no attempt to introduce direct democracy in Europe after whatever experiments with it had occurred in ancient Greece and Rome. (In the eighteenth century, even Rousseau, who advocated popular rule but not by representative institutions, considered direct democracy to be impractical except in cities and towns.) The concept of representation developed slowly during the Middle Ages and at first provided only for the representation of elites of various kinds. In France the idea of the "third estate" emerged, which meant that the rising, economically important middle classes should be represented along with the nobility and clergy, that is, the first and second estates, respectively. But Louis XIV dissolved the Estates General in 1614, and it did not reconvene until after the French Revolution, when it became the French parliament. In Great Britain the idea of a House of Commons, similar to the French idea of the third estate, arose to represent the middle classes, who were excluded from and obviously not the focus of attention in the older, aristocratic, House of Lords. After the French Revolution, the application of the principle of equality meant that elected parliaments would not represent the nobility or clergy but rather "the people," whose deputies were themselves mostly upper-middle class.

The limitations of representation in early parliaments can be seen in Great Britain. Before the first electoral reform law of 1832, only about 5 percent of the male population over age twenty could vote, while after the reform the proportion rose to a little more than 7 percent. A reform in 1867 increased the male voting population to more than 16 percent, and after 1884 about 30 percent, or about half of the adult male population, could vote. By 1921 74 percent of the adult males could vote. Women were not allowed to vote until 1925 (in most democratic states, women could not vote until after World War I; but they could not vote in France until 1944).[5] In Germany the Bismarck Reich after 1871 had a monarch who was "sovereign" in foreign and military affairs; however, there was a national parliament (*Reichstag*), which was elected by a system of universal male suffrage that was more democratic than the then existing electoral systems in either France or Great Britain; however, the largest and most populous state in the German federation, Prussia, had a three-class system for its parliament according to which the very small percentage of the adult male voters who paid the first one-third of the taxes elected the first one-third of the parliament, a larger proportion paying the second one-third of the taxes elected the next one-third of the parliament, and the large majority who paid the last one-third of taxes elected the final third of parliament. In the United States there were property restrictions in many of the subnational states and local governments after the Revolution and the Constitution of 1789, but slowly these were removed, and by 1850 universal suffrage for white males prevailed. Women were not allowed to vote in national elections until 1920, and most black Americans could not vote until 1965. One can argue, then, that if judged "by the standard of universal suffrage for competitive multiparty elections," there were, in electoral terms, no democracies in the world in 1900.[6]

Samuel Huntington, on the other hand, has suggested that modern democracies first emerged in the nineteenth century. According to him, democracies developed in three waves. The first democracies had their roots in the American and French Revolutions, but he does not classify a country as democratic until 50 percent of the male population was eligible to vote and the executive was responsible to a parliament or to the voters. The United States did not meet these criteria until 1828, followed later by Switzerland, France, Great Britain, and others. By 1920, which he sees as the end of the first wave, there were about thirty democracies. There were a number of reversals in the interwar period, and only about twelve countries were democratic in 1942. A second wave after World War II brought the number back to about thirty. Another reversal occurred in the 1960s, especially in Latin America but also in Greece and Turkey. But starting in the mid-1970s, a number of new and returning democracies emerged to constitute the third wave. Most of the states that joined this wave were able to do so as a result of the collapse of communism in 1989. By 1990 Huntington counted fifty-nine democracies, about 45 percent of the total number of states.[7]

A somewhat different perspective is offered by Freedom House, cited above, according to which 120 of the 192 states in the world were democracies at the end of the twentieth century. These states represented 62.5 percent of the world's population; however, of these 120 states only eighty-five were "liberal" democracies, representing 38 percent of the world's population.[8] The highest concentration of liberal democracies is in Europe, with twenty-seven states alone in the European Union and forty-seven in the Council of Europe (although some of these states, such as Russia, are "electoral" democracies).

Sometimes states that have at least the outward appearance of having democratic governments are accused of authoritarianism (i.e., restricted democratic practices), because they curtail or limit civil liberties, including freedom of the press, and discourage opposition without actually outlawing it. Such regimes are often referred to as "electoral," "transitional," or "emerging" democracies, states that appear to be democratic based on their constitutional arrangements, political institutions, e.g., parliaments, and relatively free elections. However, they fail to live up to the standards of "liberal" democracies, which are usually older, well established democracies that are recognized for their multiparty systems and conduct of free, fair, and frequent elections that not only hold elected decision-makers accountable but also lead to occasional changes of governments. The foundation of these characteristics is, of course, the protection of civil liberties, especially freedom of speech, press, and assembly, and the rule of law and equality under the law.

What are the distinguishing characteristics of "liberal" democracies? First, almost all of them have relatively high per capita incomes with a large middle class. India is an exception in per capita income, but its middle class is large in number and growing. All of the liberal democracies also have free market economies, although they vary in the degree to which they own parts of certain enterprises and provide public services of various kinds. In Europe, for example, most democracies are also "welfare states," which means that a large proportion of their national income is designated for public services such as health care, family allowances, nursing homes, unemployment compensation and public assistance, public housing and/or housing subsidies, public transportation, and retirement benefits. These benefits are generally more generous and more broadly based than in the United States. On the other hand, the United States—where taxes are lower than in the European welfare states—does usually spend proportionately more for education than even some of the European welfare states. While many liberal democracies are multinational states, the protections offered in the area of human rights usually keep ethnic, racial, and religious conflict in check. Therefore, there are rarely groups in liberal democracies that threaten rebellion or serious civil conflict, although Northern Ireland and Spain can be seen as exceptions. One can also note the experiences of the United States, Great Britain, France, and India that demonstrate that even liberal democracies may sometimes fail to live up to their human rights ideals regarding minority populations and experience violent demonstrations as a result.

As in the case of nondemocratic political systems, there can be significant differences among democratic governments. In some states, such as Russia, or even more, Belarus, there is evidence that the mass media are not entirely free, that the electoral process is manipulated in such a manner as to favor the government, that there is some repression of opposition elements, and that the rule of law is not entirely secured. Among "liberal" democracies there are also differences, some of the most important of which will be discussed later in this book. Whether and to what extent one liberal democracy is "more democratic" than another is, however, very difficult to assess. In one democratic state there may be an attempt to protect the rights of a defendant by restricting pretrial publicity (as in Great Britain), while in another state pretrial publicity may be protected as free speech (as in the United States). Or persons convicted of committing certain crimes may face the death penalty (United States), while in almost all other democracies the death penalty is prohibited. In terms of elections, legislators are elected in most European democracies by proportional representation, which is seen by many as fairer than the American and British winner-takes-all single-member districts; however, proportional representation usually leads to coalition governments, while single-member district usually lead to one party's gaining enough seats to govern alone, thus providing perhaps more stable and responsible government (see chapter 4). It is very difficult to argue that on balance one liberal democracy is more democratic than another, and so this author would place all liberal democracies in about the same position along the continuum of democracies.

Figure 1.2

A Continuum of Democratic Political Systems

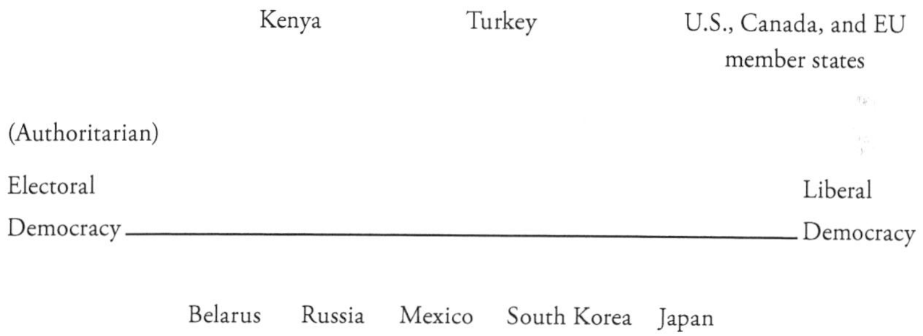

Kenya   Turkey   U.S., Canada, and EU member states

(Authoritarian)
Electoral Democracy ———————————————— Liberal Democracy

Belarus   Russia   Mexico   South Korea   Japan

Most liberal democracies are "Western," that is, they are located in Europe or have populations of mostly European origin, such as the United States, Canada, Australia, and New Zealand. India is an exception, but it was ruled by Great Britain for a century before achieving independence in 1947. One can argue that Japan is also an exception, but, again, it was heavily influenced after World War II by the United States. This book will focus on four of these states: the United States, Great Britain, Germany, and France. Each of these states, though sharing the characteristics and conditions that place them in the category of "liberal democracies," is very different in a number of key respects. These include differences regarding general type of political system, separation of powers, checks and balances, territorial organization, the organization of the three branches, party and electoral systems, interest groups, legal systems, and public policies. Becoming aware of and understanding these differences will make the reader more familiar with political systems in general and with liberal democratic political systems in particular.

The European Union, which is not a state, also will be included in our comparison. The reason is because it is a highly integrated organization of twenty-seven states (as of 2011) that has a number of characteristics that place it in a "near state" category. It plays an increasingly important role in world trade by becoming the major trading unit in the world; its bureaucratic leadership, the "Commission," rather than the individual member states, negotiates with trading partners such as the United States, Japan, and China; it is responsible for a "common agricultural policy" (CAP) that replaces what used to be individual state policies; its Council of Ministers and Parliament pass regulations that now make up a large proportion of the most important laws that apply to the member states; it has a powerful supreme court that ensures compliance with EU policies and, in some cases, can overturn laws and even constitutional provisions of the member states; it has a common currency, the Euro (used, however, by only seventeen of the member states as of 2011); it acts in unison—at least most of the time—on foreign policy issues; and it is increasingly active, though still with a somewhat modest impact, in the military—especially peacekeeping—arena.

Conclusion

The world consists of almost two hundred states, but there are important differences among these entities. Some in fact are "failed states," others are "challenged states." All states by definition are supposed to be "sovereign," that is, capable of making decisions without external interference; however, large and powerful states enjoy more independence than their weaker counterparts, and in an increasingly globalized world even large states fall under a variety of constraints that in fact limit sovereignty to some degree.

The term "states" is often used interchangeably with the term "nation," when in fact "state" refers to a population, territory, a government, and sovereignty, while "nation" refers to a "people" that may or may not be the "population" of a state. Most states are not "nation-states" but rather "multinational states" with two or more national groupings making up the population.

The almost two hundred states that exist can be classified in different ways, but the simplest is probably "nondemocratic" and "democratic." There are, however, important differences within these two categories, so that placing them on a continuum is more useful than perceiving them as dichotomous variables. In doing so, it is clear that there are subcategories of nondemocratic and democratic systems. In the latter case there are, for example, "electoral democracies" and "liberal democracies." This book focuses on four states that are liberal democracies as well as the EU, a state-like organization that is composed of liberal democracies.

There are, of course, classifications of states and political systems other than what has been discussed thus far. For example, presidential versus parliamentary democracy, representative versus direct democracy, popular sovereignty versus parliamentary sovereignty, and other terms are also confronted when one reads about different political systems. We will look more closely at a number of terms or concepts in the following chapters.

Endnotes

[1] Jimmy Kandeh, *Coups from Below: Armed Subalterns and State Power in West Africa* (New York: Palgrave Macmillan, 2004).

[2] Seymour Martin Lipset, *The First New Nation: The United States in Historical and Comparative Perspective* (New York: Basic Books, 1963).

[3] Samuel P. Huntington, *Who Are We? The Challenges to American Identity* (New York: Simon and Schuster, 2004).

[4] Robert Dahl, in his book, *On Democracy* (New Haven: Yale University Press, 1998), 2, suggests a threefold division of nondemocratic, newly democratic, and established democratic governments.

[5] Ibid., 23–24.

[6] Freedom House, a privately funded American organization that reports on the development of democracy around the world, makes this argument. See www.freedomhouse.org/reports/century.html, p. 1. Robert Dahl also writes of democracy as a "product of the twentieth century." See *On Democracy*, 3.

[7] Samuel P. Huntington, *The Third Wave: Democratization in the Late Twentieth Century* (Norman: University of Oklahoma Press, 1991), ch. 1.

[8] Dahl, *On Democracy*, 2.

Chapter 2

Classifying Liberal Democracies

Introduction

We have seen that there are two simple categories of democratic and nondemocratic political systems but that for the sake of greater precision each of these categories should be broken down into several subcategories. For the general category of democratic states, it is important to distinguish between "electoral," "emerging" or "transitional" democracies, and "liberal" democracies. Liberal democracies, however, also vary dramatically according to their institutional makeup, political processes, and public policies. The United States, Great Britain, Germany, and France are all liberal democracies, but each has a number of distinctive characteristics which are outlined briefly below. We will look at these characteristics in more detail in chapters 7 and 8.

General Considerations

Some characteristics are shared in general terms but with some variation. The United States, France and Germany are republics, while the United Kingdom is a constitutional monarchy. The difference, of course, is that the British have a hereditary head of state (see below), while the other states have a directly or indirectly elected head of state. Some definitions of "republic" also emphasize that power is exercised by representatives chosen directly or indirectly by the citizenry. This, of course, excludes dictatorships, even though they sometimes call themselves "republics," but it would include Great Britain, so a hereditary head of state is really what distinguishes Britain from our other liberal democracies.

Another general constitutional or legal question concerns popular versus parliamentary sovereignty. In most democracies sovereignty is said to reside in the people or, more practically perhaps, in the constitution; however, in the United Kingdom the parliament, that is, the House of Commons, is sovereign. In practice one can argue that sovereignty may be divided among different institutions. In the United States, for example, one could maintain that sovereignty is shared in a very complicated arrangement by the president, both houses of congress, the Supreme Court, the federal and state governments, and, ultimately, the people, or at least those who vote. If one focuses on popular sovereignty, then a further question arises that concerns representative versus direct or plebiscitary democracy. In the UK parliament is sovereign, yet there have been some popular referenda in recent decades to decide certain basic questions, e.g., devolution for Scotland, even though technically, these have been advisory only. The United States at the national level is a purely representative democracy; however, there are procedures for popular votes on bond issues in virtually all of the states, and many states, e.g., California, permit initiatives and referenda on a variety of issues. Germany, like the United States, does not have referenda at the national level, but referenda of various kinds are permitted in the *Länder* (states) and municipalities. In France the president can call for a referendum on certain important questions, but this has been done only ten times since the Fifth Republic was established in 1959. Whatever differences may exist concerning the above, it is clear that all four of our liberal democracies are representative democracies with limited provisions for direct democracy, especially at the national level.

Basic Institutional Structure: Presidential Democracies

Obvious differences in the basic institutional structure of liberal democracies are associated with the concepts of presidential versus parliamentary government. The United States is often cited as the model of the presidential system.[1] A number of other states, particularly in Latin America, have adopted presidential systems, but these have often degenerated into some form of authoritarian rule. Some presidential systems in Asia, such as the Philippines, have also had mixed success as presidential democracies. The frequent failure of presidential systems in other parts of the world to live up to liberal democratic standards suggests that the success of the American system has much to do with a unique history, traditions, experiences, and leadership that had in general a more positive effect than elsewhere on the development of the system.

While presidential systems, like parliamentary systems, vary from state to state, there are a number of features that are common to each system. Students of American government know, of course, that the American model has a single executive that combines the head of state and head of government functions (see below), separation of powers, checks and balances, direct election of the president, and a limited term of office. Other presidential systems generally share these characteristics. On the other hand, the French model, which is known as the semipresidential system, is different in some important respects. Instead of a single executive, the French model (also found in Russia, for example) has a dual executive with a separate head of state and head of government. Separation of powers and checks and balances are also different in the French model. The method of election is direct but still very different from that used in the United States, and the term of office is different.

As noted above, the classical presidential system is characterized by one directly elected executive leader who functions as both head of state and head of government. In every state in the world (excluding "failed states") the "executive" consists of a head of state and a head of government. In all states the head of state is the ceremonial leader who not only serves as a symbol of the state but also represents the state in international relations by traveling abroad on official "state" visits and receiving the credentials of newly appointed ambassadors from other states that have diplomatic relations with the head of state's country. The head of state is not typically engaged in policy making, although he or she may become involved in the political process under certain limited circumstances. Good examples of separate heads of state are constitutional monarchs, such as the current queen of England and the monarchs of the Scandinavian countries. The presidents of Germany and Italy are examples of ceremonial heads of state in a republic.

There is also a head of government in every state. The head of government is the political leader of the state, who is heavily involved in policy making. He or she is generally responsible for the major actions of the heads of various departments or ministries and, as a result, usually hires and fires high government officials, such as cabinet officers and their chief aides, to ensure conformity with his or her overall policy wishes. Examples are the prime minister of Great Britain and the chancellor of Germany. As noted above, the classical presidential system is characterized by one directly elected leader who functions as both head of state and head of government, whereas the French semipresidential model has a dual executive similar to the parliamentary system.

Separation of powers. As a general rule, there is a separation of powers between the executive branch and the legislative branch in presidential systems. This means that each branch is—or should be—*independent* of the other. This is achieved not only by separate election of the president and members of the legislature but also by separation of personnel in the executive and legislative branches. Thus the American Constitution (Article I, Section 6) provides that members of the president's cabinet may not also be members of the legislative or judicial branches.

Even though the executive and legislative branches are separate in the American model, they may not be entirely independent of each other. There are checks and balances provided by the Constitution according to which there may be some mixture or overlapping of functions, such as the president's right to veto legislation and the Senate's right to confirm the president's nominees for federal courts; however, there are also informal examples of greater or lesser independence of the executive and legislative branches. Thus independence is characteristic of divided government, i.e., when the president is of one party and the House and/or Senate are in the hands of the other party. On the other hand, when the president's party has a majority in both houses of Congress, and especially when the president is popular and enjoys widespread support in public opinion polls, he can have great influence over legislators. They bask in his popularity and want to be identified with him in the next elections. An unpopular president, in contrast, may not have the support he needs for his agenda in Congress, even if his party has a majority.

In France, there is also a separation of powers between the executive and legislative branches; however, it is not quite as straightforward as in the American model. The president and parliament are elected separately—indeed, even on different dates, though in the same year. The president, rather than parliament, also selects the prime minister as head of government, even if he is forced by an opposition majority in parliament to appoint a leader of that opposition. The government (cabinet) members are prevented by the incompatibility rule of the constitution from being members of the parliament, which strengthens the idea of separation of powers. On the other hand, the prime minister and his government are accountable not only to the president but also to parliament, which can remove the prime minister by a vote of no-confidence. In this sense the French parliament has a control over the government more characteristic of parliamentary systems that is not found in the American model except in the very rare case of impeachment.

Checks and balances. Separation of powers is closely associated with the concept of checks and balances, especially in the American presidential system. Checks and balances are means by which one branch has some influence on the personnel, procedures, or actions of the other branch that serve to control to some degree that branch. Thus checks and balances are designed to weaken somewhat the independence of the separate branches of government and their ability to act alone.

There are numerous formal and informal checks on the president in the United States. The best examples of formal checks and balances include the presidential right to veto bills passed by both houses of Congress, and the right of the Congress to override the veto with a two-thirds vote in each house; the right of the president to nominate and appoint judges to federal courts and other high officials, including members of his cabinet, but only with the "advice and consent" of the Senate; and the right of the federal courts to rule on the constitutionality of congressional enactments and presidential actions, but also the right of the president to nominate judges and the Senate to confirm their nomination. The president can be removed from office by impeachment in the House and conviction in the Senate for "treason, bribery, or other high crimes and misdemeanors." President Clinton was impeached by the House of Representatives for his affair with Monika Lewinski, but the impeachment failed in the Senate in large part because it was not clear what the *impeachable* offense was. Another example of a formal check would be the monetary policies of the Federal Reserve, because its decisions on interest rates or comments by the chairman of the Federal Reserve, for example, can have a significant impact on the president's economic policies. Another example of checks on the president's power can be found in international commitments, such as various treaties that have been signed by American presidents and ratified by the Senate, or views of both allies and potential enemies that the president must take into account. Whether the president enjoys majority support in one or both houses or whether he faces an opposition majority in both houses can, of course, be crucial in his achieving success or failure.

In the French semipresidential system, the president is the dominant figure when he enjoys majority support in the National Assembly and can appoint whomever he wishes to be prime minister. In this case the prime minister is primarily responsible for routine governmental activities and for carrying out the president's agenda. On the other hand, when opposition parties have a majority in the National Assembly and the president is forced to appoint as prime minister someone who is a leader of opposition forces or at least supported by them, the resulting *cohabitation* means that the president and prime minister must cooperate. The president cannot realistically dismiss a prime minister who enjoys majority support in the parliament, and, of course, the prime minister cannot remove the president from office. Furthermore, the prime minister must countersign most actions of the president. The Constitutional Council, a kind of constitutional court, can also rule unconstitutional certain actions of the president and prime minister, for example, a referendum proposed by the president or the conduct of an election. It must also be consulted on the arrangements for presidential elections and on the conduct of referenda or in case the president declares a state of emergency.[2]

In both the American and French systems informal checks and balances are sometimes more important in limiting presidential power than the formal ones. For example, newspaper articles and commentaries, television and radio reports, and public opinion are major checks, as are the state of the economy, views of allies as well as enemies, cooperation or lack thereof by the bureaucracy, and disagreements among leading cabinet officers and departments.

Direct election. A major characteristic of a presidential system is the direct election of the president and a separate election of the legislative branch, whether consisting of one or two chambers (houses). The direct election of a president requires a particular electoral system. One might argue that the simplest system would be one in which the candidate with the most votes wins. An obvious problem with this system is that in a contest with multiple candidates, a candidate with far less than 50 percent plus could win. This would weaken him or her in terms of electoral legitimacy. The solution adopted by many states, for example France, is to require a runoff election, usually between the top two candidates, if no candidate receives an absolute majority in the first round. That way the winner of the second round is guaranteed an absolute majority and has more democratic legitimacy than would otherwise be the case.

The United States has a unique system of direct election of the president. Because of the important role played by the thirteen original states in the Constitutional Convention in Philadelphia in 1787 and their insistence that they be given a role in the selection of the president, the United States does not, in fact, elect its president directly by a popular vote. Instead, the candidate who receives an absolute majority of votes (now 270) in the Electoral College (now 538) is elected. Votes in the Electoral College are cast by state delegations of "electors," who represent in the individual states the candidate who receives the most votes (not necessarily an absolute majority!). In other words, it is a "winner-take-all" system, with the winner in each state except Maine and Nebraska collecting all of that state's electoral votes. However, the Constitution does not require bloc voting; indeed, Maine and Nebraska allow electors to vote for the presidential candidate who won a majority in the elector's congressional district. There have also been a few instances in the past when an elector voted for a candidate who did well in certain parts of the state but did not actually win the most votes overall.

The number of electors is determined by the total number of senators and representatives from the state. Thus, Wyoming sends three electors, because it has two senators and one representative, whereas California sends fifty-five electors, because it has two senators and fifty-three representatives. There are 538 Electoral College votes: 100 senators for the fifty states, 435 for the number of representatives, and three for the District of Columbia. The Electoral College has failed only three times since 1789 to vote for the candidate with the most votes nationally. The last occasion, of course, was the election of 2000, when the Democrat, Al Gore, received five hundred thousand more votes overall than the Republican, George Bush. However, an absolute majority of 270 in the Electoral College could be secured only by a victory in Florida, and the winner of that contest was finally determined in effect by the Supreme Court in a controversial 5-4 decision.

In France, as in some other semipresidential systems, the president is elected directly by the people in a two-ballot system. If no candidate receives an absolute majority in the first round—and in France none ever has—the two candidates with the most votes face each other in the second round two weeks later.

The president of France has not always been elected by popular vote. The constitution of the Fifth Republic that went into effect in January 1959 called for election by an electoral college consisting of elected local government officials. Soon, however, the first president elected by this method, Charles de Gaulle, recognized that he would enjoy more legitimacy if elected by popular vote. As a result he had the constitution changed to provide for the current two-ballot system to take effect in the 1965 election. He was then surprised and disappointed when he did not receive an absolute majority on the first ballot; however, he did win handily in the second round. Because he lost a referendum in 1969 dealing with the reform of the French Senate and regional issues, he resigned without serving out his full seven-year second term.

Terms of office. It is clear that the system of selection is very important in presidential democracies, but the length of the term of office is also important.

In the United States, the term of office is four years, with only two terms allowed by the Twenty-Second Amendment, passed in 1961 in response to the four terms won by Franklin D. Roosevelt. It is interesting to note that many American states have no term limits for their governors, some have a two-term limit, and Virginia limits its governors to one four-year term.[3]

There are, of course, numerous arguments both for and against term limits for presidents, as for other offices. Arguments for term limits are usually based on the view that even elected leaders can serve too long and begin to treat their office like a self-understood right, that they may become entrenched in part because of media attention and/or simple lack of competition, and that new ideas and new leadership are desirable, if not necessary, every few years for a democratic system of government. One powerful argument against term limits is that they limit choice; that is, they restrict the voters' right to vote for the continuance in office of a political leader whom they have come to respect and admire. Another is that executive leaders often have long-range plans and projects that they want to see through and for which they have gained public approval over the years; continuity and stability in office may be important factors in completing the projects. A president may also have developed close personal contacts with foreign leaders and be involved in delicate and important foreign policy initiatives that might be interrupted or even defeated by a change of leadership.

In France the Fifth Republic Constitution that went into effect in 1959 provided for seven-year renewable terms for the president who was directly elected in 1965 and thereafter. Only François Mitterrand served two full terms, from 1981 to 1995. President Jacques Chirac served a seven-year term from 1995 to 2002; however, a constitutional change in the meantime provided for five-year presidential terms to end in the same year as the five-year terms of the popularly elected parliament, the National Assembly. Thus, the next presidential and National Assembly elections were held in the spring of 2007, but not on the same day, as in the United States. There are no term limits for French presidents; however, no president has served more than two terms since the Fifth Republic was established in 1959.

Basic Institutional Structure: Parliamentary Democracies

Most democracies are parliamentary systems. A much smaller number are semipresidential systems, such as France and Russia, and only a few functioning democracies follow the American presidential model. Great Britain and Germany are parliamentary systems, but their institutional arrangements are also very different in certain respects. What are the major characteristics of a parliamentary democracy?

We have seen above that in every state there is a head of state and a head of government. A major characteristic of a parliamentary system is a dual executive; that is, the separation of these two offices, each held by a different person. The head of state occupies a largely ceremonial office, although he or she may have considerable influence in the selection of a head of government. The prime minister of Great Britain, for example, who is head of government, is not elected by a majority of the House of Commons but rather is appointed by the monarch, the head of state. The monarch appoints the leader of the majority party, who undoubtedly would have been elected by the majority in parliament if there had been a vote in that body. In that sense, it can be argued that the selection process makes little difference in practice; however, it could matter if no party has an absolute majority of seats in parliament or if the leadership post in the majority party were contested. In such a case the monarch would have to decide whom to select, and that decision could be controversial.

In some parliamentary systems, such as Great Britain, Spain, the Netherlands, Belgium, and the Scandinavian countries, the head of state is a hereditary monarch. In Germany, as in most other parliamentary systems that are republics, the head of state is the president. In some states the president is selected by parliament, but in Germany he is elected for a five-year term by an electoral college ("Federal Assembly") composed of members of the *Bundestag*, which is the popularly elected parliament, and an equal number of members of *Land* (state) legislatures. The person elected is usually a prominent member of one of the leading parties; for example, the current president, who was elected in the summer of 2010, is Christian Wulff, who at the time of his election was the prime minister of Lower Saxony and a leading member of the Christian Democratic Union (CDU), a center-right party and the largest party in Germany. On the other hand, Horst Koehler, his predecessor, was the head of the International Monetary Fund (IMF) and was not active in electoral politics before he was nominated by the CDU.

In most parliamentary systems the head of government is called the prime minister or, sometimes, premier, or in Germany and Austria, the chancellor. The head of government is the other, and politically more important, part of the executive, usually elected by a parliamentary majority that consists of a coalition of two or more parties, because one party rarely receives an absolute majority that allows it to govern alone. Unless it appears that no coalition can be formed, in which case a head of state could become involved in behind-the-scenes discussions, any action by the head of state concerning the selection process for the head of government is largely a formality. As noted above, however, the prime minister in Great Britain is appointed by the monarch, who is head of state, but with the implicit support of a majority in parliament.

In contrast to France, the heads of government in Great Britain and Germany dominate the executive branch and control to a considerable extent the political agenda. France, as we have seen, has a semipresidential system in which the powers of the president and the prime minister have varied according to the majority in the National Assembly. The power of the prime minister in Great Britain and Germany also varies from time to time; however, it varies in large part based on the size of the head of government's majority, the cohesiveness or discipline of that majority, the leadership skills of the head of government, the condition of the economy, and, of course, whether, as in Germany, a coalition government can be formed without too much internal disagreement between the coalition partners.

Separation of powers. A major characteristic of a presidential system is the separation of powers between the executive, that is, the president, and the legislature (in the United States the House of Representatives and the Senate). Each branch is elected separately and is, therefore, *independent* of the other. This is not the case in a parliamentary system. Indeed, some British observers suggest that there is a *fusion* of powers between the prime minister and his or her cabinet and the parliament (House of Commons).

Even if *fusion* is somewhat of an exaggeration, when we look at either the British or the German parliamentary systems, we see that the head of government holds office only because his or her party received a majority of votes in the parliament or, in the case of Germany and most other parliamentary systems, has put together a majority coalition of two or more parties (following the 2010 parliamentary elections, the British Conservative and Liberal Democratic parties formed a coalition government, because the larger Conservative party failed to win an absolute majority of seats). Neither the British prime minister nor the German chancellor is elected by popular vote. Instead, the prime minister is appointed by the monarch because he or she is the leader of the majority party in parliament. This person is elected to the House of Commons by the voters only in his or her parliamentary constituency or district. In Germany the chancellor is selected by the *Bundestag* majority (but is elected to parliament by voters in a district *or* over the party list, to be discussed below). He or she is probably the chairman of the largest party, but this is not necessarily the case. Gerhard Schröder (chancellor from 1998 to 2005), for example, turned over his chairmanship of the Social Democratic Party to Franz Müntefering while he was chancellor, on the grounds that he was too busy to perform adequately the duties of party chair (other grounds that were not publicly announced concerned the growing opposition by members of the left wing of his party to government reforms initiated by Schröder).

In a parliamentary system, then, the government must have a majority in parliament or attempt to muddle through as a minority government, usually only for a short period of time. If the government loses its majority, it must call for new elections or be subject to a vote of confidence, which if it loses will force it from office. Government and parliament are not *independent* of each other; rather, the government is *dependent* on a parliamentary majority. The government is also made up mostly of members of parliament, who therefore serve in both the legislative and executive branches. Even if *fusion* is too strong a term, it is clear that the connection between government and parliament in a parliamentary system stands in strong contrast to the separation of government (cabinet) and legislature in a presidential system.

The relationship between government and parliament is one important reason why there are usually cohesive, disciplined parties backing and opposing the government. Especially if the government has only a small majority in parliament, it must count on the continuous support of that majority or risk being removed from office. If the failure to receive majority support for a bill or action occurs on a normal vote, the head of government might ignore it and move on to other matters. However, if the head of government and the cabinet definitely want the legislation and are willing to force a showdown, they can declare that a vote for or against the bill is a vote of confidence. Only after losing such a vote would a head of government be likely to call for new elections.

Removal of its government from office—usually by a vote of no confidence—would not just be embarrassing for the majority party or coalition; it would also make it difficult for the members of the parliamentary majority to face the voters in a new election resulting from the no-confidence vote and to argue that they should be reelected after their party has shown it does not have the discipline to keep its own government or coalition government in office. Voting against their own government in a vote of confidence is also risky for the dissidents, because they are more likely to be challenged for renomination in the next election. In some cases, however, the dissidents create problems for their parties because of dissatisfaction with government policies by many party members or voters in their constituencies.

Checks and balances. If the head of government emerges from the parliament and has a disciplined and cohesive majority supporting him or her, what checks are there on the executive in a parliamentary system? In Great Britain the monarch cannot remove the prime minister so long as he or she is the leader of the majority party in parliament, and the president of Germany does not have the constitutional authority to remove the chancellor. Only in the semipresidential system of France can the president remove the head of government at will; however, he cannot realistically remove the prime minister if the prime minister has the support of an opposition majority in the National Assembly.

There are, nevertheless, a number of checks on the head of government in a parliamentary system that are both similar and very different in certain ways from the checks found in a presidential system. It has been noted that the prime minister in Great Britain appears to have a great deal of power derived from the fact that he or she is the leader of the majority party, which is highly disciplined and cohesive. What prevents the prime minister, then, from becoming a kind of elected dictator during his or her term of office?

First, the prime minister must retain the support of the majority of the ruling party. This includes the "extraparliamentary party," that is, the party organization outside of parliament organized both at the national level and especially in the individual constituencies, and the "parliamentary party", that is, the members of parliament (MPs) who belong to the party and make up the majority in the House of Commons (often called the "party caucus" in the United States but the "party group" in much of the comparative politics literature). Margaret Thatcher resigned as prime minister in 1990 not because she lost a parliamentary vote of confidence but because she failed to retain sufficient support in her parliamentary party to withstand an internal challenge from members of her own parliamentary party. Tony Blair won three elections as leader of the Labour Party in 1997, 2001, and 2005, but growing opposition to his leadership in both the extraparliamentary party and the parliamentary party led him to announce that he would resign as prime minister in the summer of 2007.

A second important check on the power of the prime minister consists of influential rivals in the cabinet or in the House of Commons. The then popular chancellor of the exchequer, Gordon Brown, who had been identified as the government official most responsible for the overall positive state of the British economy and high employment figures since 1997, had been waiting in the wings for several years for Blair to resign, and some of his followers wanted to see him give Blair a good push. Blair saw a number of his cabinet ministers resign in his last years of office in protest over some of his policies, especially with regard to Iraq. Competition by rivals and resignations of cabinet officials place constraints on the prime minister, because he or she must be careful not to antagonize even more members of the party over controversial policy matters.

Another check, found in most democracies, is the bureaucracy. The British have a tradition of placing top civil servants, who are recruited on the basis of merit, usually from elite universities, in important positions throughout the bureaucracy. These civil servants have the reputation of serving any government loyally, whether they agree philosophically with government policy or not. The cabinet minister who becomes their boss is responsible for the actions of everyone within the ministry, so the loyalty of his civil servants is crucial to his success in the cabinet and in the House of Commons. However, the cabinet ministers are often accused of "going native", that is, of accepting the conventional wisdom of the long-serving civil servants and then resisting to some extent some of the policies of the prime minister or cabinet colleagues that would bring about change opposed by the civil servants. In Germany there is also a tradition of loyalty by civil servants, but top civil servants are usually appointed by the government in order to ensure that government policies will be supported and carried out.

The opposition in parliament, in both Great Britain and Germany, is also a check. Since it has a minority of seats and has little or no ability to influence members of the majority to vote with it, it is limited essentially to criticism of the government in debates on legislation and during question time. This criticism rarely changes the government's initiatives, but it is reported in the media and noted by the attentive public. Debates force the head of government and cabinet ministers to answer publicly sometimes embarrassing or difficult questions on politically sensitive issues. American cabinet secretaries rarely have to respond to criticism by assembled opponents, and the American and French presidential news conferences are hardly comparable to parliamentary question time in Great Britain and Germany in holding the leader's feet to the fire. The opposition might also raise questions in some of the committees that consider government legislation, and the committees might, especially if some of the members of the majority party join in the criticism, have some influence on the government; however, given the general weakness of British committees, especially in comparison to congressional committees in the United States or even Germany, committee influence in Great Britain is usually not an important factor.

In most parliamentary systems, including Germany, a coalition must be formed to create a government. This requires compromise on the part of the parties forming the coalition, and the result might mean that the leaders of the parties involved, including the leader who becomes head of government, might have to promote initiatives that are different from those announced in the party's program during the election campaign. In any case, the formation of a coalition government means that there will be internal checks of one party versus the other(s) not found in a single-party government typical of Great Britain. But even the British had to form a coalition between the Conservatives and Liberal Democrats after the election of May 2010, because no party gained an absolute majority of the seats in the House of Commons.

In Germany, as in the United States, there is a powerful constitutional court that has the right of judicial review, that is, the right to rule on the constitutionality of federal laws and acts of the executive. In France there is a Constitutional Council that may review proposed statutes for conformity with the constitution. It does not, however, have the right of judicial review once a statute has been promulgated. In France as well as in Germany, there is also a well developed system of administrative courts to which citizens can bring complaints against the state. In France appeals from these courts are heard by the Council of State, which is the highest administrative court and also an adviser to the government on draft legislation. In Great Britain, because of the principle of parliamentary sovereignty, no court can rule a law or executive act unconstitutional; however, the executive can be and is checked in certain cases by statutory law. The British, like other members of the European Union and Council of Europe, must also abide by decisions of the high courts of these two organizations.

Every democratic government, whether in a presidential, semipresidential, or parliamentary system, also faces constraints from media criticism, public opinion polls, views of allies as well as actions of enemies, domestic and international economic conditions, divisions within the government, or unforeseen and unpredictable events, such as a major flood that requires the expenditure of funds that were to be used for other purposes. The state of the economy can have a major influence on government plans and policies, sometimes undermining promises made during an election campaign. What appeared to be a period of clear sailing ahead for a party or coalition government after winning an election may, in other words, become an unexpected storm with rough seas.

Indirect election. Unlike the president in a presidential or semipresidential system, neither the head of state nor the head of government is directly elected in a parliamentary system. The head of state in a constitutional monarchy is the hereditary monarch, while this office is usually filled by election by the parliament in a republican parliamentary system. In Germany the head of state is elected by a special college of electors consisting of members of the elected house (*Bundestag*) and an equal number of members of state legislatures.

The head of government in a parliamentary system, for example in Germany, is usually elected by the parliament—but in Great Britain he or she is appointed by the monarch. In the semipresidential system of France, the head of government, the prime minister, is appointed by the president; however, this person must have majority support in the National Assembly.

The head of government is elected by the voters directly only to a seat in the parliament. In Great Britain this means winning a seat in a single-member district or constituency (in which the candidate is not required to live). Needless to say, this tends to be a "safe seat," that is, a district that is safely in the hands of the party with which the head of government is associated, often as the party leader. In France there have been a number of instances when the president appointed a person not elected to parliament (if a member of parliament and appointed, he or she must then resign the seat), such as a top civil servant or former cabinet minister, to be prime minister, but this is possible only when he has majority support in the National Assembly. If the opposition has a majority, the president must appoint an opposition leader.

In Germany there is a more complicated "mixed" electoral system that combines proportional representation (PR) and single-member districts that will be described in more detail in chapter 4. The result is that the chancellor, like other members of parliament, can enter the *Bundestag* either having won a direct seat in a single-member district or as a candidate on a party list. Half of the seats in Germany are distributed on the basis of votes in single-member districts and half through proportional representation, which means in principle that the percentage of the vote equals the percentage of the seats in parliament. In this system candidates win seats either by being placed toward the top of a party list, with the number of seats depending on the proportion of the vote received, or by gaining a majority or plurality of the vote in a constituency or district.

Simply being a member of parliament is not, of course, sufficient for selection as head of government. In Great Britain the monarch selects the person who also leads the majority party. If the prime minister should lose support as majority party leader, as Margaret Thatcher did in 1990, the new party leader—in 1990 John Major—will be appointed prime minister by the monarch. In Germany the *Bundestag* elects the person who is either *the* leader or at least *a* leader of the largest party in the coalition. (Normally the largest party in a parliamentary system becomes the leading party in a coalition government; however, smaller parties might also join together to form a majority coalition without the participation of the largest party.) In France the president may select anyone he wishes, whether a member of parliament or not, as long as he has majority support in the National Assembly; otherwise he must appoint a leader of the party that leads the majority in parliament.

Terms of office. The *heads of state* of most parliamentary democracies, as we have seen, are selected by some means other than by popular election. That is, the presidents of parliamentary republics are usually elected by parliament or, in the case of Germany, by an electoral college, for limited terms of four or five years. On the other hand, some parliamentary democracies are constitutional monarchies. While there is no election of the monarchs, who serve for life or until they relinquish the throne to a son or daughter, on rare occasions there can be problems of succession.

In Japan, for example, there were questions in 2005 and 2006 about the assumption that the successor to the emperor had to be male and, therefore, what to do about the fact that there were two daughters but no direct male heir to the throne. In 2006 a son was born, and the debate was put off until a future date.

The terms of office for parliamentary *heads of government* can vary widely over time. The official term of office for the British prime minister is five years, but the prime minister can ask the monarch to call for new elections at almost any time before the official term has elapsed (this has been changed by the current government, at least until the next elections in May 2015). This is usually done in the fourth year, but it might come in the third or fifth year, depending on the situation. For example, if the prime minister sees that the public opinion polls show his government is generally popular in the fourth year, he or she will be tempted to call for new elections. On the other hand, if the polls are not favorable, the prime minister will probably wait until the end of the five years in the hope that the public will react more favorably to government initiatives or that the economy, for example, will begin to improve. In any case the British prime minister has a considerable advantage over the opposition—and over counterparts in other parliamentary states—because of the ability to chose the time of elections.

In Germany the founders of the Basic Law believed in 1948–49 that the experience of the Weimar Republic after World War I and before Hitler came to office in 1933 suggested that the chancellor should not be able to call for new elections on his own and should not be subject to removal by a vote of no confidence unless a new chancellor is elected at the same time. This "constructive vote of confidence" is unique among parliamentary systems, which normally allow a head of government to be voted out of office without a simultaneous replacement. In most parliamentary systems the rejected head of government remains in office as the head of a "caretaker government" until a new government coalition is formed or new elections are called, which produce a new government. The constructive vote of confidence was designed to address the problem of frequent changes of government and public impatience with resulting new elections and to provide Germany with stable governments that were lacking in the Weimar Republic. As it turned out, instability never became a problem in post–World War II Germany, in large part because of a successful economy but also because of a very different party system, which did not include sizable extreme parties of the left and right that wanted to impose their own views on society.

The normal term of office for the chancellor in Germany is four years. On two occasions, however, elections occurred after three years in spite of the fact that the Basic Law does not give the chancellor the power to call for new elections. As noted above, Chancellor Kohl called for a vote of confidence in 1983, which he lost on purpose. Since the opposition did not have the votes to elect a new chancellor, the president dissolved the *Bundestag* and called for new elections. In 2005 Chancellor Schröder also called for a vote of confidence, which he lost on purpose. Again, the president dissolved the parliament, and new elections were held on September 18, 2005, a year before they were scheduled to take place. The major difference in the results of these two early elections was that Kohl won and Schröder lost; however, the loss suffered by Schröder's SPD was so close that it was able to form a coalition government with the slightly more successful CDU/CSU under Angela Merkel as the new chancellor.

Like the German Weimar Republic, problems of government instability also plagued the French Third and Fourth Republics of 1875–1940 and 1946–58, respectively. In both French republics the majority coalitions were very unstable, usually lasting only about six months, because no single party could ever win a majority of the seats, the parties that formed the coalition governments were not disciplined, and therefore they sometimes voted against their own governments. In addition, some parties were extreme and could not be included in a coalition. Often some ministers in the cabinet who were also leaders of their parties had aspirations of gaining a more important ministerial post or even of becoming premier or prime minister, and therefore they also were willing to have their parties vote against the government in the hope that a new government coalition would be formed that would include them in a more important position. This game of musical chairs disgusted much of the French population and, especially, General Charles de Gaulle.

When de Gaulle was called by parliament in 1958 to lead France at a time of great turmoil caused by the war in Algeria, he created a commission to write a new constitution for a Fifth Republic. This constitution was approved by the electorate in the fall and went into effect on January 1, 1959. It contained a number of provisions designed to correct some of the weaknesses of the previous two constitutions. In the first place, of course, was the transition to a semipresidential from a parliamentary system, which provided for a head of state who would be elected for a seven-year term by an electoral college consisting of local political elites. He would have extensive powers and would appoint the prime minister, who would be accountable to both the president and the National Assembly. It was assumed that the president would have majority support in the parliament. During his first term of office, de Gaulle had the constitution changed to provide for the popular election of the president in 1965. Later the seven-year term was changed to a five-year term to correspond to the electoral cycle of the National Assembly beginning in 2004; however, the elections for the president and National Assembly do not occur on the same day.

The presidential term of office was changed for a number of reasons, but an important one was to reduce the probability that the president would be faced with an opposition majority in the National Assembly and forced to appoint a prime minister who did not in general share the president's views. The resulting "cohabitation" meant in practice that there was a built-in system of checks and balances between the president and prime minister that did not lend itself to cooperation and efficient government. A five-year term for the president that coincides with the election cycle of the National Assembly makes it more likely that the majority of voters who elected the president will also vote into office in the National Assembly candidates who support the president.

Another provision of the Fifth Republic constitution designed to strengthen the cabinet appointed by the prime minister is the rule of incompatibility. According to this rule, members of the cabinet may not be members of the National Assembly. The purpose of the rule is to discourage cabinet ministers from playing the game of musical chairs described above. The rule is one reason, however, why the French system is not a traditional parliamentary system, which typically draws members of the cabinet from the parliament.

The European Union

The EU is not a state, but it has institutions that can be compared to some extent to those of states. Nor is the EU a presidential or a parliamentary political system; rather, it is a unique system that draws on the conventional state models of liberal democracy while also differing from them.

The uniqueness of the EU's institutional structure can be seen in several examples. Before the Lisbon treaty went into effect at the end of 2009, the EU had a presidency consisting not of a person but of a member state (in practice the head of government and his or her cabinet ministers), with a term of six months. The member states rotated in this position by alphabetical order, but the larger EU membership of recent years led to a rotation based on size of population. That is, the state that held the presidency was assisted by both its predecessor and successor, and the rotation schedule was fixed so that one of the three was always a larger state with a larger bureaucratic capability that could be useful in leading the EU. The head of government (but in France, the head of state) of the state that held the presidency was responsible for setting much of the agenda of the EU during the six months of that state's leadership. The head of government's cabinet ministers chaired the decision-making Council of Ministers and other bodies. At the end of the presidency in December and June, respectively, there was a European Summit or meeting of all of the heads of government and some heads of state (e.g., France), called the European Council, which usually made some decisions concerning the agenda of the state holding the presidency.

A European constitution, which was negotiated in 2003 and 2004, proposed numerous changes in institutional arrangements, including, for example, a president elected by the agenda-setting European Council (i.e., heads of government of the member states) who would serve a term of 2½ years for a maximum of two terms. Though approved by either the parliament or voters in more than a dozen member states, the constitution was rejected in referenda in France and the Netherlands in the spring of

2005, thus ending for the time being any progress toward new institutional arrangements for the EU presidency. In December 2007 a Constitutional Reform Treaty (Lisbon treaty) was signed by the heads of government of the EU member states as a substitute for the failed new constitution. The Lisbon treaty was much shorter than the constitution, but it was designed to provide for the key changes contained in the constitution and was therefore thought to be a satisfactory substitute. As a treaty, it could be passed by member state parliaments and did not require a referendum in states like France and the Netherlands. However, in June 2008 voters in Ireland, the only EU member state with a constitutional requirement of a referendum, rejected the treaty, thus creating a new constitutional crisis for the EU, which requires that all member states agree to constitutional changes. A new referendum, which contained some clarifications for Irish voters, was then scheduled for the fall of 2009, and it was passed.

On January 1, 2010, Herman Van Rompuy, a former Belgian prime minister, assumed the newly created office of president of the European Council. He had been nominated by the European Council, which consists of the heads of government and head of state of France, and approved by the European Parliament for a 2½ year term, in accordance with the Lisbon treaty. He replaces the rotating member state presidency of the European Council.

The new president of the European Council will not replace the individual in the EU institutional network who holds the title of president of the EU Commission. This president is elected by the heads of government of the member states for a term of five years, and he participates in the European Council meetings. He is the formal leader of the other commissioners, who are responsible for certain portfolios similar to those found in the cabinet of a state. These include commissioners responsible for agriculture, fisheries, trade, competition, environment, and so forth. The larger states, Great Britain, Germany, France, Italy, and Spain, had two commissioners each, but since 2005 all twenty-five—and since 2007 all twenty-seven—member states have one commissioner. This number will be reduced by 2014, and commissioners will rotate to provide the member states with equal representation on that basis.

The commissioners or directors general of the Commission who are responsible for the various portfolios submit drafts of legislative proposals derived in part from the agenda set at the European Council meetings, now headed by its new president, or by the Council of Ministers, which is headed by a six-month rotating presidency consisting of a member state. Who adopts, modifies, or rejects proposals made by the Commission? The short answer is the European Council of Ministers and the EU Parliament. This process—to be described in more detail later—involves approval by both the Council of Ministers and the Parliament. The Parliament cannot initiate legislation, as its counterparts in states may do (although in practice most national legislation is introduced by government ministers); however, changes in recent years have placed the Parliament increasingly in the position to modify or reject legislation proposed by the Commission and accepted or revised by the Council of Ministers. Under certain circumstances the Council can override objections by the Parliament, but this is done rarely today.

The Council of Ministers, it should be noted, is not just one body of ministers; rather, it consists of various combinations of cabinet ministers, who form subject matter councils such as ministers of agriculture, finance, transportation, and so forth. As noted above, these separate councils are headed by the state that has the presidency of the Council of Ministers on a rotating, six-month basis. In approving proposals by the Commission, the Council of Ministers shares a key legislative function normally associated with parliaments in democratic states.

The Lisbon treaty replaced the commissioner responsible for external relations with a high representative for foreign and security affairs, in effect an EU foreign minister. The UK's Lady Catherine Ashton assumed this position on December 1, 2009, after having been nominated by the European Council and approved by the European Parliament. She heads a European foreign office of about three thousand civil servants, serves as vice president of the European Commission, and chairs the EU General Affairs and External Relations Council, composed of the foreign ministers of the member states. She cannot determine foreign and security policies, because these must gain unanimous approval by the member states. She is, however, the main spokesperson for the EU abroad, and this role together with her role in the Commission may in the future make her the best known and most important person in the EU, together perhaps with the president of the Commission. The new president of the European Council may play a more important role inside the EU, but the new high representative for foreign and security affairs is probably in a stronger position in external representation.

In terms of separation of powers, some of the responsibilities of a head of state and head of government are divided in the EU between the new president of the European Council; the president of the EU Commission; and the president (in this case, a member state) of the Council of Ministers. The European Council sets much of the agenda, and the EU Commission drafts legislative proposals that are accepted, modified, or rejected by the Council of Ministers and the EU Parliament. Voting procedures in the Council of Ministers vary, however, depending on the subject matter, and generally a "qualified majority" (more than just a majority) or even a unanimous vote is required. In other words, minority positions in the Council of Ministers cannot be easily overcome.

It is clear that the complicated decision-making procedure provides for many checks and balances, because a number of institutions and individuals must act in order for legislation to emerge and pass. Once legislation is passed, it must be administered by the bureaucracies of the member states, which sometimes means very uneven administration across the EU. A major responsibility of the EU Commission, therefore, is to check on the quality of administration and, if necessary, take an offending state before the European Court of Justice (ECJ) in order to force compliance. The ECJ, then, is another check on the behavior of the EU member states and the actions of the Commission in carrying out EU regulations.

Conclusion

The two basic types of democratic systems are presidential and parliamentary. A third type that has been adopted by a number of emerging democracies, especially in central and eastern Europe following the collapse of the Soviet empire, is the French model of the "semipresidential system." A fourth type, not discussed here, was the French "government by assembly," which was the characterization of the unstable system of strong parliaments and weak governments found in France during the Third and Fourth Republics of 1875–1940 and 1946–58. It was a system that could be said also to have existed in Italy from 1945 to about 1990.

The presidential model provides for a single national executive, elected directly by the population for a fixed term. The American president is not elected directly, but with some important exceptions (e.g., the presidential election in 2000) the result of the Electoral College vote is usually the same as it would have been in a direct popular election. Another key characteristic is a separation of powers between the executive and legislative branches, which means that the president and legislators are elected separately, that the president cannot dissolve the legislature and call for new elections, and that the legislature cannot remove the president in a vote of confidence. On the other hand, there are certain checks and balances that allow the American president, for example, to veto legislative acts and to nominate and appoint—with Senate approval—federal judges and high-level federal officials. The legislature, again using the United States as an example, can override the president's veto with a two-thirds vote, prevent the president from making important appointments by failing to approve nominees, and refuse to accept part of the president's agenda. The president can, of course, also be checked by decisions of federal courts, especially the Supreme Court, in his exercise of power. Other, less formal checks on the president, such as the state of the economy, the media, public opinion, the views of certain interest groups, and the international environment, can be important factors also in limiting presidential actions.

A parliamentary system has a dual executive, with a clear separation of the office of head of state and head of government. The head of state has largely ceremonial responsibilities as a representative of the state who stands above parties and politics. Americans are most familiar with the British monarch as head of state, but a number of other democracies in Europe, the Middle East, and Asia also have monarchs as nonruling heads of state. In democratic republics, which include most democratic states today, the head of state is usually a president selected by a parliamentary vote, as in Italy, or an electoral college, as in Germany. Presidents are not usually elected directly by the people in parliamentary republics, because a popular election would make the president a partisan figure and would provide him or her with a degree of legitimacy that would compete with the head of government.

Whether elected by a parliamentary majority or appointed by the head of state, the head of government (as well as all or most cabinet members) usually comes from the parliament. In that sense there is no separation of powers in a parliamentary system that is comparable to the presidential system. Even if the head of government is not a member of parliament, which is sometimes the case in a semipresidential system such as that found in France or Russia, that person is not elected by a popular vote. In other words, British Prime Minister David Cameron and German Chancellor Angela Merkel are candidates for popular election only in their individual constituencies. There is no popular vote for a head of government in a parliamentary system.

In most parliamentary systems—but technically not in Germany—the head of government can ask the head of state to dissolve the parliament and call for new elections following a lost vote on an important matter or on a vote of confidence. The parliament, for its part, can also remove the head of government in a vote of no confidence. This might lead to new elections, but it is more likely to lead to the formation of a new coalition government with a new head of government. The parliament, then, is a crucial factor in its role of keeping the head of government in office and, in the process, supporting his or her agenda. This requires disciplined majority support in order to prevent instability. The capture of the legislature by a party not in support of the head of government, as happens frequently in the American presidential system, would not work in a parliamentary system.

The EU is not a state, but it has institutions and enacts policies that are similar in important respects to states. It does not have a head of state or a head of government comparable to either a presidential or parliamentary democracy; however, it has a president of the agenda-setting body, the European Council, composed of the heads of government of the member states; a president of the bureaucratic EU Commission, which also drafts legislation; and a Council of Ministers that, together with the above, performs many of the functions associated with heads of state and government. To complicate matters further, the Council of Ministers as the major decision-making body also performs some of the functions of a legislative body. The EU Parliament debates and votes on issues like the parliament of a state, but it may not propose legislation.

Some observers complain about the EU as suffering from a "democratic deficit." There are a number of reasons for this complaint, including the fact that the EU Parliament is the only popularly elected body; the new president of the European Commission is nominated by the heads of member state governments and approved by the Parliament but not the citizens of the EU; the members of the Council of Ministers come from the elected governments of the member states, but they are not directly responsible to the citizens of the EU; the president of the EU Commission is selected by the heads of government of the member states; and, perhaps most importantly, the EU has become increasingly involved in a wide range of policies concerning normal citizens, policies that in the past were the responsibility of the elected governments and parliaments of the member states.

On the other hand, a parliament is generally also the only elected body in a state with a parliamentary system. The EU Parliament has always had the power to reject the EU budget proposed by the Commission, it has to approve the new president of the European Council and the high representative for foreign and security affairs, and it has been given increased powers vis-à-vis the Commission and Council of Ministers in recent years. It must also approve the nominees for posts in the Commission. In the mid-1990s it took action that led to the resignation of the entire Commission due to charges of nepotism, cronyism, and mismanagement by certain commissioners. One can also make the case that the roles of the elected parliaments of the EU member states have declined throughout much of the past several decades in favor of the powers of governments headed by leaders who usually enjoy the support of a disciplined majority party or coalition in the parliament. Finally, the EU is not a state, and some of the criticism of the EU is based on the premise that it is or should be. But the wish of some leaders and citizens in Europe to see the EU evolve into a more democratic federal state, which they see as the logical conclusion of "ever closer union," is vehemently opposed by other leaders and Euroskeptics in general.

The major structural similarities and differences between presidential and parliamentary systems that have been outlined briefly in this chapter will be discussed in more detail in chapters 7 and 8 below. First, however, chapters 3 through 6 will discuss territorial arrangements, electoral systems, and political party systems, with a special focus on the United States, Britain, France, Germany, and the EU.

Endnotes

[1] Charles Jones, *The Presidency in a Separated System*, 2nd ed. (Washington, DC: Brookings Institution Press, 2005), argues that the United States does not have a presidential system but rather a *separated* system. But he is not talking about the United States from a comparative government perspective; rather he is rebutting the assertion that the American president dominates the political system. He does not offer a generic definition of a presidential system. Nevertheless, his focus on the separation of powers is similar to mine below.

[2] For a good discussion of checks on the French president, see Anne Stevens, *Government and Politics of France*, 3rd ed. (New York: Palgrave Macmillan, 2003), chs. 2 and 3.

[3] One governor, Mills Godwin, served one four-year term as a Democrat and, after an intervening term, another term as a Republican.

For Further Reading

Mayer, Lawrence C. *Comparative Politics: The Quest for Theory and Explanation.* Cornwall-on-Hudson, NY: Sloan Publishing, 2007, 53–64.

Verney, Douglas V. "Parliamentary Government and Presidential Government." Chap. 1 in *Parliamentary Versus Presidential Government.* Edited by Arend Lijphart. Oxford University Press, 1992.

Chapter 3

Territorial Organization

Introduction

The analysis of the institutional structures of all political systems, democratic or not, involves a focus on relationships between and among the branches of government. Examples discussed in chapter 2 as well as in following chapters include the separate election of the president and the legislature in a presidential system, the relations between the head of state and head of government in a parliamentary system, the inability of a president to dissolve a legislature, the right of a parliament to vote on a motion of confidence concerning the head of government, and general checks and balances.

In all political systems, whether democratic or not, there is also a *territorial dimension*; that is, states can organize their territory according to three general categories: unitary, confederal, or federal. In a unitary state the central government is *the* government of the country. There may be regional administrative organizations that carry out central government policies or supervise local governments in their implementation of national policy, but regional administrative units and local governments operate under laws passed by the central legislative bodies and answer to central executive branch agencies. In the diagram below, one can see that there is a direct relationship between the people and the central government, just as there is also a direct relationship between the people and local governments.

It may be tempting to assume that unitary systems are nondemocratic, but this is not the case. It is true that in practice a nondemocratic regime will centralize power regardless of any decentralizing language in the constitution; however, most of the world's democracies, including Western liberal democracies, are unitary states.

A confederation consists of a central government, but one that is more or less dependent on regional governments such as provinces or subnational states. These regional governments have a considerable amount of autonomy and can control even the national political agenda to a large extent. The national government is usually in charge of foreign affairs and defense, and it encourages through its national policies economic cooperation; however, even these areas may be limited to some extent by the actions of the regional governments. Cooperation and unity of purpose may exist to a considerable extent, but in the final analysis the regional units have the last word on many key issues, that is, they are largely sovereign entities. The diagram below shows that there is a direct relationship between the central government and the regional governments but only an indirect relationship between the central government on the one hand and local governments and the people on the other hand.[1] The United States was organized as a confederation between 1777 and 1789, as was most of the South from 1861 to 1865. However, because of the inherent weakness of a confederation, no state at the present time is organized as such. Switzerland may come close in some respects, but it is still classified as a strong federation. After the demise of the Soviet Union in 1991, the Commonwealth of Independent States (CIS) was formed by eleven of the fifteen former Soviet "republics" as a loose confederation, but it was not successful in meeting minimal expectations. While the European Union, which will be discussed below, is not a state, it does have many features of a confederation—and, for that matter, a federation.

A federation can be seen as a complicated compromise between a unitary state and a confederation. There is a strong central government, but it is limited by the constitution to certain powers that it carries out on its own, such as foreign affairs, defense, the regulation of commerce throughout the federal territory, and the protection of certain basic rights common to all citizens; it shares some powers with the regional governments (states, provinces, *Länder*, cantons), and some powers are carried out alone by the regional governments, e.g., regulation of local governments, schools, streets and local infrastructure, and local/regional planning. As seen in the diagram below, in a federation there is a direct relationship between the central government and the more or less autonomous (but not sovereign) regional governments *and* a direct relationship between the central government, local governments, and the people.

Figure 3.1

Territorial Organization of States

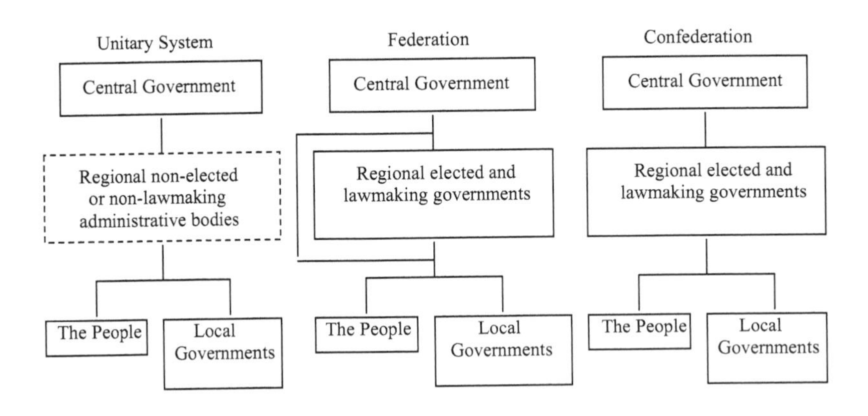

Federations and confederations are more likely to be found in certain kinds of states. One common example is multiethnic states in which the population speaks two or more languages and is generally concentrated in specific regions. Good examples would be Russia today, which has about a hundred different ethnic groups and is divided into eighty-nine "subject" territories; India, which is divided by language and religion (Hindu and Muslim); and Canada, with its English- and French-speaking populations, the latter of which are concentrated in the province of Quebec. Most federal states with very diverse populations are large in geographical size, but there are exceptions, such as Switzerland, a very small country with four language groups generally divided into cantons, or Belgium, with two major language groups. That ethnic tensions can overwhelm federal structures and procedures designed to foster unity can be seen in the failed federation of Yugoslavia, which collapsed when civil war broke out in the early 1990s. The Soviet Union was also a federation before it broke into fifteen separate, independent states in 1991; however, federalism in the USSR was a mere facade for the actual rule of a centralized state that was completely penetrated by a highly centralized and disciplined communist party.

Other states have become federations because of history. Certainly the United States is an example, because the original thirteen states would never have agreed to be subsumed under a central government in a unitary system and lose the autonomy to which they had become accustomed. It also makes sense for the United States, like Australia, Canada, Brazil, and Russia, to be a federation because of its large geographical size. Washington, DC, is too far removed from the various regions and localities to govern efficiently and effectively by a policy of "one size fits all."

History is also the major explanation for federalism in Germany. Outside of Europe, Germany is not a large country, and it does not have serious ethnic and religious divisions, at least not today. But there is a very long history of fragmentation of German-speaking territories going back to the Holy Roman Empire, with a tradition of independence and self-government under a variety of kings, princes, dukes, bishops, and, in some cities, of local merchants and guilds.

Unitary States

Great Britain and France are good examples of centralized democratic unitary states, although less so today than in the past. In Great Britain, Parliament is sovereign and therefore ultimately responsible for all lawmaking, including passing laws under which local governments ("local authorities") operate. The British "Quangos" (quasi-autonomous nongovernmental organizations), "appointed bodies which carry out public functions, ranging from major executive bodies such as the Arts Council to small advisory groups such as the Expert Advisory Group on AIDS,"[2] may have assumed many responsibilities and act with a considerable degree of autonomy, but they can be disbanded or reformed at any time by Parliament. In 1997 referenda in Scotland and Wales led to *devolution*, that is, the transfer of a number of responsibilities, such as local government and education, to elected assemblies in these two regions in Britain. In Northern Ireland, in contrast, the continuing tensions between the large Catholic minority and the Protestant majority have interfered with and even prevented the application of real self-government. In any case, though devolution in Scotland and Wales has brought about considerable decentralization in the British unitary state, the Parliament retains the legal right to change the conditions of devolution at any time; that is, devolution does not enjoy constitutional protection.

France has a long tradition of highly centralized government. The monarchy that was deposed by the French Revolution in 1789 was one whose bureaucracy in the provinces had penetrated the entire state to carry out the king's policies loyally and effectively. During the nineteenth and much of the twentieth century, the revolutionary principles of "liberty, equality, and fraternity" were seen to require the same laws and enforcement procedures throughout the state. The state was divided into departments (*départements*), which are regional administrative units somewhat comparable to many American counties in geographical size, headed by a prefect (*préfet*) after a Napoleonic reform in 1820. The prefect implemented central government policies and supervised those carried out by local governments. The local governments, or *communes*, and especially departments, were seen more as administrative than as self-governing units. In spite of a departmental assembly—elected after 1871—and executive council, "the prefect still wielded the full power of the state."[3] The anecdote that the French minister of education could tell a visiting foreign delegation on what day and time the rigorous national high school (*lycée*) qualifying exam would be held in every school in the country and which question the students would be answering at 11:15 a.m. may have been an exaggeration, but it served to demonstrate the control central ministries had—or were reputed to have—over their domestic activities throughout the land.

In the decades before 1982, the elected general council of the departments gained some powers, but the prefect still had to approve the decisions taken, and he still prepared and implemented the budget, even though he often had to reach compromises with the general council. In 1982 and 1983 the president, François Mitterrand, and the government he appointed, pushed through the National Assembly and implemented reform legislation that began a process of decentralization. These reforms established a three-tier system of subnational units: the *communes* and *départements* that already existed and the new regions. The departments now number ninety-six, excluding the four overseas departments. The reforms transferred the most important powers of the prefect to the chair of the general assembly of the department, and they transferred powers to the *communes*, thus increasing the power and influence of mayors, but they failed to provide for a fiscal reform or increased popular participation.[4] More obviously, they failed to rationalize the more than thirty-six thousand local governments, while in other European states, including Great Britain and Germany, significant and wide-reaching territorial reforms of local units occurred in the 1970s.[5] In preserving the *communes*, the term used for all local governments of any size, they mollified the local *notables* (local elites), but the problems of small size, insufficient administrative capability, and inability to deal with many local social and economic problems were left unresolved. However, in 1999 legislation was passed that was designed to encourage joint projects among *communes* and that created new territorial designations—*agglomerations* and *pays*, terms now used for various cooperative arrangements.[6]

At the same time that central state powers were decentralized by increasing the competencies of the general councils in the department and the mayors in the communes, the reforms of 1982 and 1983 also brought about some deconcentration, that is, a transfer to the prefects of some additional authority for remaining central state functions. Thus the prefect now heads in his or her department a number of social services of the ministries and remains a powerful and influential figure in the department.[7] He or she is also the government's public relations officer in the department and is responsible for public order.

The regions, of which there are now twenty-two, are made up of several departments headed by the chairperson (*président*) of the regional council. But the departmental prefect is the government's representative at the subnational level. The regional *président* is responsible above all for coordination in the implementation of national policies and for planning. He or she is in effect the representative of the European Union in the region, in part via membership in the EU's Council of Regions, and is responsible for applying for and administering EU funds; the chairperson is a problem solver and mediator in the region. On the other hand, the departmental prefect is responsible for the local implementation of national and EU policies.[8]

While Great Britain and France are still classified as unitary states, it is clear that in recent decades both states have become more decentralized in different ways. The UK has devolved a number of important competencies to Scotland, Wales and Northern Ireland, all of which now have their own regional parliaments. The French have created regions made up of the ninety-six departments, and both administrative units have been given certain competencies by the central government. However, France remains a more centralized state than the UK. Anything approaching federalism, like British devolution of competencies to Scotland, for example, would not be acceptable to the French, because of the strong tradition in the country favoring equal treatment and uniformity in the application of important policies.[9]

Federal States

In contrast to Great Britain and France, the United States and Germany are federations. The United States has been a federation since its inception in 1789. The founding fathers in Philadelphia were made up of delegates from thirteen largely independent states that had formed a confederation in 1777 in their struggle for independence from Great Britain. But it was in large part because of several serious institutional weaknesses in the provisions of the Articles of Confederation that the founding fathers decided in 1787 that a new constitutional order was required. From their own experience, they had the British unitary model and the American model of confederation to draw on. Indeed, the American territorial organization that emerged can be seen as a compromise between the British unitary state and the Articles of Confederation of 1777–89. However, the *Federalist Papers*, written by Alexander Hamilton, James Madison, and John Jay, show clearly the influence of the writings of Locke, Montesquieu, Hume, Hobbes, and other philosophers as well as the history of Greece and Rome in their thinking.

The result was the first *federal* system of territorial organization that provided not only for a *division of powers* or responsibilities between the central (or national or federal) government and the state governments but also a system of presidential government that established an institutional *separation of powers.* In general terms, the federal government is responsible for foreign affairs, defense, interstate commerce, and "all Laws which shall be necessary and proper for carrying into Execution the foregoing Powers [those listed in Article I, Section 8] and all other Powers vested by this Constitution in the Government of the United States or in any Department or Officer thereof." A problem in the American federal system, however, can be seen in differences in the interpretation of just what powers the interstate commerce clause, the necessary and proper clause, and other provisions of the Constitution give the federal government and which powers are to be retained or given to the states. The answers to these questions have emerged over the decades and have depended on the time, circumstances, and, of course, the individual interpretations of members of the executive branch (e.g., Franklin D. Roosevelt), the Congress, and, especially, the Supreme Court. During some periods of history, such as in the decades between about 1937 and 1990, the Supreme Court has generally had an expansive or more liberal view of federal powers, whereas before the New Deal and since about 1990, the Supreme Court has generally taken a more restrictive or conservative stance that has included more sympathy for states' rights.

German federalism differs in some key respects from the American model. For many centuries, hundreds of territories made up the Holy

Roman Empire in central and southern Europe. In 1789, the year of the French Revolution and the beginning of the United States under its current constitution, the German Empire, including Austria, consisted of 314 secular and church territories and "free" cities as well as almost fifteen hundred special knightly estates, which enjoyed a measure of autonomy from higher authority.[10] Under the pressure of Napoleon, the Holy Roman Empire ceased to exist in 1806. By 1815 what was the old Holy Roman Empire consisted of a German Confederation of thirty-nine states, excluding the eastern territories of Prussia and Austria. In 1866 the German Confederation was dissolved, and in 1867 the North German Federation was formed. It included all but the four south German states and Austria.

Germany did not become a "nation-state" until the states in the North German Federation and the four south German states, again without Austria, joined in 1871 following the victory of these states in the Franco-Prussian War under the leadership of Prussia. The new Germany was formed as a federation of twenty-five states, but, unlike the United States, one state, Prussia, had a large majority of the population and territory of the new country. As a result, of course, it played a dominant role in the formation and development of Germany until World War I, as can be seen by the fact that the head of state in Germany, the kaiser, was the king of Prussia, and the chancellor of Germany was the prime minister of Prussia. However, the other states in the new federation did retain some autonomy, which was reflected in the second legislative chamber, the *Bundesrat*, which represented the *governments* of the subnational units. These were "states" until they became *Länder* after World War I. The German federation until 1918 was not, however, a liberal democracy. Its parliament, the *Reichstag*, was elected by universal male suffrage, but the Kaiser's powers regarding foreign and defense matters were not subject to sufficient political checks, and he could retain a head of government of his choice even without parliamentary support. In other words, the first German state was a federation but, at best, an electoral democracy with a strong monarch as head of state.[11]

After World War I, Germany became a parliamentary democracy. It remained a federation, but the federal features were weakened in order to provide the central government with the powers and authority deemed necessary at the time to deal with the numerous and serious crises facing the country. There was only a brief transition of "normalcy" between the devastating inflation of the early 1920s and the disastrous depression after 1930. These developments were in large part responsible for the rise of the National Socialists under Hitler, who became chancellor and then dictator in 1933. Hitler's rise to office was also the end of German federalism.

After World War II, a new constitution, the Basic Law, was introduced in 1949. It provided for a new federal system and a parliamentary democracy. In accordance with the pre-Hitler German tradition, two legislative chambers were established: a popularly elected parliament, the *Bundestag*, and a second chamber representing the *Länder* (states). Unlike the popularly elected U.S. Senate, however, the elected *Land* governments send their delegations to the *Bundesrat*. This body approved about 60 percent of all legislation until September 2006, when reforms were introduced that are designed to reduce this figure to about 35 to 40 percent. Even with the reforms, however, the *Land* governments, and especially the individual prime ministers of the *Länder*, have an important voice in national legislation. A major reason for the role played by the *Land* governments is the German tradition of division of powers. The division between the national and state governments in the United States and Germany can be seen in both countries in the separately elected officials, administrations, legislatures, and courts; however, the division of responsibilities is quite different. In the United States, the national government has its own separate administration or bureaucracy, its own laws, and its own taxes to pay for its activities. In Germany the federation, that is, the national cabinet and parliament, is responsible for most legislation, while the *Länder* are responsible for most of the administration of laws. The *Länder* and their local governments have very little authority to raise taxes on their own. Instead, they share taxes distributed by national laws that, however, must be approved by the *Bundesrat*, which represents the *Land* governments. In other words, the *Länder* usually participate in the making of federal laws, but they do not control the process. Thus, when Americans speak of "dual federalism," they mean that the national government has its areas of responsibilities and the states have theirs; each level is generally autonomous of the other. In Germany, however, dual federalism means in general legislation at the federal level and administration at the *Land* level. One result of this difference, along with other factors, is that some observers suggest that Germany has a *unitary federal system* in which the *Länder* may be important units but far less autonomous than, for example, American states.

The European Union

Though not a "state," the EU comes closer to being a state than any other international organization. It has a number of characteristics that we identify with states, such as executive, legislative, and judicial institutions; it carries out certain policies normally associated with states, such as a common agricultural policy and a common trade policy; it has a common currency, the Euro, that has been adopted by seventeen of the twenty-seven member states; and it has to a considerable extent—but with some important exceptions—common foreign and security policies. In other words, the member states of the EU share a good deal of their sovereignty, because they recognize that especially in a globalized world more uniform decision making is desirable and even necessary to compete and protect European interests. Nevertheless, they often disagree among themselves about how much more of their sovereignty to grant to central institutions in Brussels, and all of the EU member states are wary in varying degrees even if generally supportive of the regulatory reach of the EU.

So what is the EU? Is it a nonstate confederation or federation? Or something in between? The somewhat unsatisfactory answer is that it is a unique international organization *with a territory* that has both confederal and federal features that, taken together, are without parallel in history. It is far more than a conventional trading bloc, such as the North American Free Trade Association (NAFTA), because it enacts policies administered by the EU member states, and many of these policies go beyond trade relations; it includes an elective body (the EU parliament); it has a council of heads of government led by the newly created position of president; it has a council of ministers as well as a commission with a sizeable bureaucracy; and it has a high court that not only interprets the laws passed by EU institutions but also requires member states and their courts to abide by EU decisions. One could argue, then, that it is at least a confederation of twenty-seven European states. The member states retain some of their sovereignty and share the rest; and decisions of the EU do not apply directly to citizens of the EU but only to them through the institutions of the member states. But it is more than a confederation in the extent to which the central institutions pass legislation and write regulations that account for more than one-half of the domestic total legislation of the member states. It is more like a federation in the extent of its legislative rules and the regulation of foreign and internal trade, environmental issues, human rights, education, a common currency, and other important matters. However, as noted above, it does not act directly on the citizens of the EU, and direct action is a characteristic of a federation. It is less than either a confederation or a federation in its inability to act in unison in certain "domestic arenas," such as immigration policy, and especially in foreign and defense affairs, in spite of the fact that a common foreign and security policy is a major goal of the EU. This is not to deny that on most issues there is something approaching a common foreign and security policy; however, the responses to the conflicts in the former Yugoslavia during the 1990s, the American invasion of Iraq in 2003, and actions taken against Libya in 2011 demonstrated that there are limits to EU unity in matters that the member states see as affecting directly their vital national interests.

One might be tempted to see the EU as a kind of revived Holy Roman Empire. Many of the member states that comprise the EU today were at various times parts of the hundreds of political units that made up the empire. The empire, however, was also a unique combination of states and state-like entities different in key respects from the EU. The generally small territories provided the actual government over their subjects, but the rulers were not sovereign and enjoyed their power only as a part of the empire and in alliance with the emperor. The emperor ruled through the "princes," who in turn ruled through the lesser nobility. In the imperial cities, small groups of oligarchs, usually from the guilds, were in charge. There was no capital city, and the emperor traveled from place to place with his entourage to demonstrate his authority. His territorial base consisted of his own lands, over which he ruled directly. By the end of the fifteenth century, the lack of imperial territory meant that only an emperor with extensive holdings could afford to accept the crown. Thus the Austrian Habsburg line became the dynastic rulers, even though some of the Austrian domains were not in the empire. By 1500 the empire was a patchwork of dynastic and ecclesiastical territories and free cities organized in a *Reichstag*, which was equal to the emperor and consisted of three chambers representing different sets of rulers and their territories. There was also an imperial court to resolve differences among the entities of the empire.

The emperor and central institutions were relatively weak, however, and unable to prevent conflicts and even war within the empire. The Reformation served to strengthen the territorial princes even further, as could be seen especially in the decision of the Augsburg *Reichstag* of 1555, which gave the princes the right to decide which religion their subjects would embrace. The Thirty Years' War of 1618–48 represented the greatest failure of the empire to enforce internal peace, and after 1648 the empire, though not irrelevant, became more of a loose alliance of increasingly independent-minded territories, which were dominated by absolute monarchies. The war between Prussia and Austria in 1740 and the Seven Years' War between Prussia and Austria and their respective allies from 1756 to 1763 (in the American colonies, known as the "French and Indian War"), were serious blows to the cohesiveness of the empire, but the French Revolution and the wars that resulted between the empire and France led to the final demise of the empire in 1806.[12]

Some scholars have argued that the empire after 1648 was severely weakened and of relatively little significance. Others, however, have noted that the empire possessed a "grandiose historical mystique" as a "living and legitimate successor of the ancient western and Christian Roman Empire as renewed by Charlemagne and his successors."[13] This "mystique" is undoubtedly one of the strengths of the EU, as can be seen especially in the idealism of the founders after World War II and in the general enthusiasm today of the eastern and southern European states in their efforts to become members of the EU.

Setting aside the crucial fact that the EU is not a state, it is interesting to compare it with the two federations discussed in this book, the United States and Germany, in which case one can see immediate parallels as well as significant differences. Similarities include the division of powers or responsibilities between central and regional institutions (American states, German *Länder*, and EU member states). In each case each level has important powers, and there is continuing controversy over the appropriate amount of power each level should exercise. In all three political systems, there is a high court that rules on such controversies, and in each system the high court has generally promoted the powers of the central authorities. Indeed, there are a number of parallels between the American Supreme Court and the European Court of Justice in overturning certain policies and actions of the member states in a process of increasing unity and integration.

While American states have always enjoyed a considerable amount of autonomy, they were never entirely sovereign. Some of the *Länder*, e.g., Bavaria, Hamburg, and Saxony, were sovereign—at least until German unification in 1871, when they became parts of the new German federal state. On the other hand, most German *Länder* today emerged after World War II as former Prussian provinces or parts of former states. In contrast, all of the member states of the EU were and still are sovereign, in spite of the many powers that are now shared by these states.

Another important difference is language and culture. Though a country of immigrants, the United States has seen English become the first language of the vast majority of the population. Americans also had a tradition of local self-government, a relatively open social and political class system, and shared common moral values derived mostly from Protestant Christianity.[14] Since the Civil War, American federalism, with the exception of racial attitudes before the 1970s, has not been subject to some of the highly divisive regional conditions that have plagued a number of other federal states with strong language and cultural divisions. Such divisions, of course, exist in the multilanguage EU; however, the role of English as a common language of European elites and youth and the weakening of nationalism as a result of World War II, close economic ties, widespread travel, study abroad, and other factors have reduced the effects of language, religion, and other cultural divisions.

There are more parallels to the EU in German history than in the American experience. In 1871 twenty-five formerly sovereign states joined together to form the Bismarck Reich. The new state, a federation, had a common language—if one ignores the numerous dialects that competed with the "official" high German—and a diverse but still largely common culture. It was, however, divided by regional differences, including the Catholic West and South and the Protestant North and East. The German Confederation of 1815 and the Customs Union of 1834 promoted a limited degree of cooperation among the dozens of German states, including Austria, but did not prevent a brief war in 1866 between Prussia and Austria and its allies, which Prussia won. The federation formed by Bismarck, first in 1867, then in 1871, provided for a division of power but not for a democracy. A parliamentary system was formed under the rule of law with a parliament (*Reichstag*) elected by universal male suffrage, but it was not a liberal democracy. The kaiser remained a kind of absolute monarch in the areas of defense and foreign affairs and appointed a head of government (chancellor) who was not accountable to the *Reichstag*. The Federal Republic of Germany, formed in 1949, stands in sharp contrast to the Bismarck Reich in that dialects are less important than in 1871, Protestant-Catholic tensions have been sharply reduced in a much more secular society, regional differences have declined, and, most importantly, the current political system is not only a federation but also a liberal democracy.

The EU was founded in 1957 (Treaty of Rome) by six states (France, Germany, Italy, the Netherlands, Belgium, and Luxembourg). In 1973, 1980, 1986, and 1995, nine other European states joined. In 2004 ten central and eastern European states joined, and Bulgaria and Romania joined in 2007. Negotiations over Turkish membership (projected to last about ten years) began in the fall of 2005, but Turkish membership is highly controversial. In the meantime Croatia's application is under review, and its Balkan neighbors have expressed an interest in becoming members. Iceland is also in the process of applying for membership. In order to qualify for negotiations for membership, each state had to be recognized as being a liberal democracy with a free market economy and agree to accept the tens of thousands of pages of EU regulations. Most, but not all, members of the EU are also members of NATO; all are members of the Council of Europe, an organization of forty-seven states concerned above all with human rights and "low politics," such as education, culture, and transborder cooperation on numerous issues. All EU member states have a Judeo-Christian (Roman Catholic, Protestant, Greek Orthodox) heritage, although religion has never been a formal criterion for membership.

Controversy over Turkey's application for membership revolves around both official and unofficial criteria: liberal democratic, European, and Christian. Turkey can make a good case, but not one convincing to everyone, that it is or is quite far along toward becoming a liberal democracy; it can argue that if not traditionally a part of Europe, it has been oriented toward Europe since World War I and is a member of NATO; while generally poorer than most other EU states, it has experienced impressive economic growth in recent years; and it is clear that Turkey is a generally secular state, even though its population is mostly Muslim. Thus Turkey offers Muslims in a number of neighboring states an attractive alternative to anti-Western Islamic governments like that of Iran. But Turkey has a large and growing population of more than seventy million, not all of which favors a secular European-oriented democracy, and it would be the largest state in the EU if admitted, probably at the earliest in 2016. Needless to say, whether the EU can admit and integrate Turkey in spite of significant popular opposition in the current EU member states and general concerns about its impact on the traditional culture, institutions, and policies of the EU will remain a major and divisive question for many years.

Conclusion

In our discussion of presidential and parliamentary systems, we could see that these are very broad categories and that many differences, some far-reaching and others rather minor, exist within each general system, in spite of certain basic common features. In looking at unitary and federal systems—there are no states organized as confederations at the present time—we can also see considerable variation within each category. Unitary systems differ in the amount of decentralization and deconcentration they provide. Great Britain and France are now far more decentralized than they were two or three decades ago, and increasing decentralization seems to be a general trend among democratic states. Federal systems also vary dramatically in the actual powers the national and regional levels exercise. The ethnic composition of the federal state, the geographic size of the country, and history and tradition are all important factors in understanding the differences among federations. Another difference today is the degree to which the federal state has assumed the many social responsibilities of the welfare state. Because the welfare state is based in large part on the concept of equality, there is great pressure in such a state to coordinate policies and procedures with national legislation and to pay for them with nationally imposed taxes. Differences based on separate regions become difficult to accept, given the idea of a national, rather than a regional, citizenship and the demand for equal protection and services. Other challenges, especially in federal states less economically developed than Western federations such as the United States and Germany, seem to be arising more in the form of ethnic and religious differences among the citizens inhabiting various parts of the country. In any case, the welfare state and ethnic and religious tensions will continue to challenge the twenty to twenty-five federations in the world today.

Though not a state, the EU is responsible for many activities and policies normally associated with states. "Ever closer union," the goal repeated in the Treaty of European Union (Maastricht treaty of 1991), means to many Europeans a nonstate political system becoming increasingly more like a federal state. The so-called Euroskeptics, who are especially strong in Great Britain and Denmark, but are found as a minority throughout the EU, reject this goal and even see federalism as a dirty word. They prefer a Europe focused on a free market and a common trading policy that would preserve the sovereignty of the member states rather than promote more integration. They generally favor a larger membership, not only in order to enlarge the common market, but also because more members make political integration more difficult. They do not even favor a confederation and would be perfectly happy with an EU more like the NAFTA that serves merely to promote trade between Canada, the United States, and Mexico.

Endnotes

[1] Wilfried Swenden provides a formal definition of a confederation in his book *Federalism and Regionalism in Western Europe: A Comparative and Thematic Analysis* (New York: Palgrave Macmillan, 2006), 13: "Compared with a federation, a confederation provides for a stronger position of the compounded entities. First, the entitites that form a confederal arrangement retain their character as *sovereign states*. Second, in contrast with federal structures, confederations do not rule out the unilateral exit or secession of one or several of the federated entities. Third, confederal centres do not act directly upon the people, but prescribe the consent of the political institutions of the confederal entities first (for instance the member-state legislatures or their populations). Finally, decisions of the centre require the consent of *all* the states. Hence, the principle of unanimity fully applies."

[2] Tony Wright, ed., *The British Political Process: An Introduction* (London and New York: Routledge, 2000), 277.

[3] Olivier Philip, *The Prefet (1)*, www.ambafrance-us.org/atoz/prefet.asp.

[4] Ibid. and Anne Sa'adah, *Contemporary France: A Democratic Education* (New York: Rowman & Littlefield, 2003), 214.

[5] See Arthur B. Gunlicks, *Local Government Reform and Reorganization* (Port Washington, NY: Kennikat Press, 1980).

[6] Sa'adah, *Contemporary France*, 214

[7] Anne Stevens, *Government and Politics of France*, 3rd ed. (New York: Palgrave Macmillan, 2003), 145–47, 155–58.

[8] Ibid., ch. 6.

[9] Ibid.; Philip, *The Prefet*.

[10] Franz-Ludwig Knemeyer, *Regierungs- und Verwaltungsreformen in Deutschland zu Beginn des 19. Jahrhunderts* (Cologne: Grote'sche Buchhandlung, 1970), 21.

[11] For a discussion of the origins of German federalism, see Arthur B. Gunlicks, *The Länder and German federalism* (Manchester and New York: Manchester University Press, 2003), Chapter 1.

[12] Ibid.

[13] Quoted from John G. Gagliardo, *Reich and Nation: The Holy Roman Empire as Idea and Reality, 1763-1806* (Bloomington: Indiana University Press, 1980), p. vii.

[14] Larry Siedentop, *Democracy in Europe* (New York: Columbia University Press, 2001), pp. 9-14; see also Samuel P. Huntingon, *Who Are We? The Challenges to America's National Identity* (New York: Simon and Schuster, 2004), Foreword.

Chapter 4

Elections and Electoral Systems

Introduction: Electoral Systems

Elections are the most important means by which democratic governments secure their legitimacy, i.e., public acceptance of their right to rule for a limited time. In fact, however, elections alone are not necessarily proof that a state is democratic. They must be free, guaranteeing freedom of speech, press, and assembly; fair, providing opposing candidates with real opportunities to compete and win seats without manipulation by the government or by certain groups; and they must take place on a regular basis. In chapter 1 we distinguished between liberal and "electoral" democracies, the latter sometimes also referred to as "transitional" or "emerging" democracies. The distinction is between states that have free, fair, and regular elections and those that have elections that do not meet liberal democratic standards.

There are, however, almost as many ways of electing candidates as there are democratic states. There is no consensus on which method is more or less democratic, in part because different electoral systems have different goals. These goals may include, first of all, "one person, one vote," which is common among electoral systems; fairness in the sense that all or most votes count and are not wasted; simplicity, that is, that the system is easily understood; or they may be designed to encourage a two-party system or a multiparty system. According to a major study, there are three main families of electoral systems around the world: plurality-majority systems, proportional representation (PR) systems, and semi-PR systems.[1] Variations of each system result in electoral procedures that are sometimes very different even in neighboring liberal democracies

The United States has been an exception among democratic states in that it has always had a two-party system with an occasional third party emerging for a brief period but then fading away because some of its main positions were adopted in one form or another by one of the two large parties or the issue that was its primary focus receded into the background. The two-party system, however, is found more at the national and state levels than at the local level, where, because of local election laws, many or most candidates for local office are "independents" elected in nonpartisan elections. It is also the case that many regions of the United States are dominated by one party.

We have seen that the British Westminster system is based in large part on one party's gaining an absolute majority of seats in the House of Commons, which makes it possible to form single-party government in the UK. While there may be three or more parties that win seats, only two parties, the Conservative and the Labour parties, are able to gain a majority by themselves. On the other hand, all continental European democracies have multiparty systems that usually require coalitions of two or more parties to form a government with a majority of seats in parliament. In the EU Parliament there are also numerous party groups, and two of these are much larger than the others; however, parties in the EU Parliament do not form a "government," which is a major difference between it and parliaments in the EU member states.

Why is there a two-party system in the United States and, in terms of forming governments, in Great Britain? (Following the parliamentary elections of 2010, the Conservative and Liberal Democratic parties formed a very rare coalition government.) Why do all of the continental European states, including Germany and France, have multiparty systems?

There are a number of reasons why a few democratic states have two-party systems but most have multiple parties. Some of these reasons have to do with religious and ethnic minority populations, strong regional differences, ideological divisions, history, and, at least in the United States, separation of powers. The most important reason in most states, however, is the electoral system.[2] That there is a wide variety of electoral systems is demonstrated clearly when we look at our four liberal democracies and the EU. Indeed, it is demonstrated when we look at the different electoral systems found just in the UK.

Elections in the United States

The United States holds general elections on the first Tuesday after the first Monday in November with a *single-member district, single-ballot, plurality electoral system.* This means that candidates for office at the national and state levels are elected in single-member districts, and that the candidate with the most votes, or a plurality (simple majority), not necessarily an absolute majority, wins the seat. This is called a winner-take-all system. The number of districts for state legislatures and the US House of Representatives depends on the number of seats. For the House of Representatives, the 435 seats are distributed among the states on the basis of population. Thus California has fifty-three seats while Wyoming has only one. For the Senate, in contrast, each state has two seats regardless of population, and the entire state is the electoral district.

Because of this "winner-take-all" system, a premium is placed on getting the most votes. This requires the nomination of a candidate who can appeal to the broadest cross-section of voters in the district, and it means that candidates that are identified with minorities, whether they be racial, ethnic, regional, economic, partisan, or ideological, have less chance of being elected. If they want to ensure that their views or interests will be represented, they must either join forces against the dominant candidate to improve their chances of defeating him or her or somehow cooperate with the dominant candidate. There is no hope for direct representation so long as the various opposition groups are fragmented. They could, of course, give up and become a part of the candidate's voting coalition, which in effect would mean becoming supporters of the candidate's political party, since independent candidates have little or no chance of being elected at the national and state levels. But one party and its candidate cannot realistically represent all interests in a district, and so those that are not represented must support an alternative party. It is clear, then, that the American electoral system strongly encourages a two-party system in spite of the many divisions in society that could be bases of a multiparty system.

This electoral system can result in some serious distortions of actual voting support. Let us take as an example a state with ten congressional districts in which the Republicans and Democrats are divided overall at 48 percent Republican, 47 percent Democratic, and 5 percent other. Let us assume that the votes in each district are distributed in such a way that the above distribution is reflected in the actual election results in each district. The result would be ten seats for the Republicans and none for the Democrats. This does not happen in reality, because voter preferences are not evenly distributed across district lines, but there are in fact many outcomes that are highly unsatisfactory from the perspective of electoral fairness and the principle of equality.

Another example of inequality was the sizeable difference in the population numbers that existed in rural and urban districts in many states until the 1960s, when the Supreme Court ruled that congressional and state legislative districts had to have close to equal populations. This meant that some districts with small populations had the same representation as districts with large populations. This is called malapportionment. Today only very small differences in population are allowed, which can make the drawing of district boundaries even more complicated than would be the case otherwise.

The problem today is not malapportionment, but rather maldistricting or "gerrymandering." State legislatures are responsible for drawing the boundaries of election districts for both state and congressional districts, and, with the aid of computers, legislative majorities in most states in recent years have drawn the boundaries in such a way that one party has an advantage over the other. For example, we might find that in a large metropolitan area one district in the center of the city has been created with an overwhelming majority of poor (mostly Democratic) voters, while two surrounding urban districts have a slight majority of more affluent (mostly Republican) populations. All three districts would be "safe" for the incumbents, who could focus attention on their voters and ignore the others. On the other hand, if the boundaries were drawn in such a way that the populations were mixed, all three districts might be competitive, with candidates being required to appeal to a broader cross-section of racial and economic groups in order to win more support. In almost all states, districts are drawn to make them safe for incumbents who represent particular populations, thereby producing safe districts in which there is little or no prospect of serious opposition in any election. The result is that about 95 percent of the seats in the US House of Representatives are safe seats with very little turnover (except in special circumstances, such as a scandal involving the incumbent or "wave" elections—see below). Competitive races are usually found only when a seat is "open," i.e., when there is no incumbent running for reelection. At least two-thirds of Senate seats are safe seats, because the state as a whole tends to be Republican or Democratic; again, however, open seats are usually more competitive. (Sometimes, however, as noted above, "wave" elections may change normal calculations because of widespread dissatisfaction with the candidate or party that occupies a safe seat, as in the congressional midterm elections in 2006, when Democrats won control of the House of Representatives and the Senate, or in 2010, when Republicans won back control of the House and gained several seats in the Senate.)

The system used for the presidential election is more complicated. In this case the president is not elected directly by the voters but rather by an absolute majority of the Electoral College. The Electoral College has a total of 538 electors, who are technically elected by the general voting population in the various states and districts based on 435 seats in the House of Representatives, one hundred seats in the Senate, and three seats from the District of Columbia. An absolute majority of 270 votes is required to elect a candidate. If no absolute majority can be secured, the decision goes to the House of Representatives, where every state has one vote. In the 2000 presidential election, Al Gore won the popular vote by five hundred thousand votes, but neither he nor George W. Bush had 270 votes without the Electoral College votes from Florida. The candidate that would win *all* of Florida's Electoral College votes, even by the thinnest of margins, would win the presidential election. In a highly contested process, it was left to the Supreme Court to decide who had won, and a 5-4 majority of the court decided in favor of Bush.

There have been a number of proposals for changing the electoral system used for selecting the president and for making congressional races more competitive. One suggestion is to follow Nebraska and Maine in electing members of the Electoral College from congressional districts rather than from the state as a whole. In this case the candidate with the most votes in California would not win all of the Electoral College seats but only those from congressional districts in which he or she had won a plurality or majority. This would require presidential candidates to campaign across the country rather than focus their attention on the states with a large number of Electoral College votes. Objections to this proposal that would require a constitutional amendment to go into effect come from a variety of sources, including those who tend to benefit from the current system and those who believe the founding fathers were right in giving states such an important role in electing the president.

In the case of congressional and state legislative districting, the parties that have benefited in each state from their right to draw boundaries that result in significant advantages for them are not likely to give up the opportunity to continue doing so. Popular support for reform may also be uncertain. In 2005 voters in a referendum in California rejected a proposal by the governor, Arnold Schwarzenegger, to have a commission of retired judges draw the boundaries of election districts. Probably the only way that the drawing of district boundaries will be reformed in most states is through a ruling by the Supreme Court that the current system is a violation of the equal protection clause of the Fourteenth Amendment.

Elections in the United Kingdom

The British hold elections on Thursdays and also have a single-member district, single-ballot, plurality electoral system for the House of Commons, which they call the "first past the post" system (FPTP). Unlike the United States, however, more than two parties have some success in parliamentary elections and in the devolved regions such as Scotland. Looking at the election results in the country as a whole, the Labour and Conservative parties usually receive by far the most votes (between 70 and 80 percent) and seats (between 85 and 95 percent), but during the last three decades the Liberal Democrats have been receiving between 15 and 25 percent of the vote and other parties up to about 10 percent. The most important of these have been the nationalist parties, which have received around 15 to 20 percent in Wales and Scotland, respectively, in recent elections.

The Liberal Democrats have been disadvantaged the most by FPTP. In 2010, for example, they received 23.6 percent of the vote and 8.8 percent of the seats (fifty-seven of 650). The main reason they received so few seats in relation to their vote is that their support is widely dispersed among the constituencies, and they came in second or third in many of them. In 2010 the nationalist parties in Wales and Scotland received together 2.3 percent the total vote and 1.4 percent of the seats (nine); other parties received 7.6 percent of the vote and 0.31 percent of the seats (two). The only reason these smaller and other parties received seats is because they had a sufficient number of supporters concentrated in the districts that they won. Thus the Welsh and Scottish nationalist parties won three seats in Wales and six in Scotland with pluralities, i.e., simple majorities, in those nine single-member constituencies. Needless to say, they did not even bother to run candidates outside of Wales and Scotland.

For our purposes the most important effect of FPTP is that only one of two parties in the House of Commons can gain an absolute majority of *seats* and, therefore, is in a position to form a single-party government. But no party has received an absolute majority of *votes* since 1945. Indeed, the largest parliamentary majorities (between 61 and 63.4 percent of the seats) have been won with less than 45 percent of the vote (Labour with 40.7 in 2001 and 43.2 percent in 1997), which means that in most cases there were three or more parties contesting the seats, and the party with the most votes—Labour—won.

In the 2010 parliamentary election the Conservative and Labour parties not only failed to win an absolute majority of the votes; for the first time since 1945, neither party won a majority of *seats*. As a result it was necessary to form a coalition government in order to obtain a majority of seats in the House of Commons. After some maneuvering, the Conservatives, who had received 36.9 percent of the vote and 305 seats (47 percent) formed a government with the Liberal Democrats, who, as noted above, had 23.6 percent of the vote and fifty-seven seats (8.8 percent). Some Liberal Democrats had preferred a coalition with the Labour Party, which had received 29.7 percent and 258 seats (39.7 percent), but these two parties would not have had a majority in parliament without the support of some smaller parties.[3]

There is much dissatisfaction with the FPTP system in Britain. It rewards the larger parties and works to the disadvantage of the smaller parties that are not spatially concentrated. Thus the Scottish National Party, which is concentrated in Scotland, can win a plurality of votes in a number of constituencies. On the other hand, the Liberal Democrats, who compete nationwide, have suffered the most from this system, winning usually 15 to 20 percent of the vote but only 3 to 8 percent of the seats in parliament. Individual constituencies can be won by less than 50 percent, i.e., a plurality, of the vote, and there have even been a few occasions when the party with the larger share of the vote did not win the larger share of seats in the House of Commons. The emergence of smaller parties, not only the nationalists but also the Greens and some others, has made victories by plurality even more likely. There are also complaints that the Westminster system, which features a single governing party and a large opposition party, has encouraged an adversarial party-dominated system that discourages cooperation and consensus.

On the other hand, there are significant advantages of FPTP for the British political system. The system is easy for voters to understand, and it probably promotes a closer contact between the member of Parliament (MP) and the constituency. Most important for the functioning of the political system, however, is the fact that the electoral system makes it possible for one party to gain an absolute majority in parliament and form a single-party government. Thus the UK stands almost alone in Europe as a country that can hold one party accountable for its successes and failures in government (the Swedish Social Democrats—but no other single party—have held office alone much of the time during past decades).

But change may be coming. As one of the conditions for joining the coalition with the Conservatives, the Liberal Democrats insisted on a change in the electoral system to the *single transferable vote* system. The Conservatives resisted, but they did offer to pass a law authorizing a referendum in May 2011 that would offer the voters the opportunity to vote on a proposal to change the voting system for the House of Commons to the *alternative vote* system. This system would still call for single-member districts, but an absolute majority would be required to win the seat. In casting a ballot, the voter would vote for a first and second choice. If no candidate won an absolute majority, the votes of the candidate with the fewest first-place votes would be ignored and the votes for the second, or alternative, candidate distributed among the remaining candidates. This procedure would be repeated until a candidate received an absolute majority.

The Conservatives, and some Labour MPs as well, indicated they would oppose the change during the campaign concerning the referendum, and it was clear that broad public support was lacking. Unfortunately for the Liberal Democrats, who hoped to win more seats under this system in future elections, the referendum failed.

It should be noted that FPTP is not the only electoral system currently found in the UK. Indeed, there are separate systems for elections to the EU Parliament and for Scotland, Wales, and Northern Ireland. For the EU Parliament, there is a proportional representation (PR) system based on party lists. Voters cast their ballots for parties rather than individual candidates, and the parties receive seats in proportion to their vote. A still more complicated system, very similar to the German electoral system to be discussed below, is what the British call the "additional member system" which is a mixed system of FPTP and PR used for the parliaments of Scotland, Wales, and the Greater London Assembly. Still another electoral system, the single transferable vote, is used for the assembly in Northern Ireland.[4]

Elections in France

So far we have looked at two states with the same electoral system for their national legislatures: the single-member district, single-ballot, plurality system. France has a different version of this system: *a single-member district,* ***two-ballot****, majority-plurality system*. For elections to the National Assembly, there are generally two ballots on two successive Sundays. On the first Sunday any party candidate (independents have little or no chance of being elected) with an absolute majority wins the seat in the district. Because this happens in only about 10 percent of the districts, a second runoff election is held the following Sunday in which only those party candidates who received at least 12.5 percent of the vote on the first round may participate. In this case the candidate who wins a plurality on the second round wins the seat. Because there can be only one winner, some parties that failed to receive 12.5 percent on the first round or that see little chance of winning a plurality on the second round may openly support other parties that are reasonably close to them ideologically. The French Communist Party, for example, may ask its voters to support the French Socialist Party on the second Sunday in hopes of preventing a right-of-center party from winning. The Socialists have sometimes thrown their support to the Greens and other left-wing parties for the same reason. Thus the second round of elections has the effect of encouraging a two-bloc system of parties on the center-right and center-left.

As in the UK, parliamentary elections must be held every five years, but five elections were held earlier than scheduled since 1959 because the president dissolved the National Assembly and called for new elections. That this can backfire was demonstrated in 1997, when the results of new elections called by President Jacques Chirac led to the opposition's gaining a majority and Chirac's having to appoint an opposition socialist leader as his premier.

Like the United States with its procedures for the presidential election, the French semipresidential system has a somewhat different system for the election of the head of state. But unlike the United States, presidential and legislative elections are not held on the same day. As in the case of parliamentary elections, there are two rounds of presidential voting. On the first Sunday voters cast ballots for a number of candidates; however, only the candidate who wins an absolute majority wins the election. This has never happened, so all presidents have been elected on the second round, in which only the top two candidates from the first round participate.

Normally these are candidates from the two major blocs representing center-left and center-right parties. However, in 2002 the French were embarrassed when an extreme right candidate, Jean-Marie Le Pen, was second with 16.9 percent of the vote on the first ballot in comparison with the 16.2 percent received by the Socialist candidate, Lionel Jospin. Therefore, Le Pen ran against Jacques Chirac on the second ballot, which was held two weeks after the first ballot. Chirac had won a plurality of only 19.9 percent on the first round. He won easily on the second round, because even voters who disliked him intensely disliked Le Pen (who received 17.8 percent on the second ballot) even more.

The French electoral system does not, of course, lead to a two-party system, as does FPTP in the United States and, to a lesser extent, in the UK. The two-ballot feature provides a greater, though limited, opportunity for multiple parties. Traditional ideological divisions also help sustain a multiparty system, which flourishes in many local governments. In contrast to the United States, however, the French system guarantees that the president is elected by an absolute majority of voters. And in contrast to the U.S. and British FPTP system, the French two-ballot feature in parliamentary elections gives parties that fail to win an absolute majority on the first round a second chance.

It should be noted that the French also have a second chamber, the *Senate*, which is not elected by popular vote. Rather, one-third of its 321 members are elected every three years by an electoral college consisting of the popularly elected members of local communal councils, departmental councils, and members of parliament. This system of election means that the *Senate* represents above all the views of local councils, which can be quite different from those of the electorate in elections for the National Assembly. The Senate cannot be dissolved, and it must approve all legislation passed by the National Assembly for it to become law; however, it functions mostly as an amending body.

Elections in Germany

Germany, which, like most continental European countries, votes on Sundays, has experimented during the last one hundred years with three basic kinds of electoral systems: a single member district system (FPTP) in the Kaiserreich of 1871–1918, proportional representation (PR) in the Weimar Republic of 1919–33, and a mixed system of FPTP and PR in the Federal Republic after 1949. The mixed system, which the British call the "additional member system" and have adopted for their parliamentary elections in Scotland and Wales, is designed among other things to combine some of the advantages of FPTP and PR.

The principle behind any PR system is that the *percentage of the vote equals the percentage of the seats*; however, this principle needs some elaboration. The multimember district in which the voting takes place can vary in size from a few seats to hundreds of seats. In Germany the multimember districts for the national elections are the sixteen German *Länder* (states); the number of seats for each *Land* varied in the 2009 election from six in the city state of Bremen to 130 in the largest *Land*, North Rhine-Westphalia. But the total vote in all sixteen *Länder*, i.e., the nationwide vote, determines the number of seats won. The total number of seats in the *Bundestag* is 598, which means that a party with only 1 percent of the vote should receive six seats. In order to prevent too great a fragmentation of parliament into many small parties, most countries that have PR have a minimum percentage requirement for obtaining seats. In Germany this is 5 percent. The votes cast for parties that do not win 5 percent are placed in the pool of votes for the parties that do qualify for seats. This means, for example, that if a party wins 4 percent, it wins no seats and its percentage will be shared by the qualifying parties. It also means that the parties that win more than 5 percent benefit slightly from the percentages won by parties that fail to achieve this minimum goal.

Seats are not distributed in a PR system merely by ascertaining the percentage each party wins. Indeed, there are numerous mathematical formulae used to determine the exact number of seats a party should receive. In Germany the d'Hondt method of calculation was used for many years, but it was replaced in 1987 by the Hare-Niemeyer method. This method was replaced in turn by the Sainte-Laguë/Schepers procedure for the 2009 elections. Each of these complicated methods of calculation is designed to produce numbers of seats that are fair both to the larger and the smaller parties, based on their proportion of the vote. Nevertheless, there are differences in results that lead to considerable controversy, especially regarding the "surplus seats" described below. Due to pressure from the Federal Constitutional Court, the *Bundestag* is supposed to enact a new method of calculation in 2011 in order to deal with this situation

If the voters vote for parties rather than candidates, as in FPTP, who gets elected? In most cases the parties select candidates and place them on a list, with the top candidate in first place, the next candidate in second place, etc. In the German case, each *Land* party provides a list of candidates, who are elected in order based on the method of calculation unless they are elected in a single-member district.

If Germany had a PR system only, as is the case in many democracies, the 598 seats would be distributed among the various parties that receive 5 percent or more of the vote, and the parties would then distribute the seats by *Land* list. This would be a fair application of the principle of equality; however, the Germans have also wanted to have the close relationship between the voters and candidates that is promoted in a FPTP system. Therefore, the 598 seats in the *Bundestag* are divided so that one-half of the seats are filled by candidates on the lists made up in the various *Länder* and the other one-half by candidates that run in winner-take-all single-member districts. Thus the German voter has two votes, one for a direct candidate in one of the 299 single-member constituencies and one for a party in one of the sixteen multimember districts (in this case, one of the *Länder*) mentioned above. Seats are distributed according to the proportion of the vote received as calculated by the particular method, described above, that is being used for that election. In any case any single-member district seats won are subtracted from the total number the party is to receive based on its proportion of the party vote. Thus in 2009 the Christian Democrats (CDU/CSU) with their 33.8 percent of the total vote won 239 seats overall, the vast majority of which were won in single-member districts. On the other hand, the Free Democrats (FDP), who joined the CDU/CSU to form a coalition government, gained 14.6 percent of the total vote and won ninety-three list seats but no single-member seats. Because the FDP did not win in any of the 299 constituencies, it would not have won a single seat in a FPTP system. The results of the 2009 election are shown below.

Table 4.1

Results of the 2009 *Bundestag* Elections

	Direct Seats	Surplus Seats (Überhang- mandate)	List Seats (with Surplus Seats)	Total Seats	Total Vote
Christian Democrats (CDU/CSU)	218	24	21	239	33.8%
Social Democrats (SPD)	64	0	82	146	23.0
Free Democrats (FDP)	0	0	93	93	14.6
Left Party (Linke)	16	0	60	76	11.9
Greens	1	0	67	68	10.7
Others (21 small parties)	0	0	0	0	6.0
Totals	299	24	323	622	100.0
Turnout					70.8

Source: www.Bundeswahlleiter.de; *Das Parlament* (Nr. 41: 5 October 2009), *Zeitschrift für Parlamentsfragen* 41, No 1 (2010), *German Politics and Society* 28, No. 3 (Fall 2010).

A close look at the table reveals that there are more than 299 list seats and more than 598 total seats. Where did the additional twenty-four seats—a record—come from? These are "surplus seats" (*Überhangmandate*) that result when a party wins more direct seats than it "deserves" based on its proportion of the vote. In 2009 the CDU won many direct seats by narrow margins, in some cases with less than 30 percent of the district vote. As a result the CDU won twenty-four "surplus" seats by winning ten more direct seats in Baden-Württemberg and from one to four more direct seats in six other *Länder* than it "deserved." The CSU, the CDU's sister party in Bavaria, won an additional three seats.

In terms of fairness, it is clear that the German electoral system goes much further than either the American or British FPTP systems or the French alternative. Voters can vote for a direct candidate in a single-member district, but they also have a second vote for a party. If their party receives at least 5 percent of the total vote, their individual vote will count toward the proportion the party receives for its party list candidates.[5] Partly for this reason the German system has been closely studied by a number of other states, and it has been adopted with some alterations in Russia, New Zealand, and the UK (for regional parliamentary elections in Scotland and Wales only). On the other hand, the German system promotes a multiparty system, which means that coalition governments are the norm, and due to its complexity it is not well understood by many German voters.

Like France, Germany also has a second legislative chamber, the *Bundesrat*, which is not considered to be a part of parliament. The reason is because it is not popularly elected but rather consists of members appointed by the governments of the sixteen *Länder*. Therefore, it is considered to be a chamber of the *Länder*, not an "upper house" of parliament (even though it is often referred to as an "upper house" by many journalists and other commentators). The delegations range in number from three to six, depending on the size of population in the *Land*, but votes are cast as a bloc by each delegation. Until recently the *Bundesrat* had the power to amend or even veto about 60 percent of the legislation passed by the *Bundestag*, which gave the *Land* prime ministers and their cabinets significant influence in the federal legislative process. A reform in 2006 was designed, among other things, to reduce the potential veto power of the *Bundesrat* over legislation from about 50–60 percent to 30–40 percent, but it was not clear by the end of the decade to what extent this goal had been achieved.

Elections in the EU

Elections for the EU Parliament are held every five years. The Parliament was an appointed body until 1979, when the first popular election was held. All of the then nine member states except the UK agreed to use a PR party list system for the election of the members of the European Parliament (MEPs). France, of course, continues to this day to use its single-member district, two ballot, majority-plurality system for its National Assembly elections, but it agreed from the beginning to use PR for electing its MEPs. Until the end of the 1990s, the UK was still the only member state with FPTP for the EU elections; however, after its victory in 1997, the Labour Party under its leader, Tony Blair, introduced PR for the election of British MEPs. The result in both France and the UK is that some parties that win few or no seats in the national parliamentary elections do much better in the EU elections, because they receive seats in proportion to their votes. Today all EU member states use PR for the election of their members of the EU Parliament; however, EU elections take place over a four-day period—on Thursdays and Fridays in some countries and on Sundays in most.

As noted in chapter 2, there are no executive offices in the EU subject to popular election.

Other Differences among Electoral Systems

It should be noted that there are also other aspects of electoral systems that can have important effects on election outcomes. Registration procedures, terms of office, campaign financing, and electoral turnout are also important features of any democracy.

Registration procedures. Registration procedures in the UK, France, and Germany are quite different from those in the United States. These states do not have a history of discrimination based on race; however, workers, especially those without property, were given the vote much earlier in the United States (excluding black workers). Like the United States, they did not allow women to vote until after World War I; indeed, France did not enfranchise women until 1944! But today registration is generally automatic for all citizens eighteen and above. In the UK, for example, names of eligible voters are published and listed in public libraries and other public buildings, based on an annual canvass of households in each locality. Eligible voters may also register themselves and change their registration information at any time. This provides for a rolling register that is updated monthly. In Germany all residents of a town or city have to register with local authorities; those who are citizens of voting age and not ineligible for certain legal reasons receive a card in the mail that admits them to the polling place indicated on the card.

In the United States voters must take the initiative in registering to vote. In past decades some registrars, especially in the South, used different criteria for accepting or rejecting registration by black Americans. In some states a poll tax had to be paid in order to vote, which discouraged low-income voters of all races. These and other egregious means of discouraging voting were not made illegal until the 1960s. However, registration procedures remained restrictive by requiring prospective voters to register in person at a particular office at particular times that were often not very convenient. In the past this was thought to be a major reason for the low voter turnout at all levels of government, and in recent years registration has been made easier by permitting citizens to register when obtaining a driver's license (motorvoter legislation) or sometimes when visiting a shopping mall or, for students, by stopping at a registration booth on campus. The result is that there has been an increase in registration but not in voting participation. This raises other questions, such as whether setting the deadline for registration weeks before the election, just when some voters are beginning to take note of the election campaign, or whether having elections on a weekday (Tuesday) rather than a Sunday as in almost every other democratic state, depresses the vote. In any case, voting turnout in the United States is among the lowest in the democratic world, and the various explanations for this fact remain numerous and controversial. It should be noted that parliamentary elections in the UK are on Thursdays, and turnout is lower in the UK than on the continent. Some experts therefore argue that the day on which elections are held matters. It is also worth noting that the FPTP system in Great Britain and the United States may discourage voting, because voters who do not support the majority party and its candidates in noncompetitive districts, of which there are ever more in the United States due in part to maldistricting (gerrymandering), can see that their votes will be wasted in the winner-take-all single-member district.

Registration procedures mean that we have to distinguish between eligible and registered voters when we talk about turnout, especially in the United States. Reports of turnout do not always make clear whether the statistics are based on one or the other set of figures or, indeed, on the voting-age population, which is yet another standard. Obviously, turnout figures for registered voters are much higher than for all of the eligible voters or the voting-age population, which includes the prison population, noncitizens, and other ineligible persons. Turnout figures for our four democratic states, using the same standards for comparison, make clear that there are significant differences among them in terms of voter turnout . Turnout in American presidential elections in recent decades has been from somewhat less to somewhat more than two-thirds of the registered voters but only about 47–57 percent of the voting-age population (the highest turnout since World War II was 63.1 percent in 1960). Turnout for midterm elections, i.e., congressional elections between the presidential races, is even lower: usually about half or more of the registered voters and 34–39 percent of the voting-age population. Turnout in Germany is highest, ranging between 82.2 and 77.7 percent of the registered voters from 1998 to 2005 and from 70 to 75 percent of the voting-age population. Turnout in the 2009 election was a low of 71 percent. In the UK from 72 to 59 percent of registered voters turned out in 1997, 2001, and 2005, whereas the voting-age turnout was 70 and 58 percent in 1997 and 2001, respectively. France is considerably behind Germany but about the same as the UK in voter turnout in parliamentary elections; however, the turnout for presidential elections, which neither the UK nor Germany has, is higher.[6]

Why is turnout lowest in the United States and highest in Germany, with France between Germany and Great Britain in presidential elections and between the United States and Great Britain in parliamentary elections? One hypothesis that might explain these differences is the electoral system. In the United States and the UK, votes cast for the losing candidates in the FPTP or single-member district system are wasted. Germans, on the other hand, cast two votes, one for a direct candidate by FPTP, the other for a political party that gains seats based on the proportion of its national vote. For the PR portion of the German electoral system, all votes count for seats on the party list unless the total vote for the party falls below 5 percent. Knowing that at least the second vote will count probably increases voter turnout to some extent in Germany. Other hypotheses would have to include the registration procedures; the day of election; and historical, social, economic, and racial factors. In the United States some religions discourage voting, but the numbers involved are small.

Frequency of elections. The frequency of elections, that is, the terms of office, is another aspect of elections that deserves mention. For example, the fact that members of the US House of Representatives must run for reelection every two years—as opposed to senators, who run every six years—has certain consequences for the political system. One is the low turnout discussed above in midterm or off-year elections, i.e., elections between presidential races. Presidential elections in recent decades have garnered a considerably higher percentage of the voting-age population and about two-thirds to three-fourths of registered voters. The low turnout in midterm elections is somewhat puzzling, however, given the fact that many states hold state elections at the same time. In any case it is clear that presidential races draw more voter interest and thus participation than midterm congressional races.

Another aspect of frequent elections concerns the attention those elected to the legislative body can devote to the numerous, often complicated and controversial, political issues that face them. It is relevant here to note that no other national legislative body in the democratic world has as short a term as the US House of Representatives. Indeed, in Europe the trend is from four- to five-year terms for parliamentary bodies at all levels of government, including local councils.

Elections for the House of Commons must be held within a five-year term, but the prime minister can call for new elections just about whenever he or she wants. This usually means sometime in the fourth year or before the middle of the fifth year, depending on the prime minister's assessment of the party's chances based largely on opinion polls or certain events. Some observers suggest that the right of the prime minister to call for elections gives his or her party an unfair advantage. While this may be true in most cases, it does not guarantee by any means the results the prime minister was hoping for. It should be noted that the coalition government that was formed in 2010 has agreed to hold elections in May 2015, thus waiting until the five-year term of office is over. Early elections can be held now only with a 55 percent majority vote in the House of Commons. This could change again, however, after the 2015 election.

The traditional right until recently of the prime minister to call for new elections contrasts sharply with parliamentary elections in our other three democracies. As in the UK, parliamentary elections in France are supposed to be held every five years, with the difference that early elections in France have been relatively rare. In Germany parliamentary elections are every four years; however, a five-year term, which is now common for the regional parliaments in the *Länder*, is under consideration. In France the president is now elected every five years, as is the National Assembly; however, as we noted above, the presidential and parliamentary elections are not held on the same Sunday but rather a few weeks after the presidential election.

Campaign finance. It is well known that US senators and, especially, representatives, must begin soliciting campaign contributions almost immediately after their election, so there is little or no time when they can concentrate on their main duties without thinking about money. Money is so important because election campaigns are so expensive, in large part due to television advertising costs. It may be true that normally about 95 percent of congressmen do not face serious opposition in the general election, due in large part to their safe districts, but most congressmen still spend large amounts of money (often in many millions of dollars) to discourage potential opponents and to overwhelm those who do oppose them. Regardless of the honesty and integrity of a congressman, he or she must engage in continuing fund-raising activities that attract many lobbyists and interest groups that have money to give to political campaigns and that expect consideration for their views in return.

The United States has by far the longest and most expensive election campaigns, and at the national level the only public financial subsidies available are for presidential elections. While nominated candidates for the presidential race may receive public *matching* funds to supplement their private funding, some candidates that can expect generous contributions have in recent years refused these matching funds for their primary campaigns so they could spend more than the maximum amounts set in return for public financing. Thus George Bush refused public financing in 2000, and John Kerry as well as Howard Dean rejected public financing in their 2004 primary election campaigns. Because he was so successful in raising private contributions, Barack Obama did not accept public funding in his presidential primary campaign in 2008; however, John McCain did. The funds for this public financing are derived from a *voluntary* checkoff of $3.00 per taxpayer that costs the taxpayer nothing; nevertheless, only about 10 percent of taxpayers now check the appropriate box on their forms. Polls show that public support for taxpayer- or government-subsidized public financing in general is low, which is one reason why there is no public financing for Senate and House candidates.

As noted above, the official term of office of the British House of Commons is five years, even though it has generally been somewhat less than that until recently. Election campaigns are very short, especially by American standards. From the time the prime minister announces new elections, only seventeen days, not counting weekends, go by before the election takes place. This cuts down considerably on costs, which are significantly lower than in the United States in any case, due, in part, to much less reliance on television and radio commercials and because of restrictions on the amount of money the MPs and parties may spend. Indeed, free television time is allocated by the state based on the past electoral success of the party, with new parties receiving a minimum amount of time. There is some dissatisfaction with the influence of interest group contributions and influence in the UK, but this is not as problematic as in the United States. On the other hand, a serious scandal erupted in 2009, when little-known provisions were revealed concerning subsidies for various expenses, including for "second homes" in London. Further revelations showed that many MPs had abused their legal right to receive these subsidies, which led to the resignations of a number of cabinet ministers as well as MPs from the House of Commons.

Election campaigns for the French National Assembly are also very short, i.e., three weeks from the time of nomination to the election. Party commercials on TV are banned six months before an election, not just during the three weeks of the campaign, and expenditures by candidates are limited. Public financing has been increased in recent years. The French president is now elected every five years, as is the National Assembly; however, as we noted above, the presidential and parliamentary elections are not held on the same Sunday. Campaign finance in presidential campaigns is an issue, but again it pales in importance to the United States. Television time is also allocated to the parties by the state.

As a rule, German parliamentary elections are held every four years, although there is a proposal to lengthen the term to five years. Election campaigns in Germany are longer than in the UK and France, but they are not as long as in the United States. Germany has a well developed, generous system of public financing for parties and elections at all levels; indeed, Germany and the United States are at opposite ends of the continuum measuring public financial support for parties and elections.[7] As in the UK and France, free television time is made available to all competing parties—not individual candidates—and paid commercial TV political ads are not allowed.

Conclusion

As noted at the beginning of this chapter, there are many electoral systems that have many different consequences for the political system. The American single-member, single-ballot plurality system is probably the most important reason why the United States has a two-party system. There are some serious problems of fairness in this system, because all of the votes that go for losing candidates do not count. This fact has led to more dissatisfaction in the UK than in the United States, perhaps because relatively few Americans are aware of alternative systems.

On the other hand, a two-party system, whether in the United States or the UK, does simplify the choices the voters have. In the case of the UK, having just two major parties in the parliament makes it possible to have single-party government, which in turn makes it possible for the voter to hold the one governing party responsible for its actions. All of the continental European states have coalition governments, which means that more than one party gets to share in governing but also that no one party can be held accountable for government actions or inaction.

In the case of the United States, a multiparty system that would probably result from changes in the electoral system would make the presidential system of separation of powers and checks and balances even more complicated and difficult to operate. Imagine what difficulties would be encountered if no presidential candidate could receive an absolute majority of the electoral college, if no one party had an absolute majority of either the House or Senate, if some parties were stronger in one region and different parties were stronger in other regions, or if some parties were based on religion, race, or economic standing.

The multiparty systems of Europe are more representative of the divisions that exist in society than are the two major parties in the United States and the UK. But it seems clear that a multiparty system would make far more difficult the operation of both the American and British models of government. In other words, electoral systems matter, just as constitutional arrangements of institutions matter.

Other issues as well, such as registration procedures, frequency of elections, campaign finance, historical and social factors, and perhaps even the day of election, can be important variables in helping to explain why and how elections in different democratic systems differ in a number of ways.

Endnotes

[1] Andrew Reynolds and Ben Reilly, eds., *The International IDEA Handbook of Electoral System Design* (Stockholm: International Institute for Democracy and Electoral Assistance, 1997).

[2] Indeed, Maurice Duverger, a well-known French political scientist, wrote in his book *Political Parties* (London: Methuen & Co., 1954), 217, that "the simple-majority single-ballot system favors the two-party system," a hypothesis that "approaches the most nearly perhaps to a true sociological law."

[3] For an analysis of the 2010 elections, see David Denver, "The Results: How Britain Voted," *Parliamentary Affairs* 63, no. 4 (October 2010), 588–606.

[4] For a discussion of electoral systems and elections in Great Britain, see Bill Jones and Philip Norton, eds., *Politics UK*, 7th ed. (London and New York: Pearson Education, 2010), ch. 7.

[5] If a candidate is elected in a single-member district but the party does not receive 5 percent of the vote, the direct candidate retains the seat won. If a party wins three or more direct seats and still fails to receive 5 percent of the total vote, it then qualifies for the proportional distribution by party list as if it had won 5 percent.

[6] Center on Democratic Performance, Election Results Archive, SUNY Binghamton (http://cdp.binghamton.edu/era/index.html).

[7] For a somewhat dated but still useful comparison of campaign finance, see Arthur B. Gunlicks, ed., *Comparative Party and Campaign Finance in North America and Western Europe* (Boulder: Westview Press, 1991; now iUniverse.com, 2000); for Germany, see Arthur B. Gunlicks, "The New German Party Finance Law," *German Politics* 4, no. 1 (April 1995), 101–21.

Chapter 5

Political Parties: Systems, Families, and Structures

Introduction: The Origins of Party Families in Europe

There are a large number of parties in European democracies. Indeed, some individual European states have at least a half-dozen parties that compete on a regular basis, and all of the states have at least three or four parties of varying size and importance that win seats in parliament. According to one famous interpretation offered in the 1960s by Lipset and Rokkan, these parties are based on a number of cleavage lines that developed as a result of certain historical events and were "frozen" in place by the 1920s. The first of these cleavages occurred as a result of the reformation and counter-reformation in the sixteenth and seventeenth centuries. The result was a center-periphery cleavage reflected in a national versus supranational religious conflict accompanied by a national language versus Latin. The second cleavage followed the French Revolution of 1789, which led to a conflict between state and church and the struggle of secular versus religious control over mass education. The third cleavage came out of the Industrial Revolution in the nineteenth century that resulted in tensions between landed interests and industry, for example agricultural protectionism and the freedom of industrial enterprises. The fourth cleavage occurred even before but especially as a result of the Russian Revolution of 1917, which reflected the conflict between owners (capitalists) and workers and raised questions about the integration of workers into the national political system as opposed to a commitment to an international revolutionary movement.[1]

The authors of this interpretation note briefly the relevance of electoral systems in encouraging the growth and persistence of parties based on these cleavages, and they discuss fascist, national socialist, and other nationalist reactions in "fully mobilized polities." These nationalist elements accept and even "venerate the historically given nation and its culture" and "reject the system of decision-making and control developed through the process of democratic mobilization and bargaining."[2] As we will see below, this interpretation emerged before the rise of green parties in the 1980s, anti-immigrant parties in the 1990s, and the often related antiglobalization parties and protest movements that emerged in the 1990s and at the beginning of the twenty-first century. In spite of not including these more recent cleavage structures in Europe (and elsewhere), the original Lipset-Rokkan approach is a useful way of thinking about party systems in Europe.

The Conservative, Liberal, and Socialist Traditions

Another way of looking at the origins of European as well as American parties is to think of major social and economic conditions and changes over time that led to the development of certain party families or traditions. This approach posits three *general* political/philosophical traditions in Europe: conservative, liberal, and socialist. Each of these traditions developed from certain periods of European history and became the dominant tradition or struggled for dominance for several decades until a new tradition challenged it and earlier traditions.

The conservative tradition is derived from the Middle Ages, which can be distinguished by a number of characteristics. One was its corporate structure, i.e., the division of society into specific groups that made up the parts of the social and economic order. One might picture society as consisting of an aristocracy representing the head, the clergy the heart and soul, the guilds the arms, the merchants the torso, and the peasantry the legs of the corporate whole. People in general were born into each corporate group with little or no chance of moving into a different group. This is especially true of the aristocracy and the peasantry. The guilds were made up of various craftsmen who passed their skills and positions on to their sons, just as the merchants passed their shops on to their sons. The clergy was more open to entrants from various backgrounds, but this depended on time and place, and the higher clergy were generally of higher social status. The economic system was based on feudal land ownership or, to put it in Marxist terms, land was the major means of production, and members of the nobility were the major beneficiaries. Religion was very important, and there was a close association between the princes and the church. Political systems were at first rather fragmented, and decentralized feudal monarchies with many powerful princes, lords, barons and bishops were followed in the seventeenth and eighteenth centuries by absolute monarchies that exercised more centralized power over a strong, often expansionist, state.

The conservative tradition began to be challenged in the eighteenth and nineteenth centuries by the European Liberals, often referred to as *classical Liberals* as distinguished from American "liberals." The Liberals[3] emerged during the Enlightenment (e.g., John Locke, Adam Smith) and the Industrial Revolution and differed from the conservatives in a number of important ways. The key characteristic of Liberalism is individualism, from which most of the Liberal values are derived. Thus the political focus of Liberalism is on civil liberties, legal equality, and self-government. "The people" or citizens should replace the monarch as the sovereign, i.e., the final source of legitimate authority. They should govern through elected representative institutions that decide public policy. The economic system identified with Liberalism is individual or free enterprise, i.e., a capitalistic system with private ownership of the industries that were replacing land ownership as the major source of wealth. In order to expand the markets for their factory-produced goods, Liberals favored free trade. The "people" were considered to be especially the entrepreneurial or property-owning middle classes, who were more numerous in the United States because of widespread land ownership. In Europe until the latter half of the nineteenth century, generally only men with property (thus excluding women as well as the working class) were considered capable of being responsible voters, and only after World War I were women enfranchised (after 1944 in France). In order to protect individual property and civil rights, including freedom of religion, Liberals believed the government or state should be limited in scope and subject to various constitutional provisions, including checks and balances and separation of powers, e.g., independent courts. In effect, Liberal government was limited democracy of, by, and for the middle classes.

European socialism can be seen as a reaction in the nineteenth and early twentieth centuries to both the conservative and Liberal traditions. The Industrial Revolution, associated with the Liberals, had brought about a massive shift of population from the rural to the urban areas, and what had been a majority of peasants became a majority of workers. These workers obviously lacked the security, status, and prestige of the old land-owning aristocracy and the money and influence of the entrepreneurial middle classes and came to rely instead on class solidarity as promoted by socialist parties and labor unions. The leaders of the workers were almost all socialists, and most of them were Marxists of varying kinds. They believed in an industrial society with public, i.e., state, ownership of the means of production, in a state monopoly over trade, and in a parliamentary democracy dominated by political parties representing the majority of the population, i.e., the working class. Public policy was to be focused on improving the conditions of the working class and peasantry as collective entities, not on the protection of individual property rights. Religion was considered by many socialist leaders to be too closely associated with the conservative tradition and therefore to be treated with some distance or even hostility. The socialists represented a revolutionary movement in some European states, but in others, such as in Great Britain, France, and Germany, they were generally more in favor of significant reforms of the political, economic, and social systems rather than revolution.

During and after World War I, the more radical socialist elements broke off from the reformist socialist parties and formed communist parties. The communists were first able to assume power in Russia, and it soon became apparent, first under Lenin, then under Stalin, that the communists were very different in some important ways from the traditional socialists. They were far more extreme and militant, for example, in terms of their demands that not just the major industries but virtually the entire economy be in public hands, which meant in practice ownership by the state and the governing communist party. In contrast to the socialists, they also insisted on one-party rule and the elimination of "bourgeois" civil liberties that were not deemed essential or even relevant to the working class and peasantry. They were hostile to religion (the "opiate of the masses") and actively discriminated against it. They were more loyal to the Soviet Union than to their own country, as was demonstrated especially before and during World War II. Although communist ideology and electoral support in Western Europe generally weakened during the decades after World War II, it was not until the collapse of the communist regimes in Eastern Europe in 1989–90 that communist parties either disappeared or changed their names and revised their policies.

Table 5.1

The Development of Political Traditions in Europe

	European Socialism	European Liberalism	European Conservatism
Period of Origin	Late 19th and 20th Centuries	18th and 19th Centuries	Middle Ages
Basic Unit of Society	Class	Individual	Corporate Units, e.g., Aristocracy, Clergy, Peasantry
Economic System	Socialist or State-Owned Industrial	Capitalisit or Privately-Owned Industrial, Free Enterprise Market	Feudal-Agrarian
Trade Policies	State Monopoly	Free Trade	Customs, Mercantalism
Property Ownership	Public Ownership of Basic Enterprises	Private	Corporate Units (Aristocracy, Church, Guild, State)

	European Socialism	European Liberalism	European Conservatism
Political Sovereignty	"The People" (Party)	"The People" (Middle Class)	Monarch or Princes
Representation	Party and Unions	Elected Representative with "Free Mandate" (Independent)	Prince and Corporate Units
Religion	Anti-Religion or Indifferent	Freedom of Religion; Separation of Church and State	State Religion
Political System	Party State, Concentrated Power	Parliamentary Democracy, Separation of Power, Checks and Balances	Feudal Monarch, then Absolute Monarch
Selected Values	**Collectivism**; Cooperation; Anti-Capitalism; Internationalism; Equality of Result	**Individualism**; Limited State; Rule of Law; Nationalism; Free Market; Politial/ Legal Equality; Separation of Church and State	**Corporatism**; Tradition; Status Quo; Hierarchy; Church; Order; Rural Orientation; Privilege; Paternalism
Main Beneficiaries	Working Class	Middle Class	Aristocracy

If we look at table 5.1, it is clear that there was a movement from right to left in the major European philosophical traditions during the past centuries, a movement from a very hierarchical corporatist tradition with no or little idea of equality to a Liberal individualistic tradition with *political* and *legal* equality, at least for the propertied middle classes, to a socialist tradition with equality for all, including especially the workers and peasants as collective entities. There are dimensions of competition other than "left" and "right," such as race, gender, and region, but economic policy tends to be the dominant factor: government regulation versus free enterprise. As one prominent scholar has noted,

This is not surprising. All governments and all parties, of whatever party system type and of whatever genesis, are obliged to formulate policies—whether more to the left or more to the right—on the welfare state, on taxation, on employment policy, on industry, on farming, on the environment, and so on. And while the various parties may differ substantially on what they consider to be the best approach to be adopted *vis-à-vis* these concerns; and while these differences may be associated with particular trans-national party families on one hand, or even with particular types of party system on the other; there nevertheless exists a sufficiently common core of concerns, as well as a sufficiently limited range of options relating to these concerns, to allow one to speak legitimately of uniformity rather than diversity in western Europe.[4]

Party Systems

The philosophical traditions outlined above were not reflected in political parties until the nineteenth century. One might argue that the British Tories (Conservatives) and Whigs (Liberals) were the first opposing parliamentary parties; however, they were *internal* to the House of Commons and did not develop an *external* organization until after the extension of the franchise, especially after 1867, to a broader electorate whose votes were needed to elect and maintain members of parliament and their parties. The *external* organization of the Conservative and Liberal parties remained very modest, however, until they were confronted by the superior organization of unionized workers by the Labour Party that emerged around the turn of the nineteenth to the twentieth century.

Table 5.2

Political Philosophical Traditions in Europe and Party Families

Socialist Tradition (Highpoint late 19th to late 20th centuries)			"Classical" Liberal Tradition (Highpoint late 18th to early 20th centuries; revived late 20th century)		Conservative Tradition (Highpoint Middle Ages to early 20th century)		
Communist	Socialist	Social Democratic	Left Political Liberal	Right Economic Liberal	Christian Democratic	Agrarian	Monarchist
PCF (France)	SFIO/PS (France) Labour (UK)	SPD (Germany)	Liberal Democrats (UK)	FDP (Germany)	CDU/CSU (Germany)	Conservative (UK)	DNVP (Germany, 1919-33)

The Social Democratic Party of Germany was founded earlier, in 1863, and it became the leading, but not majority, party of the Bismarck Reich and the largest socialist party in Europe. The French socialists (SFIO) emerged at the beginning of the twentieth century as a more doctrinaire Marxist party than its British and German counterparts. In reaction to the German and French social democratic/socialist parties, conservative and Liberal parties that had already existed in the parliament tried to improve their organization and broaden their base, although none of them ever came close to attracting the numbers of members enrolled by the socialist parties.

The socialist parties in Europe came to be characterized as mass parties, i.e., parties that enrolled large numbers of mostly working-class members organized in "branches," whose dues provided almost all of the financing of the parties.[5] The socialist mass party,[6] which Duverger thought was the "modern" model, stood in contrast to the far more limited membership and organization of the middle class Liberal parties, the peasant-based agrarian parties, and the large landholding, big-business-oriented, and/or religious-based conservative parties that relied more on financing by individuals and business interests.

Table 5.1 does not account for one type of party that emerged after World War I and grew rapidly in Europe in the 1920s and 1930s: the fascist party and its numerous variations. These variations could be found in most European states, but they enjoyed their greatest success first in Italy and then Germany. The Italian Fascist and German Nazi movements can be seen as fiercely nationalistic reactions against certain changes in social and economic conditions, but they were especially concerned with national honor and the "rightful" place of their states in Europe and the world. German fascists were appalled in particular by territorial losses suffered after World War I, and they became obsessed with the idea of racial superiority and the humiliations suffered after World War I at the hands of their enemies. These views and others are not easily derived from table 5.1. However, one can argue that from the conservative tradition fascists took the idea of a strong, authoritarian state; an appeal more to rural and small town than large urban populations; and a romantic orientation toward national history. They accepted industrial capitalism from the Liberal tradition but only so long as the capitalists served the interests of the state, and above all they adopted an exaggerated form of the nationalism characteristic of the conservatives in Great Britain and the Liberals in Germany. From the socialist tradition the fascists took the idea of collectivism, or solidarity, but only for the "true and rightful" members of the "nation." In general it is clear that the fascist ideology was at its core a vicious form of extreme nationalism and an aberration from and a gross distortion of the major political traditions in Europe.

Table 5.1 can be used as a basis for explaining the numerous party families that emerged during the nineteenth and twentieth centuries following the broadening of male suffrage in general and the growing enfranchisement of the working class in particular. In table 5.2 we can see that from the conservative tradition there is a large family of parties ranging from reactionary parties clinging to the past to moderate right-of-center parties with a focus on certain traditional conservative values, such as social hierarchy, religion, agricultural protection, respect for the national heritage, and a strong military.

An example of a conservative party on the far right that was willing to work within a democratic framework, though with reservations, was the monarchist and reactionary German National People's Party (DNVP) in the Weimar Republic before the Nazi takeover in 1933. Of our four liberal democracies, the party that would best exemplify the conservative tradition would be the British Conservative Party, also known as the Tories. At first promoting policies supporting established interests—crown and aristocracy, landowners, agriculture, and the church—it has evolved over the past century toward more economic Liberalism and even acceptance of much of the welfare state introduced by the Labour Party after 1945. It remains, however, a staunch supporter of the crown, the established protestant Church of England, and a defender of agricultural interests, free enterprise, a strong military, and an interpretation of British national interests that is skeptical of European integration. At the "left" end of the conservative spectrum, the German Christian Democratic parties (CDU/CSU) share many of the values of the British Conservatives, but monarchy is irrelevant; they are more closely identified with Roman Catholicism and its family-friendly social doctrines, and they are strong supporters of European integration. The French Gaullists, who have been associated with numerous party names since World War II, also share many characteristics with the British Conservatives, but they are very fixed on a strong military, an important role for France in international affairs—and therefore a strong Europe (under French leadership where possible) that does not undermine French national sovereignty in defense and foreign affairs.

The classical Liberal tradition, especially in its *political* form, emerged in the late eighteenth century in the United States at the time of the American War of Independence and in France during the French Revolution. *Economic* Liberalism is associated more with the rise of the Industrial Revolution, first in Great Britain, then in continental Europe and in the United States during and after the Civil War. In Europe this revolution was led by private entrepreneurs who gained wealth not by owning land but by owning and operating factories and engaging in large-scale trade within the country as well as increasingly with other parts of the world.

Both forms of Liberalism brought about significant economic, social, and political changes that became identified with increasing democracy.

The Liberal parties that emerged during the nineteenth century from this new tradition differed to some extent from state to state, but they also had a number of common characteristics. They represented the entrepreneurial middle classes who demanded more political and legal equality. Political equality meant the right to vote—at least for the middle class—in parliamentary elections, and legal equality required rule of law. Liberals demanded individual freedom from the state in the form of procapitalist *laissez faire* economic policies as well as civil liberties, such as freedom of speech, press, and assembly. Religious freedom meant opposition to a state religion, freedom of belief, and separation of church and state. On the continent of Europe, Liberalism was associated with nationalism, which in turn was associated with the French Revolution of 1789. The nation state was largely the product of Liberal agitation against the monarchies that had put together multinational states or empires in which national feelings were discouraged due to their often separatist potential, e.g., the Austro-Hungarian Empire or, in the case of Germany and Italy, where monarchies had discouraged national unity in order to protect their small state autonomy. Even though the Liberals did not advocate voting rights for peasants and workers, on the grounds that they were uneducated and/or did not own property, which was required of "responsible" citizens, they are identified with the rise of parliamentary democracy and the civil liberties that promote democracy.

Socialist parties emerged largely as a working-class reaction against the negative effects of the Industrial Revolution. Peasants fled the countryside to work in the new factories in the cities. Overcrowded living quarters, pollution from factory smokestacks, and inadequate medical facilities awaited them. Low wages, long hours, poor and often unsafe working conditions, and lack of a social security or any safety net led to the organization of unions and socialist movements or parties to represent their interests. These unions and parties were fiercely opposed by the capitalists. Socialists agitated in favor of voting rights for workers and peasants, and in some cases their more radical elements promoted revolution and the overthrow of the capitalistic economic system and "bourgeois" parliamentary state that in their view was a government of, by, and for the middle and upper classes. In Great Britain, France, and Germany, the socialist parties were dominated by reformists who, though generally in favor of nationalization of basic industries and redistribution of income, also supported a parliamentary democracy that they assumed would be dominated by the parties that represented the popular majority of workers and peasants. There were differences, however, in the role of ideology and ultimate goals, including demands for nationalization of industry, so that one could distinguish between the somewhat more radical French socialists, the more union-dominated British socialists, and the somewhat more moderate mass membership German Social Democratic Party.

In Russia, reform socialists (Mensheviks) and revolutionary socialists (Bolsheviks) battled each other before World War I, with the Leninist Bolsheviks, later called communists, outmaneuvering the Mensheviks and taking power in a revolution in 1917 against a newly established Liberal government that had in turn taken power only months earlier from the conservative Czarist regime. The actual establishment during World War I of a militant socialist regime by revolution was, of course, a dramatic historical development in Europe, and it had a major impact on European socialist parties. Socialist parties in most European countries, including France and Germany, split into reform socialist and revolutionary communist parties. After World War II the states in central Europe that had been carved out of Russia and the Austro-Hungarian Empire after 1918, i.e, Poland, Czechoslovakia, and Hungary, along with Bulgaria and Rumania, became communist satellites of the Soviet Union. The split between socialist and communist parties in Western Europe persisted until the collapse of communism from 1989 to 1991, but there were significant differences among the various states. The French communists remained an important party, largely loyal to the Soviets, until the 1980s, while the Italian communists remained strong but became increasingly independent and critical of Moscow after the Soviet invasion of Czechoslovakia in 1968. With the help of the Soviet

Union, the communists governed East Germany after World War II until 1989, when the Berlin Wall fell. The communist party in West Germany, outlawed from 1956 to 1968, suffered badly from its association with the ruling communist party in East Germany and was never a serious factor in West German politics after 1945.[7] The communist party and its allies remained a very small if sometimes noisy part of the British political landscape until the 1980s.

The United States

The three European political traditions discussed above did not have the same impact on the development of the American party system as they had in Europe. In the first place, there was no hereditary aristocracy in the American colonies, although there were large landowners, especially in the South, who also owned many slaves. The political elites in the North were not slave owners but rather entrepreneurs, traders, and professionals, i.e., those associated with typically Liberal occupations. There was no peasantry but rather mostly small, independent farmers. Religion was important, but there was no established church in the European sense (although there were more or less established churches in the colonies and states before 1789). The American Revolution was to some extent a conflict between the new ideas of Liberalism, such as broadly based representative government, civil liberties, and nationalism, against the old ideas of British conservatism, such as monarchy and hierarchy, very limited representative government, and empire. This became especially clear with the writing of the American Constitution, which reflected many of the ideas being promoted by European Liberals, such as Montesquieu, John Locke, David Hume, and Adam Smith. The European conservative tradition, then, lacked deep roots in America, and these were weakened further after independence was achieved. Liberalism became the core of the American creed, although it differed to some extent from European Liberalism due to different conditions. Thus, for example, the Liberal demand that only property owners should have the right to vote was generally accepted in the United States in the first decades after the Constitution, but a much larger proportion of

Americans owned property, and settlement in the regions west of the Appalachians by mostly land-owning farmers made the requirement irrelevant. The result was that property ownership as a requirement for voting was repealed by the last state holdout, South Carolina, in 1849. In contrast, universal male suffrage was not achieved in most European states for another fifty years or more. Of course, voting rights for blacks were not secured in the United States, in spite of the Fifteenth Amendment passed after the Civil War, until the 1960s, and the franchise for women in the United States as well as in most European states was not granted until after World War I.

The Liberal tradition came to dominate political thinking in the United States, but, of course, this did not mean that Americans were or are not divided in their political philosophies. There may have been general agreement on the civil liberties guaranteed by the Bill of Rights, but did they apply to slaves, who were not citizens? And after the end of slavery, to what extent did equality under the law apply to black Americans or other minorities, e.g., Chinese workers in the West? If equality were required, could it be *separate* and equal? Free enterprise was generally supported, but what about monopolies that controlled certain economic sectors such as steel, oil, and railroads? A limited state was commonly accepted, but what about government regulation of child labor, poor and unsafe working conditions, polluted air and water, unregulated meatpacking plants, unemployment, or poverty in old age? Should free education be provided to everyone equally, and what about medical care? In other words, there were and are many issues that can divide people within even the Liberal philosophical tradition, and these can be subsumed in very general terms under a left and a right perspective.

Table 5.3

The Liberal Tradition in the United States

Left or "liberal"	Right or "conservative"
Focus on civil liberties and equality secured largely by the state	Focus on free enterprise and freedom from state regulations
Generally supportive of government programs that assist people in various ways	Generally opposed to big government and taxes for government programs
Generally supportive of separation of church and state	Increasingly identified with religious influence in the public arena
Orientation toward internationalism	Orientation toward nationalism
Genrally identified as Democrats	Generally identified as Republicans

Traditional Liberalism is a philosophy that nurtures, sustains, and promotes individualism. We often think of individual freedom as freedom *from* government. Thus freedom of speech, of the press, or of assembly generally mean noninterference by the government. In the United States, left Liberals are designated as "liberals," most of whom are Democrats who usually emphasize civil liberties. But they also demand equality, which often requires government regulation and programs of assistance, such as laws against racial segregation, age and gender discrimination, affirmative action, or a limited welfare state that provides basic services and a safety net. However, liberal support for the separation of church and state, again, requires freedom *from* government.

A free market for entrepreneurs generally means freedom *from* government regulation, or *laissez faire.* Entrepreneurial freedom in the economic arena is perhaps the most important goal of right-of-center American Liberals, or "conservatives." The bias against government regulations in the economic arena also makes these conservatives skeptical about regulations in other areas—especially if they require more taxes—for example, in policies designed to promote equality. On the other hand, they see the need for government regulations to protect private property, promote fair business practices, open markets, and provide a stable currency. The "conservative" Republican Party has also seen the growing influence of fundamentalist religious groups among its supporters that has led to demands for a weakening of the principle of separation of church and state.

The socialist tradition never developed deep roots in the United States at the end of the nineteenth century and thereafter as it did in Europe. There are numerous reasons for this American "exceptionalism," including the broad ownership of private property, the extension of the franchise to all white males by the middle of the nineteenth century before socialist parties made voting rights for workers a major issue, the American frontier and the opportunities it offered to millions of European immigrants, and the ethnic and later racial divisions in society that served as barriers to the collective solidarity characteristic of socialist movements and parties. Unions did emerge and grow during the first half of the twentieth century, and they became identified with the Democratic Party by the 1930s; however, their leadership was never influenced strongly by Marxist and socialist ideology. In recent decades, due in part to major economic changes in the steel, coal, and manufacturing industries, union membership in the private sector has declined dramatically to 7.2 percent, while union membership among government workers increased to 37.4 percent for an overall unionization rate of 12.3 percent.[8] Union membership has been declining in Europe as well, but it is still much higher than in the United States.

Party Systems Today

The role of numbers. Party systems are frequently described in terms of numbers, e.g., one-party, two-party, and multiparty systems. There are many criticisms of this simple classification. It is sometimes argued that a one-party system cannot exist, because "party" suggests that there must be two or more "parts"; however, even a totalitarian party is "part" of a larger whole,[9] and the concept of a single party has become well established in the twentieth century. A more common objection is that "one-party system" is too imprecise. There is a huge difference, for example, between the one-party fascist or communist system and the one-party American South before 1960. Giovanni Sartori suggested a useful classification scheme that improves upon the older, simpler classification that is presented in an altered form in table 5.4.[10]

Table 5.4

Party System Classification (Based on Sartori)

One-party, e.g., USSR, Nazi Germany, North Korea today; China as a special case with entrepreneurial freedom but political repression.
Hegemonic party, e.g., East Germany until 1989 with the communist SED as hegemon and several small, noncommunist parties offering limited alternatives but not opposition; Mexico until the 1980s.
Predominant party, e.g., the Democratic "Solid South" in the U.S. until the 1960s.
Two-party, e.g., United States and, in terms of forming a government, the UK.
Limited pluralism, three to five parties, e.g., Germany today.
Extreme pluralism, six to eight parties, e.g., France and Italy.
Atomized, ten parties or more, e.g., some central European states after the collapse of communism.

The party systems in our four liberal democracies are the two-party, limited pluralism, and extreme pluralism systems. The United States, of course, is the model of the two-party system where, in spite of the occasional emergence of a third party or independent candidate, the same two parties have dominated elections at the national level since the Civil War. While there are multiple parties in the UK, the British do meet

Sartori's criteria for a two-party system (though with some modifications after the election of May 2010—see chapters 4 and 6):

> (i) two parties are in a position to compete for the absolute majority of seats; (ii) one of the two parties actually succeeds in winning a sufficient parliamentary majority, (iii) this party is willing to govern alone. (iv) alternation or rotation in power remains a credible expectation.[11]

Germany is the model of the three- to five-party system of limited pluralism. Indeed, it has changed from a 2½-party system (two large parties, one small party) throughout the 1960s and 1970s to a four-party system (two large parties, two small parties) in the 1980s and 1990s and to a five-party system in 2005 and 2009 (two large parties, three small parties). In the sixteen *Länder*, or states, a somewhat different party system prevails: a four-party system in the former western ten *Länder* and a three-party system in the former eastern six *Länder* (including eastern and western Berlin), with only the two large parties prominent in both East and West.

The French party system is an example of "extreme pluralism," in spite of the left-right bloc that usually forms on the second ballot of presidential elections (though not in 2002) and the second ballot of parliamentary elections. In the 2002 presidential election there were twelve parties that received from 2.31 to 19.88 percent of the vote on the first ballot. In the presidential elections of 2007, there were again twelve candidates, but bloc voting resumed, and the top four candidates received from 11 to 31 percent. The other eight candidates received together 15 percent as opposed to 40 percent in 2002. In the parliamentary elections of 2002 and 2007, eleven and twelve parties, respectively, won seats in the National Assembly; however, one party (UMP)—actually a federation of several parties—received 355 seats in 2002 and 313 seats in 2007 in the 577-member parliament.

The role of party structure. In an influential book published in the early 1950s, the French political scientist Maurice Duverger discussed not only numbers of parties but also their internal structure. He developed a party typology that focused on three basic types of parties. The first kind of party he described as *middle class* conservative and Liberal parties—including, with some reservations, the two American parties—with origins in the nineteenth century. These were *caucus* parties, based on a small membership (in the United States, membership usually refers to supporters who contribute money and time, not formal dues-paying members as in Europe) of "outstanding people" (in French, *notables*) organized in rather independent and decentralized structures. Their activity was directed toward elections and therefore was somewhat seasonal, and their leadership was mostly from elected members of the legislature. They were not generally interested in ideology, but personal rivalries among leaders could be divisive. In West Germany this kind of party was often referred to as an "electoral party" (*Wählerpartei*).

The second type of party was the socialist Mass parties—what the Germans call a "membership party" (*Mitgliedspartei*)—which, as the term implies, was interested in mobilizing and claiming as dues-paying members a large proportion of the working class. Rather than caucuses, the party was organized into *branches*, organizations in which political education as well as electoral activities were important. The number of members, the collection of dues, and the activities associated with the branches required a party bureaucracy[12] consisting of permanent officials that exhibited certain oligarchic tendencies. Doctrine and ideology were important, and rivalries were based more on opinion than personality.

The third general type of party included both the communist and fascist parties of the twentieth century, which were characterized in organizational terms by the formation of *cells*. Both parties were very centralized, with strict discipline and leadership based on autocratic methods. Their focus was less on elections than on propaganda, agitation, incidents, and violence. Their ideology was totalitarian, with no distinction between private and public life, and was based on irrational attachments resulting in a religious-like faith and the discipline of an army. Nevertheless, major organizational differences existed, with the communist parties based on cells in the workplace and the fascist parties based on some kind of militia organization. Communist parties claimed to represent the working classes, while fascist parties focused on the peasants and the community of race, blood, and soil.

Duverger noted that some parties did not fit into his first three types. These "other" parties included the Catholic and Christian Democratic parties that occupied a position somewhere between the caucus and mass parties in organizational structure. He suggested that the British-type Labour Party was not a typical continental socialist mass membership party but one consisting above all of trade unions and cooperative societies; in other words, its membership was mostly indirect. He also included in his "other" category agrarian parties, found, for example, in Scandinavia; and he cited parties no longer in existence or found only in regions outside of Europe and North America.[13]

Given the growth of socialist mass parties in the first half of the twentieth century, Duverger argued that a "contagion from the left" was taking place that would force other parties to copy the more "modern" structure of the mass parties or perish. What he did not realize in the early 1950s was that socialist mass parties would be and already were being challenged by a new kind of "catch-all party."[14] This type of party, best represented in Europe first by the Christian Democrats, was less a class-based ideological "membership party" like its socialist and social democratic rivals than an "electoral party" which was a leader-oriented, broadly based, pragmatic party that appealed especially to Catholics, including workers, farmers and small-town inhabitants, and middle-class and more religious Protestants. The Christian Democrats were also "membership" parties, but their focus was more on attracting strong candidates and winning elections. American parties were also examples of "catch-all parties," a designation that seemed more appropriate than Duverger's "caucus party." By the 1960s it was becoming clear that the "contagion" of which Duverger had spoken was not from the left but from the center-right catchall parties, as social democratic parties became more like catchall parties. The Social Democratic Party of Germany, for example, introduced major reforms in 1959, de-emphasizing its Marxist ties and proclaiming its acceptance of Christian social values and a regulated, but capitalist, welfare state. Parties were seen increasingly as bargaining agents that accommodated independently organized and competing interests. Elections offered "choices between teams of leaders rather than contests among closed social groupings or fixed ideologies."[15]

While the 1960s saw a decline in the socialist mass party in favor of the broadly based "catch-all parties," these parties were in turn under increasing pressure to become "cartel parties." Membership was declining—and continues to drop—and ideology was waning even among socialists. With the collapse of communism in the late 1980s, the parties on the far left were severely weakened. Parties on the far right that stressed nationalism and immigration issues generally remained small, even though they often had limited success at the national level (e.g., the French National Front) and at regional and local levels. The parties that had dominated the political scene in Europe since the 1950s were increasingly characterized by an interpenetration of party and state and by collusion and cooperation among the formally competing parties. The emerging "cartel party model" is characterized by groups of professional party leaders who compete for the opportunity to occupy government offices. Policy making is the responsibility of the professional who seeks to satisfy public wishes rather than to promote public involvement. No major party is ever really out of office; rather, elections determine the degree of influence and government actions. Generous public party financing and party patronage at all levels are good examples of this influence. In the United States, gerrymandering to protect incumbents is another example. But cartel parties are generating new forms of opposition by parties and groups that seek change in the established political system. The Greens are an example, as are the far right anti-immigrant parties in Europe.[16] The teaparty movement that emerged in the US in 2010 is an American example.

Endnotes

[1] Seymour Martin Lipset and Stein Rokkan, "Cleavage Structures, Party Systems, and Voter Alignments: An Introduction," in *Party Systems and Voter Alignments: Cross-National Perspectives*, ed. Seymor M. Lipset and Stein Rokkan (New York: The Free Press, 1967), 1-64, esp. 47.

[2] Ibid., 23.

[3] I refer to the classical Liberals as Liberals with a capital "L" to distinguish them from American liberals with a small "l," who will be discussed later in this chapter.

[4] Peter Mair, *Party System Change* (Oxford: Oxford University Press, 1997), 24–25.

[5] Cf. Maurice Duverger, *Political Parties: Their Organization and Activity in the Modern State*, trans. Barbara and Robert North (New York: John Wiley, 1963).

[6] The British Labour Party differed from its continental counterparts in that it consisted mostly of unions and their members who were automatically enrolled as party members. These worker-members did not participate as individuals but rather were represented by their union leaders, who cast votes for their membership *en bloc*. Therefore, the Labour Party was not a mass party in the sense of the German Social Democratic Party or the French SFIO, which had mass individual membership.

[7] The Communist Party of Germany (KPD) was outlawed in 1956 but readmitted in 1968 as the German Communist Party (DKP). It never succeeded in gaining more than 1 or 2 percent of the vote in West German elections.

[8] *NewYork Times*, January 23, 2010, B1.

[9] Lipset and Rokkan, "Cleavage Structures," 3.

[10] Giovanni Sartori, *Parties and Party Systems* (Cambridge: Cambridge University Press, 1976), 125.

[11] Sartori, *Parties*, 188.

[12] See Robert Michels, *Political Parties: A Sociological Study of the Oligarchical Tendencies of Modern Democracy* (New York: The Free Press, 1962).

[13] Duverger, *Political Parties*, 1–4.

[14] Otto Kirchheimer, "The Transformation of the Western European Party Systems," in *Political Parties and Political Development*, ed. Joseph LaPalombara and Myron Weiner (Princeton: Princeton University Press, 1966), 184–200.

[15] Mair, *Party System Change*, 103–05.

[16] Ibid., 116–19.

Chapter 6

Political Parties in the United States, the UK, France, Germany, and the EU

Introduction

We noted in chapter 4 that the United States has a two-party system, both in the sense that only two parties usually have any chance of winning seats in national elections and that only two parties are represented in the House and Senate (with an occasional independent member). The British also have a two-party system, but only in the sense that there are two large parties in the House of Commons, one of which almost always has an absolute majority of seats. In parliamentary elections, however, the Liberal Democrats may receive from 10 to 25 percent of the national vote (but a much smaller percentage of seats), and regional parties, such as several Northern Irish parties and the Scottish and Welsh Nationalists, win a number of seats as well. Other parties may not have much success in winning seats, but they do win enough votes in many constituencies to prevent the large parties from winning an absolute majority of the electorate. In both the United States and UK, the party system is explained in large part by the winner-take-all electoral system.

Both France and Germany have multiparty systems, although they have very different electoral systems. The nature of their party systems also varies rather dramatically. The French usually have two important parties to the right of center—one to the far right—and two or more parties to the center left to far left. These parties are often represented well in a number of the thirty-six thousand local and regional councils. They also offer candidates for election on the first ballot of the election to the National Assembly and to the presidency. On the second ballot for the National Assembly, the parties that have little chance to gain a plurality may encourage their voters to cast their ballots for a party that is relatively close to it on the ideological scale, which may then result in two-bloc voting. On the second ballot of presidential elections, the center-right and center-left also generally form two blocs. This bloc voting may give the appearance of a trend toward a two-party system, but traditional ideological divisions, regional differences, the first ballot of the two-ballot system, and the opportunities to win seats in local elections contribute to the persistence of the multiparty system.

The German multiparty system has been characterized by two large parties since the Federal Republic was founded in 1949, but in recent decades it has changed from a 2½-party system (two large parties, one small party) to a five-party system with two large parties and three small parties. This five-party system only emerged, however, in the 2005 parliamentary election, when a new far left party joined the scene. Before the 2005 election, a far left party had been an important factor only at the state level in former East Germany. Indeed, in *Land* elections since unification in 1990, there has been a three-party system in the East and a four-party system in the West, with only the two large parties playing an important role in both East and West. Some mostly short-lived protest parties and movements have won a number of seats on occasion in *Land* elections, but they have had no success in national elections.[1]

There are also multiple parties in the EU Parliament, but few of them represent only one member country. Instead, there is a European People's Party that incorporates moderately conservative parties from various states, a socialist party that represents many social democratic and socialist parties in the member states, a centrist Liberal party, a Green Party, and so forth. Member countries are therefore represented in the EU Parliament only indirectly through transnational parties that are by necessity more broadly based and less cohesive than the counterpart parties in the individual states.

The United States

During the political ferment of the revolutionary years and the period of the Articles of Confederation, numerous political groups emerged, but none of them appears to have met the definition of a political party. Even the debate between the federalists and antifederalists over the Constitution did not lead to the formation of parties. Instead, these two camps "were simply two sets of individuals holding different opinions about adopting the Constitution; they were not ... parties, because they lacked the necessary organizational structure."[2] The first political parties in the United States emerged when George Washington's secretary of the Treasury, Alexander Hamilton, and his supporters were opposed by Thomas Jefferson and his supporters in the Congress. Thus the first examples of American parties, like their British counterparts, emerged as groups *within* legislative bodies before they organized *outside* in general society.

Alexander Hamilton was the most active member of Washington's cabinet in promoting an administration agenda, and he tried to ensure passage of his proposals by drawing together those senators and representatives on whose support he knew he could depend by consulting with them regularly in a "caucus" on matters of policy and strategy. Opponents of his proposals realized that the only way to counter his influence was to organize against him those on whose support they could count. Hamilton's forces saw themselves as the true defenders of the Constitution against the radicals behind Jefferson, and they called themselves "Federalists." His opponents, under Jefferson's leadership, saw themselves as a bulwark against the restoration of some form of royalty and monarchical government in the United States, and they called themselves "Republicans"[3] (as in republicans versus monarchists).

By 1800 each party had its congressional caucus, which was used for making legislative policy and strategy and was also the device for nominating candidates for the presidency and vice presidency. Soon caucuses with the same purposes emerged in the state legislatures. By the end of Jefferson's second presidential term of office in 1809, the speakership of the House of Representatives and the membership of congressional committees were controlled by the majority party's caucus.

Extragovernmental (in Britain, extraparliamentary) party organizations, called "Democratic Societies," emerged in the early 1790s. These were the major organizational weapons used by the pro-Jefferson and pro-French elements against the Federalists. According to Ranney and Kendall,

> their characteristic feature was their crystal-clear conception of their own function, which they saw as that of launching and keeping going, each in its own county, activities likely to result in the election of Republicans and the defeat of Federalists at all levels of government. This meant, on one side, directing a steady flow of resolutions at the Congress; but mostly it meant making nominations for elective offices, and seeing to it that no Republican candidate should be beaten by a Federalist because his supporters had failed to organize a campaign of tireless and systematic electioneering on his behalf.[4]

After Jefferson's election as president in 1800, tensions between the Federalists and Republicans began to weaken, and by 1815 the contest between the two was decided with the demise of the Federalists. A second party system began to form in 1824, with the Jacksonian Democrats by the middle of the 1830s being opposed by a growing "Whig" party. During this time the caucus was replaced by the convention for the purpose of nominating candidates. Extragovernmental organization tended to become more extensive between 1800 and the 1830s through the admission of new states and changes of laws in the older states that led to increasing numbers of voters and elective offices. This, in turn, increased the rewards for effective organization. Unlike the first party system, which tended to divide the country into a Federalist North and a Republican South, the second party system was more regionally balanced. Sectional differences were apparent in the election of 1828 between Adams and Jackson, but these had disappeared by 1840. It was also not until about this time that the idea of a "loyal" opposition begin to receive acceptance by most Americans; before then each party tended to regard the other as a dangerous or disloyal faction. However, by 1850 North-South differences again became prominent, and the second party system began to decline. This became apparent with the establishment of the Republican Party in 1856, the split in the Democratic Party in the 1860 election, and the rise of the third party system.[5]

This third party system, called the "Civil War" system by one prominent political scientist,[6] lasted from 1860 to 1893. This era was characterized by Republican Party dominance until the mid-1870s and a far more competitive national political scene with a slight Democratic advantage, bolstered by a solid Democratic South, until 1893. Both parties fell largely under the control of elites who favored industrial development and private enterprise, and the Negro was abandoned by the Republicans while being expelled from the Southern polity. The fourth party system, according to Burnham "the industrialist system," existed from 1894 to 1932. The farmers and the ethnically fragmented urban working class were generally neglected after the mid-1870s, with the former in active rebellion by 1890. Shortly thereafter, an economic depression hit the cities, and the conservative Democrats lost their support throughout urban areas. William Jennings Bryan tried to appeal to both disadvantaged farmers and workers, but these proved unable to work closely together, in part due to ethnic differences as well as economic conditions. The system of party alignment that emerged in the 1890s was structured not around competition between the parties, but around the elimination of such competition both on the national level and in a large majority of the states. The alignment pattern was broadly composed of three subsystems: a solidly Democratic South, an almost equally solid Republican bastion in the greater Northeast, and a quasi-colonial West from which protesting political movements were repeatedly launched against the dominant components of the system.[7]

In part because general elections had become mere formalities in most areas, the direct primary was introduced as an alternative to the nominating convention. Electoral turnout dropped dramatically, and the political parties were increasingly discredited as an instrument of government. One of many consequences was the opposition to parties expressed in the legal requirement of nonpartisan elections at the local level, a characteristic of local politics even today in most parts of the United States that stands in sharp contrast to partisan local politics in Great Britain, France, and Germany.

A major change in the party system began with the presidential election of 1928 and the emergence of large numbers of immigrant votes in the Northeast. However, the Great Depression that started in 1929 with the collapse of financial markets led to a far more dramatic realignment and a fifth party system, which is often called "the New Deal System." This realignment took place at different times in different regions, with the South remaining largely unaffected until the 1960s. Class cleavage was added to the traditional mix of voting alignments, and the party system became nationalized. Growing industrialization and urbanization, population movements to the South and West, dramatic changes in racial policies, demographic changes, and numerous other factors helped to bring about more two-party competition.[8]

During the 1960s, especially with the candidacies of the Republican presidential nominees, Barry Goldwater in 1964 and Richard Nixon in 1968, the South changed from solidly Democratic to predominantly Republican. In the meantime the Northeast became increasingly Democratic, so that a very dramatic reversal in past sectional party voting took place. The Vietnam War, the liberal domestic legislation of Lyndon Johnson, continuing racial divisions, and a number of social and economic issues divided the two parties. But it was the strategy of uniting the traditional small-government conservative economic Republicans with those who were far more interested in opposing abortion, busing, the equal rights amendment, and promoting religion in the schools, relaxing environmental regulations, etc.—together called the "New Right"—that led to victory under Ronald Reagan in 1980 and to a new realignment of parties. This realignment, which appears to have begun in the mid-1960s and possibly reached its peak in the reelection of George Bush in 2004, was different from past realignments in a number of ways. For example, the Democratic majorities in Congress continued until 1994 and the Democratic presidential candidate, Bill Clinton, was victorious in 1992 and 1996, but the increasingly sharp divisions between the two parties and the "sorting out" of key issues along party lines certainly makes the party system in the first decade of the twenty-first century different from the New Deal party system.[9] Therefore, one can argue that the United States is now experiencing its sixth party system.

The United Kingdom

The oldest political party in Britain is the Conservative Party, sometimes referred to as the "Tories." Some observers trace the Conservatives to the reaction to the French Revolution in 1789, but they are more generally seen to have formed in the 1830s and after. The party's policies in the early part of the century were to "support established interests—Crown and aristocracy, landowners, agriculture and the church. It supported the existing constitutional order and was hostile to reform or democratization." Electoral reforms in 1832 and 1867, which brought about modest increases in the voting population, forced the Conservatives to broaden their appeal and to form an extraparliamentary party organization to mobilize new voters. By the time of the third electoral reform in 1884, the Conservative Party had a cohesive parliamentary party group in the House of Commons, an extraparliamentary party organization linking members of the constituency parties to a national organization, and a professional staff at a central office in London.[10]

After additional electoral reforms in 1918, which included extending the franchise to women (until 1930, however, only to women above 30 years of age), the Conservatives broadened their base even more, becoming (at least in their own minds) the "natural party of government." They considered themselves to be a pragmatic, nonideological and flexible party that represented the national interest, rather than class or sectional interests, and that was patriotic and in favor of a strong international role for the UK. They were also closely tied to the Church of England, so that it was sometimes said that the Conservative Party could be found on Sundays in that denomination's church pews.

In the 1970s Margaret Thatcher, who became party leader in 1975 and prime minister in 1979, was far more ideological than her predecessors and changed the party in a neo-Liberal direction that emphasized free market values, low taxation, and less state involvement in the economy and many other areas (a policy approach that she shared with Ronald Reagan). She took a hard line in the Falkland Islands dispute with Argentina, she was skeptical of European integration and the EU, and she insisted on and received a rebate from the EU for "overpayments" based on the relatively small agricultural subsidies paid to British farmers. She also imposed an extremely unpopular "poll tax" on all citizens regardless of income so that everyone would be a taxpayer and therefore recognize that public services were not free. She became so controversial in Europe and in the UK that she was forced out of office in 1990 by her own parliamentary party, which feared the Conservatives would lose the next elections because of her growing unpopularity. She was replaced by John Major, who rather unexpectedly won the 1992 elections. The government of Prime Minister Major suffered throughout his tenure from deep divisions within his own party over social and economic policy as well as policy toward Europe. By the time the 1997 elections were held, it was clear that Labour would win over the fractious Conservatives, who could no longer be seen as the "natural governing party."

The Liberal Party, often described earlier as the "Whigs," was formed in 1859 and after the electoral reform of 1867 became the major opponent of the Conservatives. Indeed, it dominated government until 1918. "It placed great importance on individualism, on rationalism and on freedom as well as on morality in the domestic and international sphere."[11] Unlike the Conservatives, it drew its support from urban and industrial areas and from religious nonconformists. With the establishment in 1918 of universal male suffrage and the franchise for women over thirty, the Liberal Party was eclipsed by the rising Labour Party and remained a small, almost insignificant party until the 1970s. In 1988 it merged with the Social Democratic Party (SDP), a break-off party from the Labour Party described below, to form the Liberal Democrats. The Liberal Democrats, like their predecessor, the Liberals, are today a party of the middle, between the Conservative and Labour parties, combining the individualistic ideological traditions of the Liberals and the revisionist, pragmatic socialism of the

SDP; however, they have been closer to "New Labour" in recent years. This makes the formation of the Conservative-Liberal Democratic coalition government in 2010 rather puzzling, but given the constellation of seats in the House of Commons there was little other choice in obtaining a majority for governing purposes.

The Labour Party was formed in 1900, largely as a result of actions taken by the trade union movement that had been promoting working-class interests in parliament since the 1870s. From its founding until the late 1990s, the Labour Party and labor unions were closely allied. At first a federation of various organizations, it became a national organization in 1918, when it also received a new constitution, which included clause 4, calling for the public ownership of the means of production, i.e., all factories and mines. Unlike socialist parties in France and, especially, Germany, the Labour Party was not a mass membership party but rather for the most part a party of unions and only indirectly of their members. It was, in the words of one political scientist, a party in which "'Labourism,' not socialism, much less Marxism, was the dominant creed."[12] Votes at the party conferences were cast by union leaders, who would cast a bloc vote for all of the union members without consulting them. Nevertheless, the party became a broad and diverse confederation of distinct groups with sometimes conflicting views. At the same time, it had a strong tradition of internal democracy, which meant that its conferences could be tumultuous affairs.

Like the Conservative Party, the Labour Party was a broadly based party, but it was a party of factions. Nevertheless, it replaced the Liberal Party as the major second party when it became the official Opposition in 1922. It formed brief minority governments in 1924 and 1929, and it joined with the Conservatives under Churchill in a coalition government during World War II. It won an unexpected majority in 1945 and introduced the British welfare state. It lost to the Conservatives in 1951 and did not regain office until 1964. It lost to the Conservatives again in 1970, won in 1974, and lost to Margaret Thatcher in 1979. Labour did not regain office until Tony Blair led them to a landslide victory in 1997.

Blair and his "New Labour" party were the result of a process of rebuilding and renewal that had taken place since 1979. Blair had persuaded the party to abandon its commitment to socialism by repealing clause 4 of the party constitution, mentioned above, regarding public ownership of key industries. He also promoted a "third way" between neo-Liberal and socialist ideology that embraced capitalism and globalization but also emphasized educational opportunities. The role of leadership was strengthened, and unions and traditional party organizations were weakened.[13] Blair's efforts to secure party cohesion in Parliament were largely successful but with some notable exceptions. The most obvious example was opposition within the party in 2003 to his decision to support the American invasion of Iraq with British troops. Since the election of 2005, when Labour under Blair's leadership again won a majority of seats in the House of Commons but with a sharply reduced majority of votes, opposition by some Labour MPs to Blair's Iraq policy and to a number of domestic measures continued. In June 2007 Blair stepped down as prime minister and was replaced by his longtime rival, Gordon Brown, the chancellor of the exchequer and most prominent cabinet member. At first Brown was very popular, and he planned to call for new elections in the fall in order to continue in office with an electoral mandate of his own and not one derived from Blair's victory in 2005; however, when the time came to call for new elections, public opinion polls suggested that his popularity had declined, and the results would be very close. Brown decided to wait until May 2010, when new elections would have to be held, but by the middle of 2009 he and his party had become so unpopular that the opposition, especially the Conservatives, was demanding that he call for new elections. He refused, in the hope that he and his party might still be able to win an upset victory.

The British have a two-party system in the sense that since the 1920s only the Conservative and Labour parties have been able to gain the majority of seats in the House of Commons necessary for the party leader to form a single-party government. The Liberals, now the Liberal Democrats, have always been a third force during this time, and they have been increasing their vote in recent parliamentary elections. Indeed, as a result of the parliamentary elections of May 2010, the Liberal Democrats joined the Conservatives to form a coalition government in order to secure a majority of seats. Other, smaller, parties may also gain some seats in the Parliament, but their chances of joining a government are small. On the other hand, the Scottish National Party, the Welsh Plaid Cymru, and the Greens win a higher proportion of seats in the parliaments of Scotland, Wales, and the Greater London Assembly. Because of the party list proportional representation system, small parties have also had some success in EU parliamentary elections. Indeed, a new far-right, anti-EU and anti-immigrant party, the UK Independent Party (UKIP), came in second to the Conservatives in the voting for the EU Parliament in June 2009.

France

Political parties in France are far more recent creations than in our other liberal democracies, but the issues that divide them can generally be traced to the French Revolution of 1789 or to the workers' movements of the second half of the nineteenth century that accompanied industrialization. The oldest of the current parties is the Socialist Party (PS), which, though not formed until 1969, was based on the older French Section of the Workers' International (SFIO), which dates back to 1905. The PS, while sometimes divided among different "currents," has been the most successful party in the Fifth Republic, second only to the various "Gaullist" parties discussed below. Several socialist leaders have served as premier, and one, François Mitterrand, was president from 1981 to 1995. The PS has also been a major force in regional and local government, especially in larger cities. In the 2007 elections for the National Assembly, the PS received 42.25 percent on the second ballot; however, the fortunes of the PS have declined rather sharply since then, due in part to internal divisions.

The French Communist Party (PCF) split from the SFIO in 1920. In part because of its leading role in the French resistance from 1941to 1945, it was an important player in the Fourth Republic from 1946 to 1958, gaining more than 20 percent of the votes in a number of parliamentary elections. Its decline under the Fifth Republic began with the first election in late fall of 1958, but it continued to win around 20 percent of the vote in parliamentary elections until the 1980s. It cooperated with the PS in the 1970s and even joined the first socialist government under the presidency of Mitterrand in 1981–83, but its electoral success diminished as communism increasingly lost its appeal in the 1980s. It continues today to win seats in the National Assembly and in many local councils in spite of the collapse of communism in central and eastern Europe. In 2007, however, it won only 2.28 percent of the vote and fifteen seats in the second ballot for the National Assembly.

Numerous other parties of the left, all of which see themselves as promoters of the "equality" part of the Revolutionary slogan, have arisen over the decades of the twentieth century to challenge the PS and PCF on some issue of ideology. Three such parties received a total of 4.1 percent of the second ballot vote and 6.7 percent of the first ballot vote in the National Assembly election of 2007.

Another party of the nontraditional left is the Greens (*Les Verts*), an often disputatious coalition of conservation and ecology movements that emerged in the 1970s. It has generally done relatively well in elections with proportional representation, such as those for the European Parliament, but, in part because of party splits as well as the electoral system, it has had much less success in elections to the National Assembly.

French Liberals, who also see themselves as the heirs of the Revolution because of their emphasis on the "liberty" part of the Revolutionary slogan as well as their anticlericalism, have gone through a number of transformations. They were never united in one party, but the most successful were the Radical Socialists (who were formed in 1901 and were "radical" in the sense that they were strong supporters of social and political freedom; they were not socialist but generally middle class, centrist, and individualistic) during the Third Republic (1875–1940) and Fourth Republic (1946–58). Though weaker than the socialists and conservatives, they played an important role as a coalition partner for larger parties on the left and right that were trying to form a government. After the establishment of de Gaulle's Fifth Republic in 1959, the party declined to insignificance by 2000. Most Liberal voters supported the center-right non-Gaullist Independent Republicans in the 1960s and the Republican Party in the 1970s, both associated with Giscard d'Estaing, who served as president from 1974 to 1981. In 1978 the Republican Party joined with some other generally like-minded groups to form a loosely organized federation, the Union for French Democracy (UDF). The UDF was internally divided during the 1980s and 1990s, and it split and re-formed on several occasions. Under the leadership of François Bayrou, it did relatively well in the first ballot of the 2007 presidential election, receiving almost 19 percent of the vote in the first ballot. However, in the parliamentary elections held several weeks later, the party split between the Democratic Movement under Bayrou's leadership, which ended up with only four seats, and a new party, the New Center, which supported the new president, Nicolas Sarkozy.

A second non-Gaullist party of the center-right was the *Mouvement républicain populaire* (MRP) that emerged as a Catholic Christian Democratic party in 1944. It was a cross-class party that stood ideologically between anticlerical socialist Marxism and anticlerical Liberalism. It tended to work with the socialists, but this was made increasingly difficult by that party's anticlericalism and cooperation with the communists. Changing its name to the Center of Social Democrats (CDS) in the 1970s, it joined the UDF in 1978.

Since the establishment of the Fifth Republic in 1959, support for and identification with General Charles de Gaulle have been the bases for the dominant party of the right. De Gaulle himself never joined, formed, or led a party, but his views on the international status and independence of France, together with his crucial roles as wartime leader of the French resistance and as political leader from 1944 to 1946 and from 1959 to 1969 (in the first years extricating France from the conflict over Algerian independence and avoiding civil war), made him a lasting rallying point for much of the French population. Starting in the late 1940s, the "Gaullists" formed the RPF, which never became a major force and steadily declined until it was disbanded in 1955. The Algerian crisis led to de Gaulle's return to power in May 1958, and in the fall a new constitution for a Fifth Republic was approved by a referendum followed by parliamentary elections. Political leaders friendly to de Gaulle formed the Union for the New Republic (UNR) to provide support for President de Gaulle and his premier in the National Assembly when the new constitution went into effect in January 1959. Later, in 1967, the UNR became the

Union for the Defense of the Republic (UDR). In 1976 Jacques Chirac founded the Rally for the Republic (RPR), and in 2002 the party name was changed again to Union for a Popular Movement (UMP), a federation of center-right forces dominated by Gaullists. The Gaullist party under its various names has been crucial in the development of the Fifth Republic, because it provided parliamentary support for the new institutions of the republic. The power of the president and the premier he appoints are largely dependent on the support of a majority in the National Assembly, and the Gaullists have usually provided the core of that majority. It also became "the first mass-based disciplined party of the French right" that focused not just on the memory of de Gaulle but also on modern organizational and marketing techniques.[14] The Gaullists, like their opponents in other parties, have often been divided internally by issues. such as the role of France in the EU, and personalities, such as the tensions between Nicolas Sarkozy, minister of Interior, on the one hand, and President Chirac and his premier, Dominique Villepin (like Sarkozy, appointed by Chirac in 2005 following the debacle of the referendum on the EU constitution), on the other. The Gaullists have also been weakened over the past years by economic issues, especially unemployment, and more recently by riots in the late fall of 2005 by young male immigrants from North and sub-Saharan Africa and by students in the winter of 2006 over a new law regulating employment conditions for young people. In spite of these challenges, Sarkozy was elected president of France in May 2007, and the UMP received 46.4 percent plurality of the vote in the June second ballot of the 2007 elections for the National Assembly. It also received again, as in 2002, an absolute majority of the seats.

The Liberals, Christian Democrats, Independent Republicans, and Gaullists are all part of the mainstream right; however, there is another party at the far right of the spectrum: the National Front (FN). This party, formed in the early 1970s by Jean-Marie Le Pen, was supported initially by those who resented the abandonment of Algeria, but it also gained adherents from antimodernization and antistate movements. Like some other fringe parties on the left and right, it also attracts anti-EU and antiglobalization elements. Above all, however, it was and remains the party of those for whom immigration in general and from North Africa in particular is a major concern. It has done relatively well in many local elections, especially in the south and east of France, and in proportional representation elections to the EU Parliament. It split in 1998, but it soon rebounded. Its most sensational success was in the presidential elections of 2002, when Le Pen won 16.85 percent of the vote on the first ballot and unexpectedly defeated the candidate of the PS, Lionel Jospin, who received a surprisingly low 16.17 percent. This gave Le Pen second place behind Chirac with 19.88 percent and, therefore, the right to compete against Chirac on the second ballot. He was soundly defeated, with a vote of only 17.78 percent, but this meant that Chirac's victory was based on votes that were more anti-Le Pen than pro-Chirac. It is clear that the overwhelming majority of French voters are opposed to Le Pen and the National Front, which receives many protest votes, but it is also apparent that the party has a core electorate of at least 10 percent. Le Pen has been replaced as leader of the FN by his daughter, Marie Le Pen, who is not quite as strident as her father on some issues, for example, she appears to reject antisemitism, but is just as staunchly antiimmigrant. In 2011 she was gaining in popularity and being seen increasingly as a threat to President Sarkozy in the first round of the presidential elections in 2012.

In spite of the fragmentation of the French multiparty system, one sometimes speaks of a division of left versus right as if France had a two-party system. For example, the various parties of the right received 49.66 percent of the total vote in the second ballot of the 2007 election for the French National Assembly, whereas the various parties of the left received 49.08 percent. This is the result of the fact that different parties of the right will often support the party on the right that has the best chance on the second ballot in parliamentary and presidential elections of defeating the leading party of the left, and vice versa. The exception is the National Front, which other right parties do not support because of its extremist views.

Germany

Unlike the United States and Great Britain, but even more than France, the party system of Germany has gone through several periods of severe disruption. The party systems of the *Kaiserreich* from 1871 to 1918, of the Weimar Republic from 1919 to 1933, of the Third Reich from 1933 to 1945, and of the Bonn/Berlin Federal Republic since 1949 have been very different in some ways, but in each case except the one-party Third Reich and communist-governed East Germany there were certain parallels consisting of socialist, Liberal, Catholic center, and conservative parties or groups.

In nineteenth century Germany, Liberal, Catholic center, and conservative party groups were active in the parliaments of the various German states and in the abortive "national" Frankfurt parliament of 1848–49. The first party to publish a program and form outside of parliament was the left-Liberal German Progressive Party in 1861. A conservative Prussian party was then formed the same year, as were other conservative parties in the following years. The right-Liberal business-friendly National Liberal Party was put together in the mid-1860s. German socialists had roots going back to the 1830s, but they did not form a party group in the 1848 Frankfurt Parliament in spite of the publication the same year of the *Communist Manifesto*, published by Marx and Engels. In 1863 the Social Democratic Party of Germany (SPD) was formed, not as a Marxist revolutionary party, but as a socialist party willing to work pragmatically within the political system in order to achieve political goals in the interest of German workers. There were, however, elements in the newly formed party that favored a more Marxist orientation.[15]

The North German Federation, which included a dominant Prussia along with more than a dozen other, smaller, German states, was created in 1867. An even larger, unified Germany was established in 1871 following the Franco-Prussian War, which incorporated the North German Federation and four south German states, including Bavaria. Four parties dominated the national parliament (*Reichstag*) during this time. From 1867 to 1878 it was the right-of-center National Liberals; however, neither it nor other leading parties could form a government, as in a normal parliamentary system, because that was the privilege of the kaiser. But the National Liberals were crucial in providing legislative support to the kaiser's chancellor, Bismarck, who could not rely entirely on the more conservative parties. At least in the first years of the new all-

German parliament, the National Liberals were often joined by the left-of-center Progressive Party, in particular in the legislative actions against the Catholic Center Party and its allies. The Center Party was formed in 1870 to represent Catholic interests in a new Reich led by Protestant Prussia. Issues such as state control of the schools divided Liberals and Catholics, as did the new dogma of papal infallibility. Conservative politicians, in contrast to the Liberals, were at first not very supportive of the unification of Germany, because they were more bound to the old particularistic order, in which mostly hereditary rulers and their conservative supporters were in control of the individual states. However, toward the end of the 1870s more nationally oriented conservative parties had formed.

By the mid-1880s the National Liberals, which had become the party of business and industry, and conservative parties, which were oriented toward large land owners, had lost their majority in the *Reichstag* to four "left" parties, i.e., two left-of-center Liberal parties, the Catholic Center, and the SPD, which had been outlawed in 1878. On the other hand, the SPD's elected candidates were allowed to serve their terms, and the party was still able to participate in elections. The antisocialist laws were repealed in 1890, and in the election of 1912 the SPD emerged as the strongest party in the *Reichstag*. During the First World War, the SPD supported the German war effort as a defensive war, in particular against reactionary Czarist Russia. However, the SPD split in 1916 over the war, and an "independent socialist" faction formed its own party.

After the war and the formation of the democratic Weimar Republic in 1919, the Independent Social Democrats split, and the more radical and revolutionary Communist Party of Germany (KPD) was formed. The SPD and Independent Social Democrats rejoined in 1924. A left-of-center Liberal German Democratic Party (DDP) and the Catholic Center Party made up the other parties from the left to the center of the party spectrum. On the right were the right-of-center Liberal German People's Party (DVP) and, to its right, the pro-monarchist German National People's Party (DNVP). This monarchist party was not, of course, a supporter of the democratic Weimar Republic constitution, but it was not as vehemently opposed to democratic government as was the even more antisystem National

Socialist German Workers' Party (NSDAP), or "Nazis," that formed in 1919. After the first election to the new *Reichstag* in 1920, it became clear that the new constitutional order faced fundamental opposition from one important party on the far left (KPD) and two parties on the far right (DNVP and, especially, NSDAP). This was especially damaging, because under the Weimar constitution (in contrast to the *Kaiserreich*), as in any democratic parliamentary system, the government was formed by the parties in the parliament. To the extent that some of these parties were antisystem and could not be included in any government, the formation of coalition governments was made more difficult. Thus the SPD, DDP, and Catholic Center parties were able to form pro-system coalitions, but when they lost seats in the parliament and were forced to join with more conservative parties, they lost even more voter support to the far left and far right. Thus in 1928 the Nazis won only twelve seats, but in the depression year of 1930 they won 107 seats. In July 1932 they won 230 seats, which, together with the Communists, gave the two antisystem parties a majority of the *Reichstag*. This meant that no pro-system government could be formed and that the government that existed at the time had to govern by emergency decrees with the tolerance of the president, former General Paul von Hindenburg. Another election was held in November of 1932, and this time Nazi support was reduced to 196 seats. But the Communists had won one hundred seats, and a pro-constitution majority still could not be formed. The old, recently reelected President Hindenburg decided to try to ask the Nazi leader, Adolf Hitler, whom he had defeated in the presidential election, to form a government with some noncommunist parties, which Hindenburg thought would be a check on Hitler's more radical ideas. But when the *Reichstag* was set on fire, Hitler was able to pass an "enabling act" that allowed him to take emergency actions, and soon he outmaneuvered the other parties and eliminated them from the parliament in order to establish one-party Nazi rule, which was made easier by the death of President Hindenberg.

The disastrous twelve-year Nazi reign that ended with a German defeat in a war started by Hitler and the Allied occupation that followed in the early summer of 1945 after the war were the low points of modern

German history. Only slowly were political parties allowed to reemerge, first at the local level, then at the state or *Land* level. A new constitution, the Basic Law, was promulgated in 1949 in the western part of Germany, which was occupied by the United States, Great Britain, and France, and the first parliamentary elections to the federal parliament, the *Bundestag*, took place in September of that year. Soon thereafter, a government in Soviet-occupied eastern Germany, which in effect was a communist dictatorship, was formed.

Numerous parties participated in the first West German elections. After a few years, however, a 2½-party system emerged.[16] The oldest of these parties, the SPD, was one of the two major parties, the leaders of which were shocked when it did not receive a plurality of the vote in the first parliamentary election in 1949. They had assumed that with their long history as a major German party, their record of resistance to the Nazis, the discrediting of the German capitalist system in the view of many voters because of its collaboration with the Nazis, and the party's nationalist stand against the occupying powers, it would be the obvious choice of a majority of voters. But for the next ten years the SPD suffered from what appeared to be a permanent position of second place, unable to gain more than one-third of the total vote in national parliamentary elections.

The second major party that did receive the plurality of votes in 1949 and was able to form the first government under Chancellor Konrad Adenauer was the Christian Democratic Union (CDU) together with its Bavarian affiliate, the Christian Social Union (CSU). The third party was the much smaller Liberal Free Democratic Party (FDP), which served as a coalition partner for the CDU/CSU for the first seventeen years of the Federal Republic. There were other small parties, including the Communist Party (KPD) until it was outlawed in 1956, but by the late 1950s they had become too small to pass the 5 percent barrier required for receiving seats in parliament under the proportional representation system.

The SPD took up a position of strong opposition to the CDU/CSU-led governments in the decade following the 1949 elections, rejecting their foreign, military, and economic policies on ideological grounds but also because it feared these policies were making reunification of the country more difficult. By 1959, however, and the failure three times in a row to exceed one-third of the popular vote in parliamentary elections, the party was ready to pass a new "Godesberg Program" that accepted the free-market system, spoke of Christian ethics, and did not even mention Karl Marx. In 1960 a party spokesman accepted the foreign policy of the government, including the reunification policy and German membership in NATO. From 1960 to 1966, the SPD, with some exceptions, became a "me too" party and engaged in a politics of consensus.

From its founding soon after the war, the Christian Democrats had a core of Catholic supporters, many of whom had been voters of the pre-Hitler Catholic Center Party, which the CDU and CSU soon replaced. However, the post-war Christian Democrats appealed not only to Catholics but also to more conservative, especially small-town, Protestants as well. In part because of its religious base, it also appealed to a large proportion of women and especially Catholic workers. It was, then, a broadly based "catchall party" that focused more on personality and economic growth and downplayed ideology. The Germans referred to it as a "peoples' party" (*Volkspartei*) or, because of its focus on winning elections, as an "election party" rather than a "membership party" like the SPD.

The FDP was the half party, i.e., the small but still important party of the 2½-party system. It was the heir of both prewar Liberal parties, which is to say that it had a left wing that was oriented toward civil liberties and a more "progressive" foreign policy and a right wing that was focused on the free-market system. (One could argue, therefore, that its two wings were somewhat like the Democratic and Republican parties in the United States.) It was generally to the left of the CDU/CSU on foreign policy and to the right of the CDU/CSU on economic policy. It was a coalition partner of the CDU/CSU until 1966, but it began to move toward the left by the parliamentary election of 1965. It joined the CDU/CSU in forming another coalition government, but the coalition soon broke up over a number of issues.

With the demise of the CDU/CSU-FDP government in 1966, the CDU/CSU turned to the SPD and formed a "grand coalition" that had about 90 percent of the seats in the *Bundestag*. This large majority made it possible for the government to pass a number of important reforms, but it also contributed to growing opposition of the far left and far right. Opposition on the left came not from the communists, who had been outlawed in 1956 but allowed to re-form in 1968 as a "new" DKP rather than KPD, but rather from an "extraparliamentary opposition" (APO) that was led especially by students and disgruntled noncommunist leftists in general. This opposition to the two major parties and their grand coalition government was similar in many respects to the student-led opposition in the United States to the Johnson administration and its Vietnam policies. The APO did not form a party, but the sometimes violent demonstrations in the universities and on the streets had an impact on the German parties and government.

Even more ominous in the view of some observers was the rise since 1964 of a new far-right party, the National Democratic Party of Germany (NPD). This party went to some lengths to dissociate itself from the old Nazis, but its strongly nationalistic, anticommunist supporters, many of whom had been Nazi sympathizers, were frustrated by a lack of progress toward unification, resentful of lost German territories in the East and problems of assimilation of some of the refugees, disaffected by the economic problems of the midsixties, and disgusted by the actions of the APO. The NPD received more than 5 percent of the vote in a series of *Land* elections prior to the 1969 federal elections, and it was feared that they would also enter the *Bundestag* and cause numerous political problems for the country. The immediate concern was that the NPD would gain enough seats to make a CDU/CSU-FDP or SPD-FDP coalition government impossible and therefore force the CDU/CSU and SPD into another now unpopular grand coalition that would, in turn, strengthen the APO in its arguments that such a large coalition was not democratic.

Fortunately, the NPD failed—barely—to gain 5 percent in the 1969 elections, which made it possible for the SPD and FDP to form a government. The CDU/CSU, which actually received more votes and seats than the SPD, was very unhappy about being thrust into the role of an opposition party, and it opposed vehemently the policies of the government to reach a negotiated accommodation with the Soviet Union, Poland, and East Germany (*Ostpolitik*). In 1972 the CDU/CSU tried unsuccessfully to pass a "constructive" no-confidence motion against Chancellor Willy Brandt. This failure was followed by new elections for the *Bundestag*, which the SPD and FDP won easily.

The SPD and FDP won the federal elections again in 1976 and 1980, by which time the FDP had begun to move politically to the right, especially on economic issues, and the SPD to the left on foreign policy. In the fall of 1982 the FDP left the coalition government and joined the CDU/CSU in forming a new government. This was perfectly legal and accepted practice in a parliamentary system, but there was criticism that the new government was not formed as the result of an election and therefore lacked legitimacy. In early 1983 Helmut Kohl, the new chancellor, was able to call for new elections in March by some creative manipulation of the Basic Law (constitution). His coalition government, consisting of the CDU/CSU and FDP, was confirmed, and Kohl and his government continued to retain their majority in the *Bundestag* through three more elections until 1998.

During the 1970s the far right NPD declined, though it did not disappear (it has since become a far-right anti-immigrant protest party that has had considerable success in recent years in *Land* elections in eastern Germany), while the APO continued its fundamental opposition to "the system." In the late 1970s, however, a new Green "movement" emerged that absorbed into its ranks most of those who had been a part of the APO. It was reluctant to call itself a party, and over the next decade and more, a bitter struggle between its "fundamentalist" wing, which rejected any cooperation with the established parties, and its "realist" wing, which urged coalition with the Social Democrats but not the CDU/CSU or FDP, was played out until the realists won, and the Greens became a formal party. This movement, then party, had started as a militant environmental group, supported above all by students and people "under thirty" who were generally better educated and middle class. They were called "postmaterialists," because they wanted to move beyond the traditional "materialist" issues such as wages, working conditions, employment, etc., and on to new issues such as the environment, women's rights, human rights, and peace. Their initial focus was opposition to nuclear power in particular but also to air and water pollution by coal-fired electricity plants, chemical dumping in rivers and lakes, etc. Their position on nuclear power led them also to oppose nuclear weapons, and therefore they were vehemently opposed to the NATO response in the early 1980s to the buildup of Soviet nuclear missiles directed against Europe. The NATO response, consisting of Pershing rockets and cruise missiles with nuclear warheads aimed at Soviet targets, was strongly supported by SPD Chancellor Helmut Schmidt, but his own party was split over this issue, in part because of the pressure from the left by the Greens. This split in the SPD was one of the causes of the collapse of the SPD-FDP government coalition in the fall of 1982.

The Greens were not only proenvironment and strongly opposed to nuclear power and nuclear weapons. They were also a militantly pro-feminist party, very sympathetic to the third world, and pacifistic. They were especially critical of the CDU/CSU and FDP, but the SPD was also seen as having compromised on too many principles and having moved too far to the center of the political spectrum. On the other hand, in the 1980s the Greens did join with the SPD in forming governments in a number of the *Länder*, and coalitions with the established parties, especially the SPD, at the local level were not uncommon. They received more than 5 percent of the vote in the federal elections of 1983 and therefore entered the *Bundestag* as the fourth German party. They gained seats again in 1987, but they failed to win 5 percent in the federal elections of 1990 (their counterparts in the East did gain seats under special provisions for eastern parties). They reentered the *Bundestag* in 1994, and, finally, in 1998, the Greens joined with the SPD in forming a national government under Chancellor Gerhard Schröder. This coalition lasted until the fall of 2005, when the elections led to the formation of a grand coalition, as in 1966–69, with the CDU/CSU and SPD. During the years of the SPD-Green coalition government, the Greens moderated their position on a number of issues, namely the sending of German troops abroad on peacekeeping missions in Kosovo, Macedonia, Afghanistan, and elsewhere.

The communists had always been a negligible factor in West German politics, whereas they ruled East Germany as a dictatorship. The communist East German Socialist Unity Party (SED) did allow a Liberal party, a

Christian Democratic party, and a farmers' party to exist; however, these parties were always a small part of the East German legislature, and they were expected to support the regime in any case. After the East German regime collapsed in the fall of 1989 and Germany was united in the fall of 1990, the SED disappeared and was replaced by the Party of Democratic Socialism (PDS). This party, consisting mostly of "reform" Communists, participated actively and successfully in East German politics and even joined with the SPD in forming governments in a number of East German *Länder*. Together with the SPD and CDU, it became one of the three major parties in the East, while its support in former West Germany remained far below the 5 percent required to gain seats in the electoral system.

Before the *Bundestag* elections of 2005, a group of disgruntled former SPD members and supporters, who were highly critical of Chancellor Schröder's policies designed to reform the German welfare state, formed the Election Alternative for Work and Social Justice (WASG). They were led by Oskar Lafontaine, the chair of the SPD from 1995 to 1999 and a prominent SPD politician at the *Land* and federal levels for many years. He resigned from the Schröder government in 1999 as finance minister because of the chancellor's opposition to his promotion of more deficit spending and easy credit to revive the German economy. In June 2007 Lafontaine and his WASG joined with the most prominent leader of the PDS, Gregor Gysi, to form "the Left Party" (*Die Linke*). This party proceeded to receive a total of 8.7 percent of the vote in 2005 (over 25 percent in the East and 4.9 percent in the West) and therefore entered the *Bundestag* as the fifth party (together with the CDU/CSU, SPD, FDP, and Greens). It then received 11.9 percent of the vote in the 2009 federal elections, exceeding the record 10.7 percent vote for the Greens, winning sufficient support in the West to make it more a national party rather than just an eastern party.

European Union

Political parties are relevant and important actors in the EU. The leaders of the member states, including the heads of government and ministers who make decisions in the European Council and Council of

Ministers, respectively, all have party affiliations and are, in most cases, professional politicians. The parties in the national parliaments and, in some cases in regional parliaments as in Germany, must pass measures to implement EU laws and regulations passed by the Council of Ministers and European Parliament. And, since the first direct election in 1979 of members (MEPs) to the EU Parliament (EP)— they were appointed from member state parliaments from 1958 to 1979—almost all successful candidates for seats have not only been nominated by political parties; they have also formed party groups that usually comprise MEPs from a number of member states. Furthermore, some of these party groups are organized as extraparliamentary transnational federations of national parties. This means that there is some semblance of political parties acting as European-wide organizations and not merely as collections of national parties. There are normally eight to eleven party groups in the EP, and usually only a dozen or two MEPs are independents who are not part of a particular party group. While political parties are obviously most visible in the EP, they are also present in the Committee of the Regions, established in the early 1990s.

The main party families discussed in general in chapter 5 and more specifically above in this chapter are well represented in the 736-seat European Parliament (EP) of the EU.[17] Arranging these parties from right to left after the 2009 EP elections, the anti-EU or anti-integration Europe of Freedom and Democracy group, which is dominated by radical anti-EU Euroskeptics from the UK, represents 4.3 percent of the total vote and has thirty-two seats. The right-wing conservative party group, European Conservatives and Reformist Group, made up of eight parties, represents 7.3 percent of the voters and has fifty-four seats. The center-right Christian Democrats, who are assembled under the label European Peoples' Party (EPP), the largest group in the EU Parliament, received 36 percent of the vote and 265 seats. On social issues, such as divorce and abortion, the Christian Democrats are generally to the right of the conservatives, while on economic issues they are usually to the left. The Christian Democrats are different from the parties to their right due to their stands on economic issues as well as on divorce and abortion but also because they are more supportive of European integration than the more nationalist-oriented conservatives, who tend to be divided on this issue.[18]

To the left of the EPP but still generally right-of-center or center are the Liberals, who have formed the party group Alliance of Liberal Democrats for Europe (ALDE). They won 11.4 percent of the vote and have eighty-four seats. With respect to personal and social freedom, the Liberals are to the left of the Christian Democrats, but they are generally to the right on economic issues. Indeed, Liberals tend to be divided between those who focus on social and political freedom, e.g., pro-choice and civil liberties, and those who stress economic freedom (rather like traditional Democrats and Republicans in the United States). Both camps tend to be supportive of European integration. Some Liberal parties have a strong agricultural tradition and favor the EU's Common Agricultural Policy (CAP); however, support for the EU may be conditional, depending on the continuation of subsidies under CAP.

The Greens formed a party group in the EP with 7.5 percent of the votes in the member states and fifty-five seats. They focus on environmental issues and pacifism but are also supportive of radical political and economic reforms that promote their "postmaterialist" agenda. The Greens have been divided on European integration, however; they support the cross-national environmental initiatives of the EU, but they are critical of the "democratic deficit" in EU decision-making institutions.

The second strongest party group was formed by the various social democratic and socialist parties and is now called the Progressive Alliance of Socialists and Democrats (S&D). It received 25 percent of the total vote in the member states and 184 seats in the EP. The numerous socialist parties that constitute the left-of-center S&D are generally united on the core issues of moderate state intervention in the economy and political and social rights such as abortion, civil liberties, and gay rights. They are somewhat divided, however, on European integration, with internal divisions found rather consistently within socialist parties, e.g., in Great Britain, France, and the Scandinavian countries.

The radical left parties, including older communist parties such as the French PCF, former communists who changed their names such as the German PDS (now the Left Party), and some small left splinter parties, also form a party group in the EP, the Confederal Group of the European United Left/Nordic Green Left (GUE/NGL). They received 4.8 percent of the votes and thirty-five seats. They are generally opposed to European integration, which they tend to see as an antiworker capitalist organization.

The support for the many parties above varies, of course, from state to state. There are, for example, no regionalist or Euroskeptic parties in Germany, whereas the latter always receive some support in France, and both groups have elected MEPs in Great Britain, where Euroskeptics did especially well in 2009. Liberal parties exist in virtually all member states, but their support varies widely from one election to the next. The conservatives do well in Great Britain, as do the Gaullists in France, whereas their even more successful counterparts in Germany are the Christian Democrats. The Greens do not elect any MEPs in a number of member states; they do have representation in Great Britain and France, but they are most successful in Germany. The socialists generally do well in all three of our countries, but their percentage of the vote declined dramatically in 2009. Indeed, social democratic and socialist parties in the PES (now S&D) alliance did poorly in almost all of the EU member states in 2009.

The fortunes of the parties are not, however, indicative of voter approval or disapproval of EU policies so much as reactions to domestic political and economic conditions. EU elections provide voters with the opportunity to send a message to their national governments about popular concerns, so that fringe parties on the far left and far right generally do much better in EU elections than in national elections. This is not to say that EU policies are irrelevant, however. For example, the expansion of the EU from fifteen to twenty-seven member states since 2002; the perception that workers from the new member states are now free to enter the older member states and take away jobs; the widespread opposition to large-scale immigration—legal and illegal—from various third world, especially Muslim, countries; open borders that some voters fear have made it easier for criminals and illegal immigrants to travel from one country to another; and the growth of EU regulations over many policy areas that were previously the concern of national governments are the targets of attention for many Euroskeptics and nationalists throughout the EU.

From the brief overview above, it is clear that the various "party families" in Europe are well represented in the EP. Indeed, four of the "families" are organized in European party federations: the Christian Democrats (with some conservative parties) in the EPP; the socialists and social democrats in the S&D; the Liberals in the ALDE; and the Greens in the European Green Party/European Free Alliance. It is also clear that in addition to a left-right division in the EP party system, there is also a division between those in each camp who emphasize European integration as opposed to sovereign national rights. There are some issues in the EP that cause a general division between left and right parties, but about three-quarters of the members vote together most of the time. This is because the two major party groups, the right-of-center EPP and the left-of-center PES (now S&D), make up about two-thirds of the EP, and they are both generally supportive of a strong role for the EU. In spite of some internal divisions within the party groups, because of certain national perspectives and ideological differences, party group cohesion tends to be quite strong. This means, of course, that voting is mostly along party lines rather than by national delegation and alleged national interest. It can also be seen, however, as a reflection of "the well-known EP party group tendency to present a 'united front' in a common struggle against member-state governments and other EU institutions."[19]

As noted briefly above, the other EU institution that has a formal organization of European-wide parties is the Committee of Regions (CoR). The parties in the CoR are not as well organized or cohesive as in the EP, however, because—as in the case of some of the representatives from the German *Länder*—the regional delegations may see a commitment to their regions that has precedence over party discipline. Another difference is that the parties in the CoR do not receive financial support from the EU budget as do the parties in the EP.[20]

Conclusion

In chapter 5 we saw that there were three philosophical traditions in Europe, which were described as conservative, Liberal, and socialist. These traditions had their origins in the feudal era of absolute monarchies, in the Enlightenment and Industrial Revolution beginning in the eighteenth and continuing into the nineteenth century, and in the massive changes in agricultural to factory work and resulting population shifts from rural to urban areas in the nineteenth and twentieth centuries. In the United States, which was the first of the Liberal democracies to promulgate a constitution that provided for a popularly elected legislature and a head of state and government elected indirectly by the people, political parties developed as early as the 1790s, during the first government of George Washington. Because the United States lacked a feudal tradition and a well-established aristocracy, there was no real philosophical foundation for a conservative party with roots in that tradition. Jefferson's state-oriented Republican-Democrats may have suspected and accused Hamilton's Federalists of being pro-monarchy, but the Federalists were really more in favor of a stronger federal role in promoting trade and the economy. From that time to the present, with the exception of the era from about 1815 to the 1830s, one can say that the United States has had two major parties that were reflections of left and right versions of the Liberal tradition that was dominant in the colonies and was the general belief system of the founders of the republic and authors of the American Constitution. It gained strength after the Constitution went into effect because of the growing acceptance of greater social and political equality that favored Liberalism.

Later in the nineteenth century, socialist parties emerged in Europe in response to the industrialization of the economy, the rapidly growing working class and their working conditions, and potent ideological critiques of capitalism. However, for several reasons socialist movements and parties in the United States enjoyed only limited success at best: universal (white) male suffrage had been secured everywhere in the United States by 1850 and was not an issue that socialists could exploit as in Europe; property ownership was widespread; opportunities for settling the American West existed throughout most of the nineteenth century; the American standard of living was relatively high in comparison with Europe; and, perhaps most importantly, ethnic, racial, religious, and regional tensions discouraged class solidarity. As we saw in chapter 4, the single-member district electoral system also made it more difficult for a socialist third party to challenge the established parties.

The United States, then, started with a two-party system and, with some brief exceptions, has had two major parties ever since. On the other hand, the names and overall goals of the two parties have changed on occasion, so that one can speak of six different party systems throughout American history.

In Great Britain political parties outside of parliament did not come into existence until after the electoral reform of 1867. In the following decades the Conservative Party (Tories) and the Liberal Party (Whigs) dominated parliamentary politics and elections. By the turn of the century, socialist movements were stirring, and in 1900 the British Labour Party was formed. The Labour Party benefited from further electoral reforms, and by the 1920s it presented a serious challenge to the Liberal Party, soon replacing it as the second major party. The Labour Party won the election of 1945, and for the first time it was able to form a Labour government.

Since then the Labour and Conservative parties have been the two major parties in Britain; however, the Labour Party suffered from deep divisions in the 1970s that led to the formation of the more centrist Social Democratic Party (SDP).This led to an almost even division of votes for Labour and the SDP in the 1980s. By the early 1990s, the SDP and the Liberals had joined to form the current Liberal Democratic Party, which has since become a major third party, running only slightly behind the Conservatives and Labour. The Conservatives, under the leadership of Margaret Thatcher, won three elections in a row starting in 1979; however, after more than ten years, Mrs. Thatcher had become unpopular even among many members of the Conservative Party, and she was replaced by John Major as prime minister in 1990. The Conservatives under Major's leadership won the election of 1992, but they lost to Tony Blair and the Labour Party in 1997. After that election, the Conservatives began to decline in popularity and to see the Liberal Democrats and even Blair's moderate "New Labour" pick up many of their former voters. By 2008–09, however, the Conservatives received more public support in opinion polls than Labour, and this trend was confirmed in the parliamentary elections of 2010, when the Conservatives won the most votes.

The British still have a two-party system in the sense that only the Labour and Conservative parties are likely to receive a plurality of votes in parliamentary elections and therefore the majority of seats required to form a government. On the other hand, the growth of the Liberal Democrats in recent years and the emergence of the Scottish National Party and small parties from Wales and Northern Ireland forced the Conservatives and Liberal Democrats to form a coalition government in 2010.

If the need to form a coalition were to persist for more than a few years, the British "Westminster system" of government would change rather dramatically and become more like some of the continental European parliamentary systems.

French political history reflects clearly the influence of the conservative, Liberal, and socialist traditions. The conservative tradition is associated with the *ancien regime* that was overthrown by the French Revolution of 1789. This was a Liberal revolution that promoted liberty, equality, and separation of church and state as major goals. The old conservative values associated with religion, hierarchy, and tradition remained in tension with the new Liberal goals throughout the nineteenth century. By the end of the century, both of these philosophical traditions were being challenged by new socialist movements. The political parties that were formed from these traditions struggled for influence and power throughout the twentieth century, with right and left extreme parties often complicating the functioning of the third, fourth, and fifth French republics that served as the political frameworks from 1875 to 1940, from 1946 to 1958, and after 1959.

Today the French party system consists of parties on the far left, i.e., the communists (PCF); the left-of-center to right-of-center socialists (PS), Liberals (UDF), and conservatives (UMP); and the far right National Front (FN) along with a number of much smaller parties that usually come and go at the time of presidential, parliamentary, and EP elections.

Since the 1870s, the Germans have lived under five different political systems: the *Kaiserreich*; the Weimar Republic; the Third Reich; after the war the West German democratic and East German communist systems; and, since 1990, the united German system, which is basically the West German system established in 1949. Excluding the Third Reich and the East German communist dictatorship, the three European political traditions have been clearly represented in the party systems of each regime.

In 1949, when the first postwar national parliamentary elections were held in West Germany, a multiparty system seemed to have reemerged. On the other hand, two parties were dominant: the Social Democrats (SPD), who were expected to but did not receive a plurality of the votes, and the newly formed Christian Democrats (CDU and, in Bavaria, the CSU), who did receive a plurality. A Liberal party, the FDP, was an important but much smaller third force, as was the conservative German Party (DP). A small Catholic Center Party received some seats but was later absorbed by the CDU and CSU. The communists (KPD) were also represented in the first *Bundestag*, but they soon declined as the economy improved and the negative example of East Germany became apparent. A number of other small parties were also represented, but the elections of 1953 and 1957 showed a dramatic decline in the fortunes of all of the smaller parties except the FDP, which, though suffering a decline, was still holding on with more than 7 percent. The results of the elections in 1961 made it clear that Germany had a 2½-party system consisting of the CDU/CSU, SPD, and the smaller FDP. A far right party, the NPD, threatened to enter the *Bundestag* in 1969, but it failed to win the required 5 percent, and the 2½-party system lasted until the 1983 elections.

In 1983 the Greens entered the *Bundestag* for the first time, at first as an antiparty movement, but later as a potential partner of the SPD. By the time West and East Germany united in 1990, a four-party system had become established in West Germany. At first it appeared that this system might be simply absorbed by East Germany, but after a few years it was clear that East Germany had a three-party system consisting of the CDU, SPD, and mostly former communists organized in the PDS. Due to special arrangements for the East in the elections of 1990, a sizable PDS party group was formed in the *Bundestag* that year, but after the elections of 1994 and 1998 only a few directly elected individual PDS representatives remained in office. In 2005 the PDS joined with some dissident elements in the SPD to form the Left Party, which received almost 9 percent of the vote; in 2009 it received even more support, 11.9 percent. As of the 2005 election, then, Germany has two large and three small parties at the national level. The far-right NPD is not represented in the *Bundestag*, but it has gained seats in a number of *Land* legislatures and local councils in East Germany in recent years.

The European party families derived from the conservative, Liberal, and socialist traditions are well represented in the EP. The "postmaterialist" Greens are also represented, as are some regional parties and Euroskeptics that object to centralizing tendencies in the EU. These parties that come from individual member states have formed from eight to eleven party groups in the EP since the first popular election in 1979.

While these party groups have much in common internally, the issue of national sovereignty divides to a greater or lesser extent almost all of the numerous parties that have gained seats in the EP. This issue is related to the question of majority decision-making (deepening), according to which individual state interests can be overridden. The issue of expanding membership (widening) is also a cause of division.

In spite of divisions between and among parties of the same family, e.g., British and German socialists, not only over issues of national interest but also over deepening and widening in the EU and other matters, party group cohesion in the EP is strong. Indeed, general agreement among party families in the EP tends to be rather high, in part apparently because of parliamentary solidarity vis-à-vis the other institutions of the EU and the national parliaments. The fact that the EP is not responsible for forming a "government," has only limited legislative powers, and remains rather distant from the voting population in the EU also affects the amount of partisanship found in the EP.

The numerous parties in the EP are a reflection not only of the fact that there are twenty-seven member states, each with a somewhat different party system, and a proportional electoral system that gives representation to small parties; they are also a result of the nature of EP elections, which are "second-order" elections.[21] This means that as in some regional and local elections, many voters do not vote for the parties they normally support in national elections but rather express their dissatisfaction with the governments and parties in their countries by casting a "protest vote" for an extremist party or in any case for a non-establishment party. Thus voting in EP elections reflects to some extent domestic political conditions as well as views toward the EP and EU. It also reflects the fact that the parties in the EP do not form a "government" that controls EU decision-making. In this sense the EP is in a position somewhat similar to the German *Reichstag* before 1918.

Endnotes

[1] Arthur B. Gunlicks, "Elections in the Länder, 1990-2002," in *Germany at fifty-five*, ed. James Sperling (Manchester and New York: Manchester University Press, 2004), 302–21.

[2] Austin Ranney and Willmoore Kendall, *Democracy and the American Party System* (New York: Harcourt, Brace and Company, 1956), 96.

[3] Ibid., 97.

[4] Ibid., 102.

[5] Ibid., 110; see also the chapters by Paul Goodman and Richard P. McCormick in *The American Party Systems*, ed. William N. Chambers and Walter Dean Burnham (New York: Oxford University Press, 1967).

[6] Walter Dean Burnham, "Party Systems and the Political Process," in Chambers and Burnham, eds., *The American Party Systems*, 295–98.

[7] Ibid., 300.

[8] Ibid., 302–04.

[9] For detailed analyses of party realignments in the United States, see Wilfred E. Binkley, *American Political Parties: Their Natural History* (New York: Alfred A. Knopf, 1964) and James L. Sundquist, *Dynamics of the Party System: Alignment and Realignment of Political Parties in the United States* (Washington, DC: The Brookings Institution, 1983).

[10] Gillian Peele, *Governing the UK: British Politics in the 21*st *Century*, 4th ed. (Oxford: Blackwell Publishing, 2004), 275.

[11] Ibid., 302.

[12] Ibid., 287.

[13] Ibid., 288–89.

[14] Anne Stevens, *Government and Politics of France*, 3rd ed. (New York: Palgrave Macmillan, 2003), 211.

[15] Ludwig Bergsträsser, *Geschichte der politischen Parteien in Deutschland*, 11th ed. (Munich: Günter Olzog Verlag, 1965), 97–118.

[16] For a review of political parties from 1949 to the early 1970s, see Arthur B. Gunlicks, "Opposition in the Federal Republic of Germany," in *Political Opposition and Dissent*, ed. Barbara N. McLennan (New York: Dunellan Publishing Company, 1973), 185–227.

[17] For an excellent overview of parties in the EP, see Simon Hix and Christopher Lord, *Political Parties in the European Union* (New York: St Martin's Press, 1997), from which much of the discussion in this section is drawn.

[18] For the results of the 2009 EU parliament elections, see http://www.europarl.europa.eu/parliament/archive/staticDisplay.do?language=EN&id=213

[19] Luciano Bardi, "Parties and Party Systems in the European Union," in *New Parties in the New Europe*, ed. Kurt R. Luther and Ferdinand Müller-Rommel (Oxford: Oxford University Press, 2002), 303–04.

[20] Hix and Lord, *Politcal Parties*, 61–62.

[21] Bardi, "Parties," 301.

Chapter 7

The American Presidential and French Semipresidential Systems

Introduction

In chapter 2 we saw that there are significant institutional differences among liberal democracies in terms of presidential versus parliamentary systems and in their separation of powers, checks and balances, selection of leaders, and terms of office. Within the general category of presidential systems, the United States has the single executive characteristic of such systems but with a number of unique features; France, on the other hand, has a semipresidential system with a dual executive. We also saw in chapter 3 that the United States is a federation, while France is a unitary state. Great Britain and Germany have parliamentary systems with dual executives typical of such systems, but each country has very different selection procedures for both the head of state and head of government. Great Britain is also a decentralized unitary state, while Germany is a federation.

There are also significant differences among legislative bodies in each of the four liberal democracies. These differences include the number of chambers and their methods of selection, the role of political parties, the importance of committees, their independence from and ability to check the executive branch, and the power of the executive to call for new parliamentary elections.

The Presidential System: The US Model

The single executive: the president. The first American constitution, the Articles of Confederation, did not provide for an executive to implement the laws; nor did it have a national court system or supreme court. The "president" was merely a presiding officer of Congress, the states were responsible for judicial functions, and the Congress was left to settle disputes between the states. In the very different Constitution of 1787 that replaced the Articles of *Confederation* with a *federation* in 1788, three separate branches of a national government were provided to help establish a stronger *union*: a legislative branch in Article I, an executive branch in Article II, and a judicial branch in Article III. The Constitution does not provide for the direct election of the president by the people but by an electoral college, the members of which are elected by the people. Normally the candidate who wins the popular vote is also the one who receives the required majority in the Electoral college; however, the election of 2000, when Al Gore received five hundred thousand more votes than George W. Bush, is a reminder that this is not always the case. The president and the vice president are elected for a four-year term. George Washington set the precedent of serving no more than two terms; however, Franklin D. Roosevelt was elected four times. He died in office at the beginning of his fourth term and was succeeded by Harry S. Truman. In 1951 the Twenty-Second Amendment to the U.S. Constitution limited the president to two terms of office.

Head or Chief of State. The framers of the Constitution considered the option of having separate executives as the head of state and head of government, but they created a single executive who would serve both functions. The title "chief of state" is not found in the Constitution, but several roles given the president make it clear that he is the ceremonial leader and symbol of the nation. These include his oath of office taken at an inauguration ceremony, the state of the union address (which was delivered in person only by Presidents Washington and Adams and not again until Woodrow Wilson in 1913), his responsibility to receive foreign ambassadors and other public ministers, and the fact that he is the only official selected by a national electorate. As a result, he is also the focus of public attention and is expected to speak and act on behalf of the nation. The president can delegate some of his ceremonial duties to his family, the vice president, or cabinet members, but he remains the most prominent political and symbolic figure in the nation.

Head of Government: Chief Executive. Article II, Section 1, of the Constitution states that "[t]he executive Power shall be vested in a President of the United States." The "executive power" is not defined clearly in Article II, and the Supreme Court has been called upon on numerous occasions to interpret this provision. Article II, Section 3 helps somewhat by stating that the president is responsible for the execution of federal laws, and the ambiguity of the provisions of Article II have made it possible for presidents over time to interpret their functions as "chief executive" in an expansive manner.

As "chief executive" or "chief administrator," the president appoints numerous officials to the executive branch but with the check of Senate confirmation of many of the nominees. He administers federal laws through his cabinet secretaries and various agencies, but Congress passed the laws and can change them at any time. Congress can also eliminate as well as create federal agencies, and it can make agencies independent of the president. On the other hand, Congress often delegates to the president and other executive officials the power to issue regulations and programs. Overall, the role of the president as chief administrator has increased dramatically in recent decades.

There are a number of offices and agencies that assist the president in administering the laws of the land. One of the most important of these is the Executive Office of the President, which includes the White House Office, the Council of Economic Advisers, the National Security Council, and the Office of Management and Budget. The president's closest advisers, such as his national security adviser and chief of staff, work in the White House Office.

Another important body is the president's cabinet, which consists of the secretaries of the major departments of government, such as the secretary of state, secretary of defense, secretary of education, and the secretary of homeland security, a new position created in 2002. Unlike the close advisers of the president in the White House Office, including the national security adviser, the fifteen cabinet secretaries need Senate approval to serve. Only on very rare occasions have the president's nominees failed to gain Senate approval. The role of the cabinet varies, with some presidents, such as Eisenhower, having frequent cabinet meetings to discuss important issues and seek advice. Other presidents, such as Kennedy, had few cabinet meetings and met with cabinet secretaries individually when their advice was sought. Still other presidents, such as Carter, started with weekly cabinet meetings but later met much less frequently. President Reagan divided his cabinet into councils along subject lines, but he and his successors continued to make most important policy decisions with his senior advisers. President Clinton paid special attention to promoting diversity by appointing more women and minorities, a policy followed by George W. Bush and Barack Obama.

Though the cabinet secretaries preside over the largest part of the federal bureaucracy, there are a number of executive agencies, such as the CIA, NASA, the Environmental Protection Agency (EPA), and others that are not part of the cabinet. Most of these are "independent agencies" whose heads are appointed by the president and are responsible to him. Nevertheless, they do operate without some of the constraints of the cabinet departments and often are associated with special interests. Government corporations, such as the Tennessee Valley Authority (TVA) and Amtrak are controlled by boards of directors that are appointed by the president.

Other important parts of the federal bureaucracy concerned with the economy are the regulatory agencies, some of which, such as the Food and Drug Administration, are part of a cabinet department (the FDA is part of the Department of Health and Human Services). However, most regulatory agencies are independent agencies. Examples are the Federal Reserve Board, the National Labor Relations Board, the Consumer Product Safety Commission, and the Federal Trade Commission. They are led by independent boards of commissioners, who are appointed for overlapping terms by the president but cannot be removed by him.

Head of Government: Commander-in-Chief. There was a consensus among the Founding Fathers that the military should be under civilian control, and the Constitution (Article II, Section 2) makes the president "Commander in Chief of the Army and Navy of the United States, and of the Militia of the several States, when called into the actual Service of the United States." This power has always been very important and is today also very controversial.

Controversy regarding the president's role as commander-in-chief arises in part from the tension between the president's role and congressional power to declare war and "raise and support Armies." In fact, Congress has declared war only five times in the history of the United States and not since World War II. Thus President Truman sent American armed forces to Korea immediately following the invasion of South Korea by North Korea in June 1950 without a declaration of war or even congressional authorization after the fact. Therefore, the Korean War set a major precedent for presidential power in emergency situations.

Since the Korean War presidents have sent troops abroad on a number of occasions. The United States was already heavily involved in South Vietnam when President Lyndon Johnson received congressional authorization in the Tonkin Gulf Resolution of August 1964 to take military actions in Southeast Asia and to attack North Vietnam in retaliation for an attack against an American destroyer. Later it was discovered that apparently there had been no attack by North Vietnam, and the resolution was repealed in 1971. In 1973 the War Powers Act was passed over President Richard Nixon's veto. The act limits the power of the president to wage war without the approval of Congress. While this would seem to be a logical extension of the power of Congress to declare war, President Nixon and other presidents since Nixon have resisted such congressional restraints on the grounds that they are an infringement of the president's executive powers. The most recent example is congressional reaction to President Obama's limited military response to the uprising in Libya. The act has been considered for revision or replacement over the years, but no changes have been made to date.

Congress approved military action in 1991 in the Persian Gulf War by American and a number of coalition forces, as a result of which Iraq was forced to leave Kuwait, but differences between the president and Congress were revealed in a number of other American actions, including Somalia, Haiti, and the former Yugoslavia. Congress passed a resolution in January 2002 authorizing military action against Afghanistan, and in 2002 Congress authorized the American military invasion of Iraq. By 2005 this authorization was being subjected to increasing criticism for the power it gave President Bush to wage war, and by 2007 there were even proposals to rescind the 2002 Iraq resolution. During the final years of the Bush administration, there was serious conflict between Congress and the president over the extent of the president's powers to commit the United States to military action abroad, to use military tribunals to try foreigners accused of terrorism, to incarcerate alleged terrorists without trial in Guantanamo Bay, and to secure information on potential terrorists by electronic means.

Head of Government: Chief Diplomat. As in other areas, the president shares power with Congress in his conduct of foreign affairs. He alone has the responsibility to "receive Ambassadors and other Public ministers," but he can appoint ambassadors only with the "Advice and Consent of the Senate." He can negotiate treaties, but he needs the consent of two-thirds of the Senate to ratify them. Congress can promote or frustrate the president's plans because of its power to "regulate Commerce with foreign Nations." As we saw above, the president and Congress may also be in conflict over the meaning of the president's power as commander-in-chief.

In spite of the constraints on the president's powers in foreign affairs, he is the dominant player in this area—a dominance confirmed in a number of cases by the Supreme Court. As chief of state, as the only nationally elected official, as the representative of the nation, commander-in-chief, head of numerous executive agencies (some of which provide the president with important advice and information), and with the ability to act quickly and in secrecy, the president enjoys important advantages over Congress in the making of foreign policy. These advantages are especially important given the need for effective leadership that only the executive branch can provide for a country that has become far more involved in the world than it was before the 1940s. This involvement is the result of its military role in World War II, its leadership role of the West during the Cold War, its emergence as the only superpower after the demise of the Soviet Union in 1991, and the role of the United States in world trade, commerce, services, and technological developments. The importance of English as an international language and the "soft power" resulting from American values and cultural influence are also major contributors to the impact of the United States in an increasingly globalized world.

Head of Government: Economic Leader. While Article I of the Constitution gives Congress a number of economic powers, including raising taxes to provide for the defense and general welfare of the United States, regulate commerce with foreign nations and among the states, and borrow and coin money, it often does so upon the urging of the president. The president implements the decisions of Congress regarding taxing and spending; he negotiates commercial treaties with foreign states; he can veto economic legislation; and he can make his own proposals in his State of the Union message to Congress. Indeed, over the years, as the domestic economy has grown and the United States has become a major trading partner with the rest of the world, the president has become a significant figure in economic decision making.

For many Americans, he is the person most responsible for the state of the economy, and his influence is, indeed, important. Presidents like to take credit for a strong economy, but inflation, unemployment, rising gas prices, outsourcing, low growth, deficits, and, of course, a serious recession not only weaken public support; they may also cost him or his party the next election.

In fact the president's influence over the economy is limited. He must share power with Congress, which may not agree with his economic policies, and he cannot control the Federal Reserve Board, which sets interest rates; the economic advice he receives from various sources is often controversial and even contradictory; the economic information he has may be incomplete, contradictory, or inaccurate; and the federal government cannot control or sometimes even affect policies in the American states, let alone conditions abroad, including oil prices and other commodity prices, currency manipulation, natural catastrophes, or war. Above all, however, the president has only a limited and indirect influence over the decisions of millions of businessmen and corporations in the United States and abroad who determine to a large extent the supply and costs of goods and services and over the tens of millions of consumers who affect their demand. The American free enterprise system, after all, is subject to only limited government control or influence, as was demonstrated in the recession of 2007-09 and resulting unemployment figures that remained persistently high even after the official end of the recession in 2009.

Head of Government: Legislative Leader. The president does not, of course, pass laws. The Constitution (Article II, Section 3) does, however, give him the power to recommend to Congress "such Measures as he shall judge necessary and expedient." He also has the power to veto bills passed by both houses of Congress. Many powers of the Congress and of the president are "implied," while Congress has also added to presidential powers by legislation. Many presidents have interpreted the Constitution to expand their powers, and various developments, such as economic, military, or political crises, have contributed to these interpretations. Technological developments, such as radio and television, and now the Internet, have added to his ability to present his ideas to Congress and the nation, just as they have opened opportunities for opponents to criticize as well as distort administration policies and actions.

In spite of the growth of presidential power in the legislative sphere, which occurs especially when the president has a majority in both houses of Congress and therefore has a better chance of passing his legislative agenda, his influence is limited by a number of factors. He cannot introduce legislation himself, but it is usually no problem to get a number of senators and representatives to introduce "administration bills" in their respective chambers. What happens then may or may not be in conformity with the president's wishes. Depending to some extent on the nature of the bill, whether the president's party has a majority in the chamber, and, indeed, on the president's popularity at the time, the bill may pass easily or fail to pass the numerous barriers that every bill confronts. Thus it can be changed or even killed in a House or Senate committee. The bill may pass one chamber but not the other. If passed by both, it may be changed in a conference committee charged with the task of reconciling the two versions of the bill. It may not receive the funding it needs. What finally emerges and is sent to the president to sign may be so different from what he wanted that he might veto it. The president's nominees for various offices, including judgeships, or treaties he has negotiated, may be rejected or delayed. The president undoubtedly has great influence over the legislative branch, but his agenda is likely to be followed more at the beginning of his term than later. Then the fate of his proposals will depend on many political, economic, and other factors, over many of which he has little control. It is clear from the above that the numerous checks and balances in the American presidential system contribute greatly to the barriers to "getting things done" and serve to make that system very complicated and difficult for many citizens to follow and understand.

The executive: the vice president. The American executive branch is unique among our four liberal democracies in having a vice president. This office cannot be compared to the two-headed executives in the UK, France, and Germany, because the incumbent is neither head of state nor head of government; rather, he or she is part of the single executive that is a distinguishing feature of the American presidential system.

There is little in the Constitution about this office, except that the vice president is elected together with the president for a four-year term by a majority of the Electoral College (see Twelfth Amendment, US Constitution), that he succeeds the president in case of his death or some other emergency (Article II, Section 1), and that he or she is the presiding officer of the Senate with a vote only in case of a tie (Article I, Section 3). Until a few decades ago the vice president rarely played an important role in the president's administration except in cases when the president died in office or, in the case of Richard M. Nixon, resigned. Important recent examples are the assumption of office by Harry Truman following the death of Franklin D. Roosevelt in 1945 and by Lyndon B. Johnson after the assassination of John F. Kennedy in 1963. In 1974 Gerald Ford replaced President Nixon, who had resigned due to the Watergate affair.

In recent decades the vice president has been given more responsibilities by the president and has therefore been in a strong position to run for president when the first opportunity arises. George W. Bush's vice president, Dick Cheney, was especially powerful. He had served in both President Reagan's and the first President Bush's administrations and had far more experience in and knowledge of domestic and foreign policy than the second President Bush; however, he had made it clear from the beginning that he would not be a candidate for president, in part no doubt due to his age and health. The selection by Barack Obama of Senator Joe Biden as candidate for vice president was made largely because of Senator Biden's foreign policy experience as chairman of the Senate Foreign Relations Committee. On the other hand, the surprising selection by John McCain of Sarah Palin as his running mate, who had been the governor of Alaska less than two years, was apparently made in order to help secure his Republican base and win votes among certain voting groups whose support he needed.

The legislature. That the legislative branch was to be at the center of the new political system designed by the Founding Fathers is demonstrated in the fact that it is the focus of the very first article of the American Constitution. The legislature was divided into two chambers but for reasons very different from the British system of government with which the Founders were, of course, familiar. The House of Representatives was the only elected body that was to represent the people; it could be seen as the more democratic counterpart of the British House of Commons. Article I, Section 2, calls for its members to be elected every two years, with the number apportioned among the states based on population. The Senate, on the other hand, was to represent the states. In contrast to the hereditary House of Lords, which represented the British nobility, the Senate reflected the then unique federal structure of the American system. This was underlined by the selection of members of the Senate by the state legislatures; they were not elected by the people until passage of the Seventeenth Amendment in 1913. Senators serve six-year terms, with one-third elected every two years; there are two senators from each state, regardless of population.

As a result of the 2010 midterm elections, which resulted in strong Republican gains and a majority in the 435-member House of Representatives, there were 242 Republicans (178 from 2009 through 2010) and 193 Democrats (257). There were seventy-five women (17 percent, below the record high of seventy-eight in 2008, but still a lower proportion than in most advanced democracies) and forty-four African Americans (10 percent), thirty-one Hispanics (7 percent), eleven Asian Americans (2.5 percent), and one Native American. There were 248 Protestants and 144 Catholics as well as twenty-seven Jews (6 percent), two Buddhists, and two Muslims. The average age was fifty-seven. The most common occupational backgrounds were public service and politics, followed by business and law.[1]

The more exclusive one-hundred-member Senate had fifty-one Democrats (fifty-seven in 2009), two Independents, who usually vote with the Democrats, and forty-seven Republicans. There were seventeen female senators, two Hispanics, two Asian Americans, one Hawaiian American, and one African American. There were fifty-six Protestants, twelve Catholics, and twelve Jews. The average age of senators in 2011 was sixty-two years. A majority of senators have law degrees. The salary for both congressmen and senators as of 2011 was $174,000.[2]

Elections for the House of Representatives take place every two years, while senators serve for six years; however, one-third of the senators are elected every two years. The two chambers are relatively equal in authority. To become a law, a bill must pass both houses, and a two-thirds vote in each house is required to override a presidential veto. On the other hand, all revenue bills must originate in the House, and only the Senate has the power to approve treaties and various presidential appointments. The House of Representatives brings impeachment charges against the president to the Senate, which tries the case and can convict the president with a two-thirds vote. No president has ever been removed by the impeachment process. The House of Representatives drew up impeachment charges against President Andrew Johnson in 1868, but the Senate acquitted him by one vote. The House also impeached President

Clinton in 1998, but the Senate acquitted him as well. President Richard Nixon avoided impeachment in 1974 by resigning from office.

The House of Representatives and the Senate—and American legislative bodies in most of the American states—are known as "working" rather than "talking" legislatures. This means that they spend much of their time in subcommittees and committees, including hearings of various kinds, considering legislative proposals or investigating certain actions or events. They do not spend as much time as most parliaments in parliamentary systems do in openly debating legislative proposals or executive actions, and there is no "question time" requiring the president and cabinet secretaries to submit to questions by members of Congress in the legislative chambers; however, some committee investigations can be seen as rough equivalents of question time (presidential press conferences also serve as a weak counterpart to question time). Congress can also be seen as a more powerful legislative body than almost all of its foreign counterparts because of its ability to pass legislation even without presidential approval (which, of course, he may then veto), to override presidential vetoes, and above all to revise executive proposals and even to block them. This, of course, is due in part to the separate election of the president and Congress and occurs especially during periods of "divided government" when the president's party does not have a majority in either or both houses of Congress. Unlike the head of government in a parliamentary system, the president has no power to dissolve Congress, and Congress cannot remove the president by a vote of no confidence.

The relations between the president and Congress depend on a number of factors. If the president's party has a majority in both houses, his ability to get his agenda passed is strengthened dramatically (even though there may be majority votes against the president on occasion due to a lack of party loyalty on certain issues at certain times). More recently, the filibuster, based on a Senate rule from the early twentieth century and not on the Constitution, has been used increasingly for partisan purposes, whereas in the past it was used infrequently and, when, then usually in an effort to block civil rights legislation or federal court nominations; sixty votes are required to overcome a filibuster, a majority the president rarely has. There may also be "divided government," which means the president faces majority opposition in either one or both houses of congress. If the president's party has a majority in *one* house only, it will be necessary to search for compromises, for example in the House-Senate conference committees, which may be able to resolve differences between bills passed by each house. If the president is faced by an opposition majority in *both* houses, his job is obviously much more difficult, but not impossible, as a number of presidents have shown. The president is likely to have better relations with Congress at the beginning of his term; however, if his support in the opinion polls is reasonably strong and his prospects of reelection good, his influence with Congress will still be strong. If reelected, chances are that his influence will decline as the next election calendar approaches, and he cannot run again.

The Semipresidential System: The French Model

In contrast to Great Britain, which has had a constitutional monarchy with an assertive parliament since 1689, France had a ruling monarchy until it was abolished in 1792 as a result of the French Revolution of 1789. The Estates General, which consisted of representatives of the nobility, clergy, and the rest of society (Third Estate) and which had not met since 1614, reemerged as a National Assembly that immediately abolished feudalism and passed the Declaration of the Rights of Man, the French counterpart to the American Bill of Rights. The monarchy was replaced by an unstable revolutionary republic, which in turn was replaced toward the end of the 1790s by Napoleon's dictatorship. The monarchy was restored in 1815, following the defeat of Napoleon at Waterloo. It was again abolished in 1848 and replaced by a "Second Republic." In 1852 Napoleon's nephew, Napoleon III, established an authoritarian regime based in part on universal male suffrage. He was forced from office in 1870 as a result of the Franco-Prussian War, and an unstable republican regime trying to become a monarchy was in place until 1875. The "Third Republic" lasted from 1875 to 1940, when France was defeated by Germany at the beginning of World War II. A French authoritarian government dependent on German support, named after its capital city, Vichy, while Paris was under German occupation, was formed from 1940 to 1944 under Marshall Pétain, a hero of World War I. He and his government were replaced by a military regime headed by General Charles de Gaulle, leader of the Free French forces that were allied with the British and Americans in pushing the Germans out of France. In 1946 a "Fourth Republic" was established, and General de Gaulle, who was disappointed and disgusted by the new constitutional order that in his opinion differed too little from the unstable Third Republic, retired from politics to his country home to write his memoirs. In 1958 the Fourth Republic collapsed under the pressures of the Algerian War, and de Gaulle returned to power. He had a new constitution prepared, and it was passed by referendum in September 1958. The new semipresidential "Fifth Republic" went into effect in October 1958. General Charles de Gaulle was elected president in December by a large majority of an electoral college and assumed his new position in January 1959.

The history of regime change in France contrasts sharply with the relative stability of British constitutional history and the even greater stability of the United States. At the time of the French Revolution in 1789, Britain had had already for a hundred years a constitutional monarchy that had to share or give up a good deal of power to parliament. Since then the monarch has become a head of state effectively restricted to ceremonial functions, while the head of government, the prime minister, is the most powerful political figure in the country as long as he remains leader of the majority party in the House of Commons. And while there have been numerous changes in American constitutional practices since 1789, the basic presidential system established at that time remains in effect today. France, in the meantime, has gone through about sixteen regime changes.

The dual executive: the head of state and the head of government. During the Third Republic from 1875 to 1940, the executive became so weak in comparison to parliament that the French political system became known as "government by assembly." The French president, who was head of state, became a weak figurehead unable to dissolve the parliament and call new elections. Because of the weak parties and multiparty system, the head of government, the premier or prime minister, who needed the approval of the elected parliament, the Chamber of Deputies, could never form a strong single-party government on the British model. The coalition governments that were formed were generally weakened not only by the number of parties needed to form the cabinet but also by a lack of British-style party cohesion. The result was that disagreements among and often within the coalition parties in the cabinet made it difficult or even impossible to pass much of the legislation the prime minister or his cabinet ministers proposed. This frequently led to a government collapse, which did not normally mean new elections but rather the formation of a new cabinet from mostly the same parliamentary parties and members of parliament. French government, then, became like a game of musical chairs, with ministers from one cabinet becoming ministers in the next cabinet but often rotating to a different ministry. Ministers became prime ministers, who became cabinet ministers again. The fact that there was often little change in personnel was the result in part of the composition of the parliament. Communist party deputies on the far left (with one exception in 1936) and members of groups on the far right generally were not considered acceptable for membership in government coalitions, which meant that the other parties had fewer options in forming moderate left to moderate right governments. Many observers felt that this political system had given France weak and ineffective governments that in turn weakened French resolve against the Germans in the years before the Second World War.

The Fourth Republic, established in 1946, did not bring about major changes in this system. Indeed, there were twenty-four prime ministers between January 1946 and May 1958, an average of one every six months. Therefore, when General de Gaulle returned to power in 1958, it was clear that he would call for a new constitutional order that would strengthen the executive and end "government by assembly." This was accomplished in the constitution of the Fifth Republic, which created a "semipresidential system" with a powerful executive and a much weakened parliament.

Head of State. General de Gaulle insisted on a separation of powers between the president and parliament, which meant the president would not be answerable to parliament and would be elected separately. Originally he was selected for a seven-year term by an electoral college, but since 1965 the president has been elected by a popular vote. This was done to strengthen the legitimacy of the president, who would not always enjoy the prestige and status of General de Gaulle. The term of office was changed to five years in 2002.

To avoid "government by assembly," the constitution of the Fifth Republic provides for selection of the prime minister by the president rather than by the popularly elected National Assembly. The president's appointee does, however, require majority support in the National Assembly if he is to get his or her legislation passed. The president also has the right to dissolve the National Assembly, which has occurred five times since 1959. Unlike British practice, the person selected as prime minister does not have to be the leader of the majority party (who, in recent decades, is more likely to be the president); indeed, he or she may be a high-level civil servant or a presidential supporter who is a politician but not the formal leader of a party.

The constitutional role of the president is not clear. He has always assumed primary responsibility for foreign affairs and defense, and he is supposed to "arbitrate" in the political arena; however, there is some dispute over the meaning of this term. In practice it seems to mean that he sets the guidelines for government policy. This suggests that he is not only head of state but to some extent also head of government. There was no question that de Gaulle considered himself to be in charge of general government policy, which was to be administered by the prime minister he appointed as the constitutional head of government. This presidential role, however, was based on the assumption that the president had majority support in the National Assembly. The Gaullist party that backed de Gaulle was the largest party in the National Assembly, but it was joined in its support for de Gaulle by other parties, so that the president had majority support. The party that identified itself as Gaullist did not gain a majority alone until the parliamentary election of 1968, which was called after the student revolt of that year. Though dependent to a considerable extent on majority support in parliament, de Gaulle never considered himself to be bound to a party but rather saw himself as a leader who stood above the parties. His successors have not been able to make such claims with much credibility, although they have all met rather strict geographical requirements for nomination and insisted that they served all of the people.

In 1981 François Mitterrand was elected president; however, he did not have a majority to back him in the National Assembly, so he dissolved the Assembly and called for new elections. A large majority of his supporters, especially Socialists, were elected. In 1986, after the regular five-year term, new parliamentary elections were held and Mitterrand lost his majority support. As a result he had to appoint a prime minister who had such support, because if he were to have appointed a Socialist or other candidate close to him politically, the National Assembly would not have passed government legislation and would probably have passed a vote of no confidence against the prime minister. Unfortunately for Mitterrand, the candidate for prime minister who headed the largest party in the National Assembly was Jacques Chirac, the leader of the opposition Gaullist party.

The occupation of the presidency by a leader of one party and of the premiership by a leader of an opposition party is called *cohabitation*. This awkward situation lasted from 1986 to 1988, when new presidential elections were held. Mitterrand ran against Chirac and won a second seven-year term, the only French president to do so. Following his reelection, Mitterrand again dissolved the National Assembly and called for new elections. Again he received a majority and appointed a new Socialist prime minister. In 1993 new parliamentary elections were held, and Mitterrand again lost his majority. This time not Chirac, but a Gaullist candidate promoted by Chirac, Edouard Balladur, was appointed by Mitterrand as prime minister.

In 1995 new presidential elections were held and won by Jacques Chirac. He appointed his Gaullist associate, Alain Juppé, as prime minister. Though new parliamentary elections were not due until 1998, Chirac and Juppé decided to call for new elections in 1997 in the expectation that the current solid Gaullist majority would be returned and would support government reforms planned during the next five years. This proved to be a major miscalculation, and the Socialist opposition gained an unexpected majority. As a result, Lionel Jospin, a prominent Socialist, was appointed prime minister and served until the end of the full five-year term of the National Assembly in 2002.

In 2000 the constitution was amended and the presidential term reduced to five years. That meant that the new presidential elections in

2002 would take place the same year as the parliamentary elections, though several weeks apart, for terms ending in 2007. Chirac won the elections against his former prime minister, Lionel Jospin, and the candidate of the radical right, Jean-Marie Le Pen (see chapter 4). A few weeks later his Gaullist supporters won a large majority in the National Assembly. In the 2007 elections, the leader of the Gaullist party, the Union for a Popular Movement (UMP), Nicolas Sarkozy, defeated his Socialist opponent, Ségolène Royal, for president, and four weeks later his party won a somewhat smaller than expected majority in the National Assembly. This made it possible for the new president to appoint a party supporter, François Fillon, as prime minister.

Political developments since 2002 suggest that the purpose of the constitutional amendment to make *cohabitation* unlikely or even end it has been achieved. The candidate who wins the presidential election can be expected under normal circumstances to lead his party and other supporters to victory in the following parliamentary elections. This means the end of divided government, the internal checks in the executive branch that *cohabitation* provided, and also the uncertainty or confusion between president and prime minister over responsibility for policy making. French government policy will be set in general terms by the president, who will be able to select a prime minister who will carry out his policies together with ministers who are accountable to the president and prime minister. This will make the French president more powerful for institutional reasons and not primarily due to personal charisma, as in the case of de Gaulle.

As we have seen above, the president has the power under the constitution to "arbitrate" among public authorities in order to promote their proper functioning and the continuity of the state. He also possesses emergency powers under Article 16, which means he can take measures to protect the state from domestic or foreign threats. He must first consult with the prime minister and the presidents of the Senate, the National Assembly, and the Constitutional Council, but their approval is not required. The emergency powers were actually invoked once in 1961, when de Gaulle was confronted with a military revolt in Algeria. He may also accept or reject the call for a referendum by the government (cabinet) or parliament.

In the area of foreign affairs, the president has as head of state the traditional functions of receiving the credentials of foreign ambassadors and accrediting and recalling French ambassadors. The Fifth Republic constitution not only provides for presidential ratification of treaties but also for his negotiating them. According to Article 5, he is the guarantor of national independence, of territorial integrity, and of the observance of treaties. The president plays a major role in the EU, even during cohabitation, as a member of the European Council. The prime minister also is a member of that body, which means that he and the president must cooperate and coordinate their policy goals in speaking with one voice on the European stage. The president also appoints several thousand senior civil servants, the highest level of which requires consultation with the cabinet, the Council of Ministers.

In spite of the many powers that the president as head of state has derived from the constitution and from practice over the years and the powers he usually shares with the official head of government, the prime minister, the president is subject to a number of checks. These include the constraints imposed on him by internal and external economic and political conditions, globalization, international treaties, and the EU (for example in trade, agricultural and environmental policy, and the Economic and Monetary Union [EMU]). Whether he has the support of a party majority in the parliament or at least the support of a majority coalition is important in the relationship he has with his prime minister as well as the parliament. He must be wary of policies that produce controversy before an election, and he has to keep an eye on opinion polls. The results of a referendum can also affect his policy options, as former President Chirac discovered most recently by the unexpected rejection by French voters in May 2005 of the referendum on the EU constitution. Finally, the Council of State and the Constitutional Council (see chapter 9) can check the legality of certain presidential acts.

Head of Government. The constitutional head of government is the prime minister, although, as we have seen, this appears to be the case primarily when there is *cohabitation.* Now that *cohabitation* is unlikely to occur, the prime minister will be sharing his or her functions on a regular basis with the president. The constitution calls for such sharing, but presidents have often made their prime ministers look more like chiefs of staff. This will probably become standard practice, with the unlikely reappearance of *cohabitation* in the future.

Before the first instance of *cohabitation* in 1986, the role of the prime minister was seen as directing, coordinating, and supervising the members of the cabinet, or Council of Ministers, but not as providing political leadership. This secondary role is to some extent symbolized by the chairmanship of the Council of Ministers meetings by the president rather than by the prime minister. During *cohabitation*, however, this chairmanship by the president has been basically a formal exercise. The current president, Nicolas Sarkozy, elected in May 2007, appointed as his prime minister François Fillon, a prominent member of Sarkozy's UMP party and parliamentary deputy, and reduced the number of ministers from thirty to fifteen. With the probable disappearance of *cohabitation*, the loyalty of the ministers is now more to the president than to the prime minister. Given the diversity of the ministers, who come from different career and political backgrounds (President Sarkozy, for example, appointed a Socialist as foreign minister) and the lack of a British-style tradition of collective responsibility, direction and coordination by the prime minister is important in maintaining a degree of unity among ministers.

In contrast to the parliamentary systems of Great Britain and Germany but in conformity with the separation of powers associated with presidential systems, ministers in France may not be members of parliament; however, they are frequently recruited from parliament, from which they must resign upon appointment to the Council of Ministers. Sometimes the president or prime minister will insist that ministers must have been elected to the National Assembly in order to demonstrate popular support at least in their constituency. Next to the prime minister, the most important minister appointed by current President Sarkozy after his election in May 2007, former Prime Minister Alain Juppé, failed to win election as a deputy to the National Assembly in the parliamentary election in June, and he lost his ministerial position as a result. In March 2011, however, he was appointed by President Sarkozy to the position of foreign minister.

Although they may not be members of parliament, it has been a tradition for French ministers and even prime ministers to hold positions as mayors or members of local or regional councils, thus providing them with a strong "home base." In recent years, however, ministers have been required to choose between keeping their ministerial position and holding local office.

The prime minister must have a sizable staff to assist him in carrying out his responsibilities, and this role is performed in large part by his private office, or *cabinet*, which consists of about sixty members. Most of these members are civil servants, but the director is always a person who is loyal to the prime minister. Another body important for coordination and collective action is the General Secretariat of the Government. For example, it coordinates government policy regarding the EU, policy concerning military affairs, and meetings of the prime minister and ministers or their respective staffs

Features of the constitution that promote a sharing of the functions of head of state and head of government include the requirement that the prime minister countersign presidential decisions, with a number of notable exceptions; this is important because only the government is accountable to parliament, and countersignature suggests that the president has acted on the advice of the government. It also provides for a certain amount of collective responsibility.

Cooperation is also necessary for the proper functioning of the cabinet, or Council of Ministers. For example, countersignature is required for the preparation of legislative initiatives, senior appointments, and the conduct of certain policy areas. In case of disagreement, the president has no formal right of dismissal, but in fact a number of prime ministers have resigned under presidential pressure. This has not been the case, however, in times of *cohabitation*, when the president has no choice but to work with a prime minister who has the support of an opposition majority. In some cases of prime ministers appointed by presidents who enjoyed majority support in parliament, the prime minister has become a rival in spite of presidential dominance, for example Georges Pompidou under de Gaulle. A different example is the Gaullist Edouard Balladur, who was appointed prime minister by Socialist President Mitterrand in 1993 with Chirac's support and then became Chirac's major party rival for the presidential nomination in 1995.

In spite of the influence and even dominance of the president in governmental affairs, French prime ministers have also benefited from the changes brought about by the Fifth Republic constitution. The constitutional powers of the parliament have been reduced, the powers of the prime minister and cabinet strengthened, and the party system has moved in the direction of a more stable two blocs if not a two-party system.

The legislature. The parliament of France consists of two chambers, the National Assembly and the Senate. The National Assembly consists of 577 "deputies" who are elected for a five-year term in a two-ballot, single-member district system (see chapter 4). The term may be interrupted by a presidential dissolution of the National Assembly, which happened in the Fifth Republic for a fifth time in 1997. All deputies are elected together with a substitute, who replaces the deputy in case of death, appointment to the Council of Ministers, or for other reasons. This makes British-style by-elections (elections of individual members between regular elections) or special elections, as in the United States, unnecessary.

The deputies of the National Assembly are mostly teachers (especially in left-of-center parties), civil servants (in contrast to the United States and Great Britain; but as in other continental states, there is no restriction in France on the political activities of civil servants), and business owners and managers (especially in right-of-center parties). Given the role of socialist and communist parties in French history, it is surprising that fewer than 5 percent of the deputies are white-collar or blue-collar workers. The percentage of women elected to the National Assembly has been low at around 5 to 6 percent; however, since 1997 that percentage has doubled.

A practice unknown in the United States and Great Britain, and known but not as common in some other European states, is the French tradition of combining elective offices (*cumul des mandats*). This has been especially the case for the office of parliamentary deputy and one or more local and regional offices. In recent years, however, deputies have been restricted to holding only one other office, usually that of mayor. This makes it possible for the deputy to serve as a well-connected and informed lobbyist for his or her town or city before central authorities in Paris, and, of course, it provides the deputy with a strong home base.

To avoid "government by assembly" characteristic of the Third and Fourth Republics, the constitution of the Fifth Republic places a number of restrictions on the National Assembly. Restrictions on length of sessions have been relaxed somewhat, so that the National Assembly now meets from the beginning of October to the end of June, and the workweek has been rationalized. But the government controls the legislative timetable, and it can insist on consideration of any government bills and private bills that it accepts. Oral question times take place twice a week and are divided among the political parties, with questions and answers limited to two and a half minutes each. For several reasons, question periods in the National Assembly are not as important as in Great Britain or Germany: these include the relative powers of the government and parliament, the fact that ministers are not members of parliament, and the absenteeism of deputies. Bills are considered by six large general committees in each chamber, which is in sharp contrast to the large number of committees and subcommittees in the US Congress. The size and number of French committees were designed to discourage specialization, the influence of lobbyists, and the power of committees to disrupt the legislative plans of the government. The report of the committee is discussed in some detail by the National Assembly and if passed is sent to the Senate for a similar legislative process.

If the Senate amends the bill, it is returned to the National Assembly for its reconsideration. The National Assembly can "shuttle" it back again until agreement is reached, or the government can establish a joint committee to resolve the issue. If this is not possible, the National Assembly makes the final decision. Disagreements are more likely to occur, of course, when the party majorities in the two chambers are different. This was evident during the last period of cohabitation from 1997 to 2002, when the number of laws passed by the Socialist majority in the National Assembly without agreement being reached in a joint committee increased from one in 1996 to about 20 by 2002, when a Gaullist majority regained control of the Assembly following the reelection of the Gaullist president, Jacques Chirac.

The powers or competences of the Congress of the United States are limited by the US Constitution; however, the implied powers and the commerce clauses also provide Congress with broad domestic authority to legislate. The concept of parliamentary sovereignty in Great Britain gives the House of Commons—in practice the government and party majority—even more authority. On the other hand, the constitution of the Fifth Republic limits the powers of the National Assembly and provides the government and bureaucracy with considerable authority to control the legislative process and to regulate important areas without legislative interference. The areas of legislation reserved for the parliament are broadly defined and have been expanded somewhat in recent years, but disputes regarding these powers can arise. These can be brought before the Constitutional Council by the president, prime minister, presidents of the Senate and National Assembly, or sixty members of either chamber. Overall, the role of parliament as perceived by deputies themselves may be reflected to some extent in their relatively poor attendance and participation rates.

Even though the semipresidential system of France does not provide for a vote of confidence for the president, the prime minister and his or her government are subject to such a check. The prime minister can either make a particular bill a motion of confidence, or a motion can be filed by one-tenth of the members of the National Assembly. Passage of the motion requires a majority vote of all members, which means that absentees are counted as voting against. If the motion fails, those members who filed the motion may not file a new motion during that parliamentary session. Only one motion has ever been successful, and when the government resigned in 1962 the president, Charles de Gaulle, dissolved the Assembly and called for new elections. The Gaullists won, and de Gaulle reappointed the prime minister, Georges Pompidou. With the first instance of *cohabitation* in 1986, however, it became clear that the president had little choice but to accept a prime minister who enjoyed the support of the majority opposition parties.

Conclusion

The American presidential system serves as a model of presidential systems worldwide. It is, however, much like the British model of the parliamentary system: a model against which other presumably similar systems are compared and then found to be very different in many ways. The American presidential system is in fact a unique system not replicated in other countries except in general outline. The French model of a semipresidential system is also unique in some ways, but there are a number of states in the world, most prominently Russia and some former Soviet republics, that come quite close to replicating the French system.

In the American presidential model, the president as the single elected executive leader may set much of the agenda and be primarily responsible for foreign and defense policy, but his ability to get his measures passed by Congress varies greatly from time to time. As noted above, some presidents have been far more successful than others, and all presidents have been more successful at some times than others. This success, however, has been the result not just of the skill and persuasiveness of the president; it is related also to a number of factors over which the president may have little or no control. The best example is probably the state of the economy during the president's term of office; that is, general economic growth and decline, employment and unemployment figures, the balance of international trade, the value of the dollar, and so forth. The president has some influence over these conditions through his appointments to the Federal Reserve, government purchases and spending in general, government regulations, and tax policies, but his influence is limited in fact by the free enterprise system, which operates primarily on the basis of decision making by private companies and individual consumer attitudes and behavior.

The president's power in foreign and defense affairs is usually greater than in domestic affairs. This responsibility derives from Article II of the Constitution, which states that "the executive Power shall be vested in [the] President," and from a number of Supreme Court decisions that have interpreted "executive power" in favor of the president. As "commander-in-chief" (Article II, Section 2), the president is also in a strong position to exercise leadership in foreign and defense matters. President George W. Bush claimed that this provision gave him broad powers to fight domestic as well as foreign terrorism. Even though the Constitution states in Article I, Section 8 that Congress has the power to declare war, American presidents since 1940 have been able to commit American troops in conflicts abroad without a formal congressional declaration of war. As a result of some of the actions taken regarding US military involvement in Vietnam, Congress passed legislation (War Powers Act) that restricts the president's power to commit troops without congressional approval. In fact, however, American troops have been sent for "humanitarian reasons" to Lebanon, Somalia, Bosnia-Herzegovina, Kosovo, and Haiti for limited durations without congressional action, while the more significant military engagements in the Gulf War, Afghanistan, and Iraq were approved by Congress. That questions of presidential power in committing troops are still unresolved was demonstrated in 2011 by American intervention in Libya.

As noted above, the limitations on the president in the domestic arena are far greater than in foreign and defense policy. These limitations are due especially to the fact that the executive and legislative branches in the American presidential model are far more distinctly separated than in a parliamentary system. In a presidential system, the president and members of Congress run for office in separate elections. The president has no power to dissolve the legislative body or bodies before the next scheduled election; no formal power to discipline members of Congress, for example by threatening to have their local party organizations nominate someone else for the next election; no formal power to have the national party withdraw financial or other support in the next election; no formal power to remove a disloyal member of the party from a committee. On the other hand, the president may be able to "persuade" or influence members of Congress by appealing to party loyalty or by offering various benefits to members, such as an appearance with the candidate during the next election campaign, a government building in the legislator's district, a favorable view of some project the legislator wishes to pursue, a visit with family to the White

House, or some other arm-twisting measure. But these are "informal" means of putting together or maintaining majorities for the president's agenda.

The legislature in the American presidential system usually has only limited means of ensuring presidential approval of its actions. The legislature cannot pass a no-confidence vote and force the president to resign before the next scheduled elections. The fact that the president and Congress are independently elected by different constituencies—the president's being far larger and more diverse—and at a set time every two years for members of the House of Representatives, every four years for the president, and every six years for the members of the Senate, means that neither the executive branch nor the legislative branch can formally affect the electoral process in its favor.

The idea that the president of the United States is "the most powerful man on earth" may be true in the sense that the president is commander-in-chief of the only remaining superpower. But given the constraints in the international environment, such as views of our allies, friends, and even enemies; international treaty obligations; international organizations, such as the UN; and, at home, given a possibly skeptical public, made wary by past experiences; opposition by the other party; changes or opposition to the president's agenda in Congress; divided government; negative media coverage; economic constraints brought about by domestic problems, such as unemployment, or international challenges, such as competition from the EU, China and India; and divisions within the administration, the president's efforts to achieve his foreign and domestic goals may not be successful. Indeed, during the Carter administration, some commentators argued that the American presidency was in decline and considerably weaker than it had been under Presidents Johnson and Nixon. Ronald Reagan, at least in his first term of office, made it clear that these commentators were wrong.

The French semipresidential system is similar to the American system in some key ways, especially in the separate election of the president, which the major characteristic of a presidential system. Indeed, he or she is even elected several weeks before the National Assembly elections. This represents a major change, however, that was introduced in 2002, when the presidential term of office was reduced from seven to five years, so that the president and National Assembly could be elected in the same year.

Perhaps the most important difference between the American and French systems is that in France there is not just one executive leader but two: a head of state, the president; and a head of government, the prime minister. This dual executive is actually more characteristic of a parliamentary system, which is why one speaks of the French system as "semipresidential." The prime minister is appointed by the president; however, the president must appoint someone who has the support of a majority in the National Assembly, because otherwise that parliamentary body could not only refuse to pass the president's agenda but also dismiss the prime minister by a vote of no confidence. When General de Gaulle introduced the new Fifth Republic constitution in 1959, the assumption seemed to be that the president would enjoy majority support in the parliament and would dominate the executive, especially in the areas of foreign policy and defense but also in important domestic areas. Thus, when the president has majority support in the National Assembly, he can appoint a prime minister who assists the president in carrying out his agenda and serves rather like a chief administrator rather than a policy maker.

On the other hand, if the president's party or supporting coalition of parties does not have a majority in the National Assembly, he must appoint a leader of the opposition as prime minister. This occurred for the first time in 1986, and it led to what the French call *cohabitation*, which means the president has to share power, especially in domestic matters, with the prime minister The change from a seven-year to a five-year term for the president, mentioned in the paragraph above, was designed to reduce the probability of *cohabitation*, since the political forces that elected the president are likely to support his party or allies in the elections for the National Assembly that follow in a few weeks.

There are two legislative chambers in France, the popularly elected National Assembly and the Senate, whose members are selected by a kind of electoral college consisting of elected local government officials. The Senate is not equal to the National Assembly in its competences and is similar to the British House of Lords in that its objections to bills passed in the National Assembly can be overridden by the latter body when supported by the government. The National Assembly was also weakened in several ways by the constitution of the Fifth Republic, because de Gaulle wanted to strengthen the executive branch *vis-à-vis* the legislative branch and end "government by assembly" that had characterized the Third and Fourth Republics between 1875 and 1940 and 1946 and 1958.

Endnotes

[1] For 112th Congress, see http://www.billlucey.com/2011/02/the-112th-congress-by-the-numbers.html and "For New Congress, Data Shows Why Polarization Abounds," *New York Times* (March 7, 2011); for the previous Congress, see Congressional Research Service, Membership of the 111th Congress: A Profile, http://assets.opencrs.com/rpts/R40086_20081231.pdf

[2] Ibid.

Further Reading

Hauss, Charles. *Politics in France.* Washington, DC: CQ Press, 2008.

O'Connor, Karen, and Larry J. Sabato. *Essentials of American Government: Continuity and Change.* 2004 ed. New York: Pearson/Longman, 2005.

Safran, William. *The French Polity.* New York: Pearson Longman, 2009.

Stevens, Anne. *Government and Politics of France.* 3rd ed. New York: Palgrave Macmillan, 2003.

Chapter 8

The Parliamentary Systems of Great Britain and Germany

Introduction

Great Britain (or the United Kingdom) is often seen as the model parliamentary system and the "mother" of many other parliamentary systems in former colonies, such as Australia, Canada, and India. In fact, however, this "model" is very different in important respects from most other parliamentarysystems, due in large part to its unique history and traditions. Germany is one of many examples of a parliamentary system with a history and traditions that are very different from those of Great Britain. These differences are reflected clearly in the selection procedures for the dual executive characteristic of parliamentary systems. Each country has two legislative chambers; however, the "upper house" in Great Britain and the second chamber in Germany (often incorrectly referred to as an "upper house") are very different in their origins, composition, powers, and roles. Great Britain is also a unitary state, with strong central controls over local government, while Germany is a federation, with the states (*Länder*) responsible for the largely autonomous local governments. On the other hand, decentralization in Great Britain has given Scotland and Wales more autonomy than is usually found in unitary states. Indeed, there is even a strong movement for the secession and independence of Scotland from the United Kingdom.

Great Britain and the "Westminster Model"

The Executive

The Magna Charta of 1215 placed limits on the absolute power of the monarch by requiring him to consult with his barons and abide by a charter of liberties, and it established the House of Lords; however, Great Britain did not become a constitutional monarchy until passage of the Bill of Rights after the Glorious Revolution in 1689, when parliamentary supremacy was established over the crown. We speak of a constitutional monarchy (i.e., a monarchy limited by laws and customs) even though Great Britain does not have a written constitution. It does, however, have a "constitution" consisting of statutory laws, conventions, and traditions. It should also be noted that membership in the European Union, with its various treaties and conventions, together with acceptance in 1998 of the Council of Europe's Convention for the Protection of Human Rights (CPHR) have, in effect, brought important elements of a written constitution into British political life.

Head of State. The monarch, at the present time Queen Elizabeth, is the head of state. The monarchy is hereditary, and the queen's heritage is from King George I (1714–27) and the German House of Hanover. Today the extensive powers of the crown are exercised on the monarch's behalf by the government, or cabinet. The queen exercises virtually no political power on her own. Rather, she is the ceremonial leader of the country, the incarnation of British history, traditions, and national pride. For example, she opens each session of parliament, receives visiting foreign heads of state, and gives her assent to legislation. The monarch does, however, have two important constitutional prerogatives: the power to appoint the prime minister and the power to dissolve parliament before its five-year term has expired. In fact, though, the monarch appoints the leader of the majority party to be prime minister, and the monarch dissolves parliament at the request of the prime minister. There might be some room for discretion in appointing a prime minister if no party emerged with a majority in the House of Commons or if there were a conflict in the majority party over its leadership, but these situations would be rare.

Head of Government. The head of government is the prime minister, who is always an elected member of the House of Commons, appointed by the monarch because of his or her leadership of the majority party in parliament. Once in office, the prime minister must retain the support of the cabinet and the majority party. He or she could lose a vote of confidence in the House of Commons, but this is in fact highly unlikely because members of the majority party are hardly likely to vote with the opposition against their own leader. If the prime minister were to lose a vote of confidence, he or she could resign as majority leader and allow a new leader to be elected by the party; however, the prime minister might also call for new elections, which his or her now divided party would surely lose. But an unpopular leader can be forced out of office without calling for new elections. Margaret Thatcher left office in 1990, not as a result of a lost vote of confidence in parliament but in response to an internal revolt by a number of members of her parliamentary party. She was replaced as party leader and prime minister by John Major, who did not have to lead the Conservative Party in a new election campaign until 1992.

The parliamentary party ("caucus" in the United States, "party group" elsewhere) selected the Conservative Party leader between 1964 (before that date, the Conservative leader and presumptive prime minister was selected by the monarch!) and 1998, when the procedure was changed again so that the parliamentary party now selects two candidates from which the "extraparliamentary" mass membership can choose one as the party leader.

From its beginning, the leader of the Labour Party was selected by the parliamentary party. As a result of challenges to this procedure in the 1970s, a change in 1981 led to selection of the leader by an electoral college consisting of representatives of the unions, the constituency parties, and the parliamentary party by a procedure that favored the left-wing Labour leaders by a ratio of 40:30:30 for the three groups. This was changed again in 1993 so that the ratio is now one-third for each group. Union and constituency party representatives were also required to consult their members before voting. In addition, labor union votes must now be cast in proportion to members' preferences, a change that sharply reduced the power of the unions that used to cast ballots en bloc for their members.

The prime minister is the leader of the cabinet (government). The nature of this leadership is controversial, but it is clear that the powers of the office have increased in recent decades. While legally the British have a system of cabinet government with collective responsibility, some observers now argue that cabinet government in fact has been replaced during the past several decades by "prime ministerial government" or, more recently, even by a quasipresidential system. This system, however, lacks the institutional checks and balances found in the United States: the prime minister is backed by a disciplined party majority; the House of Commons cannot vote against a government bill without risking the fall of the government; the House of Lords can delay a bill for one year at best; a government bill passed by parliament cannot be ruled unconstitutional by the high court because of the doctrine of parliamentary sovereignty.

The thesis of the quasipresidential prime minister derives primarily from experiences under the governments of Margaret Thatcher and Tony Blair, who were accused of making decisions without consulting their cabinet ministers. In addition, Mrs. Thatcher was accused of having a domineering and authoritarian leadership style. Both leaders were adept at using the media to enhance their personalities. However, as noted above, Mrs. Thatcher, facing an internal challenge for the leadership of her party, did resign from office in 1990. Tony Blair became prime minister in 1997, and during his first term he was very popular in the Labour Party, which won a huge victory in the 2001 elections under Blair's leadership. But after Blair joined President Bush in the decision to invade Iraq and committed British forces to the invasion and occupation of that country, opposition to him in the Labour Party and the general public began to rise. The Labour Party won reelection in 2005, but with a sharply reduced majority of seats in the House of Commons. While he still enjoyed a reduced majority support in the extraparliamentary and parliamentary Labour parties, Blair came under pressure to resign the party leadership, and he announced in 2006 that he would step down in 2007.

The examples of Thatcher and Blair demonstrate why some observers argue that the prime minister has more power than other cabinet ministers, but this power is in fact constrained by the need to cooperate with and accommodate a variety of interests. The leadership style of the prime minister is an important factor, with John Major (1990–97) emphasizing collegiality and Tony Blair (1997–2007) stressing his personal leadership. But Blair's eloquence and persuasiveness were not enough to protect him from serious criticism for his support of President Bush's invasion of Iraq. It was also clear that while Blair was able to dominate his cabinet with his personal style, his administration was known for the competition and tension between him and Chancellor of the Exchequer Gordon Brown. After Blair's resignation in June 2007, Brown became Blair's successor. Only months after Brown became prime minister, however, criticism and even opposition to his leadership began to develop within his own party, and by June 2008 voices were heard in the Labour Party calling for his replacement. On the other hand, Brown's response to the world financial crisis in the fall of 2008 was praised at home and abroad, and talk of forcing Brown out of office ceased for a while. Unfortunately for Brown, the continuing economic crisis in 2009 as well as a scandal involving the abuse of housing expense allowances for MPs of all parties led to increasing calls for Brown's replacement. It seems clear, then, that, as in our other liberal democracies, the strength of the British prime minister depends in part on issues confronting the government ("events," as one British prime minister noted), numerous conditions in society, the effectiveness of government responses, and the nature of those responses.

As both the leader of his or her party and the head of government, the prime minister has a good deal of patronage power. The prime minister appoints not only the members of the cabinet but also life peers, judges, and even church officials. In recent decades the cabinet has consisted of twenty-two or twenty-three ministers. There are, however, many more noncabinet junior ministers, who numbered seventy-one in 2009. Many other members of parliament (MPs) were parliamentary private secretaries who served as aides to ministers and are appointed by them.[1] These positions are unpaid, but they are seen as stepping-stones to higher office. In 2002 there were 130 members of the House of Commons (and twenty-four members of the House of Lords) in government positions. One member of Blair's cabinet even combined the positions of minister and leader (not speaker) of the House of Commons.[2] In appointing so many members of both houses of parliament to government positions, the prime minister must consider a number of factors, including competence, the expectations of party leaders, and personality. After making the appointments, the prime minister must also know when to fire ministers who are seen as undermining the unity and effectiveness of the government. This is made difficult, however, when the appointees have a sizable following of their own. Still, the relatively large number of MPs in government positions makes it unlikely that these members would vote against their own prime minister or cabinet and increases the already strong sense of discipline in the majority party. Indeed, the collective responsibility of the cabinet means that members of the government must either support government policies in public or resign.

The prerogative power of the crown that is exercised by the cabinet gives it in theory a great freedom to act without parliamentary approval, but political reality dictates that policies and actions be presented to parliament by ministers who are not only collectively but also individually responsible to parliament. Today the full cabinet as a decision-making body is less important than in the past. Cabinet committees, meetings of a few ministers outside of the cabinet, working groups, etc., are now the sources of routine decisions; indeed, many important decisions are also made by about thirty committees and numerous other subcommittees and ad hoc committees, and committee decisions are not generally reconsidered in the full cabinet. Depending largely on the leadership style of the prime minister, the full cabinet may still be used to settle political differences and to make important decisions, for example on legislative proposals. But these are generally prepared by the Cabinet Committee on Legislation.

The Cabinet Office and the Prime Minister's Office. The Cabinet Office consists of about 2,000 staff members on temporary assignment from other departments, and it is located around the corner from the Prime Minister's residence and office at No. 10 Downing Street. It is responsible for coordinating central government policy and for the efficiency of government administration. There are numerous units in the Cabinet Office, the most important of which is the Cabinet Secretariat, which is located in the back of No. 10 and ensures the smooth operation of the government cabinet and its various committees. It keeps the prime minister and cabinet committee chairpersons informed about key issues, and it provides agendas with supporting materials and keeps the minutes of cabinet and committee meetings. The two hundred-member specialized staff is divided into five different functional units. Because of his close contacts with the prime minister and his knowledge of the process of government, the cabinet secretary is likely to have considerable influence with the prime minister and cabinet.

The Prime Minister's Office, located in the office and home of the prime minister at No. 10 Downing Street, has grown in recent years to about 200 staff members, organized into various sections. These include, for example, advisers on public policy, on foreign policy, on the EU, and on communications and strategy. Under Tony Blair the principal private secretary, the head of the private office, was a key player who provided the prime minister with information and briefings on important issues and helped him keep in contact with the departments of government. One of the most important roles of the private office is to brief the prime minister before he or she appears for question time in the House of Commons. It also serves as a liaison with the monarch and arranges the weekly private meetings between the prime minister and queen. In spite of the close relationship between the prime minister and the private office, the staff members are officially neutral civil servants temporarily assigned to their duties from other departments. As a result, the prime minister has added a number of close political aides in the political office who provide advice from a party political perspective. In addition to the private office and political office, there is a press office, which is responsible for relations with the print and electronic media, and a policy unit, which provides advice from an objective but also partisan perspective. Members of the policy unit are generally outsiders rather than civil servants. Under Tony Blair, they helped provide central direction and generated ideas and alternatives to departmental perspectives. Prime Minister Blair also created the office of chief of staff to manage the general operation of the Prime Minister's Office and coordinate its activities with those of the Cabinet Office.[3]

Ministers and departments of government. It is tempting to perceive the British system of cabinet government as one in which the central government, represented by the cabinet, which operates according to a system of collective responsibility, is centralized, unified, efficient, and effectively led by the prime minister. However, given the number of departments, their sometimes large size and multiple tasks, the ministers and their departments operate with a considerable degree of autonomy. The most important ministry, however, is the Treasury, headed by the chancellor of the exchequer, whose influence is based on his control over the authorization to spend public funds.

Each department is headed by a cabinet minister, who usually has several junior ministers under him or her responsible for certain functional areas. All of these ministers are drawn from the governing majority party and are members of the House of Commons or the House of Lords. These leaders are responsible before parliament for the actions of the permanent civil servants, who traditionally have been politically neutral in serving whatever political party controls the government. The junior ministers, who are not members of the cabinet, usually have the title of minister of state, parliamentary secretary, or parliamentary under-secretary. These junior minister positions are important stepping-stones to becoming a minister in future governments. In 2003 there were twenty-three cabinet ministers; however, the total number of ministers was 114.[4]

Each cabinet minister has a private office, headed by a civil servant who is the private secretary, and a parliamentary private secretary (PPS), who is a member of the House of Commons. The PPS keeps the cabinet minister informed of parliamentary and party opinion and, though unpaid, is usually an ambitious MP hoping for later promotion to a junior minister position. The minister may also have two or more independent special policy advisers who are not part of the department and not civil servants.

Ministers in charge of departments are expected to develop policies and serve as spokespersons for their departments. They manage their departments, negotiate with other departments, and represent the interests of their departments in the cabinet and to local governments, interest groups, and the media. The complexity, size, and scope of the responsibilities of many departments mean that in fact the permanent civil servants have considerable influence over ministers, who are not specialists. They often formulate policies on their own, even if they generally inform their political superiors about their ideas that have political relevance. Ministers are, however, responsible for the actions of their civil servants and are expected to resign if and when these are seen as unacceptable for any number of reasons.

Ministers are also members of the House of Commons or, in a few cases, the House of Lords, and they must be present during debates concerning their departments and at question time when they must answer questions directed at their department's policies or actions. As MPs they must also continue to serve their constituencies, attend party functions, and deal with the media.

The Legislature

The United States has a Congress consisting of two roughly equal chambers, the House of Representatives and the Senate, both directly elected by the people in 435 congressional districts or fifty states, respectively. The UK, like France, has a parliament with two very unequal chambers, only one of which is elected by the people. Because the UK is a unitary state, like France, neither chamber represents regions; and because it has a parliamentary system, the government must have a majority in the House of Commons, from which most of the cabinet members are drawn (on rare occasions a minority government might be formed). As a result there are significant differences, especially between the United States and Great Britain, in terms of separation of powers and checks and balances. There are also significant differences between the UK and Germany, as we shall see below.

The House of Commons. The House of Commons is the "lower house" of parliament, with 650 members of parliament (MPs) elected in 2010 in single-member constituencies by the first-past-the-post method (there is a proposal to reduce the membership by fifty, and there might be a change in the voting system; see chapter 4). With a population of about sixty-one million, this gives each MP on average about 92,500 constituents to represent. In contrast, an American member of the House of Representatives represents on average about 690,000 people. While congressmen usually make an effort to visit their districts and promote contact with voters, and all representatives and senators have staffs in Washington, DC, and in their districts and states that provide numerous services to voters, it is clear that British MPs can generally maintain closer personal contacts with voters in their considerably smaller constituencies. This does not, however, make British MPs more independent of their party; indeed, party discipline is generally stronger in Britain, although voting along party lines has increased in the United States as well during the past few decades.

In the 2010 elections a record high of 143 women (22 percent) were elected, but the proportion of women in the House of Commons is still low by European standards. Nevertheless, women in the House have increased dramatically since 1992, when thirty-seven women were elected. Of the total number of female MPs, eighty-one were Labour, forty-nine Conservative, and seven Liberal Democrat; six women were in other parties. The first minorities were elected in 1987, and their numbers increased sharply in 2010 to twenty-seven. More than one-third of all MPs attended private schools, which educate 7 percent of the population. Almost one-third were Oxford or Cambridge graduates. A significant proportion of Labour MPs were former public employees (civil service and local government); teachers and professors; various white collar workers, political organizers, and publishers; and manual workers. The Conservative Party has a higher proportion of lawyers, former military officers, and especially businessmen.[5]

Most MPs are professional politicians, because the increase in specialization as MPs and the demands of their constituents and party leave little time for nonparliamentary work. In spite of a number of improvements in recent years, the salaries of MPs and their staff support are considerably lower than in the United States, France, and Germany. In 2009 the salary was £64,766 or about $100,000 plus (the value of the pound vis-à-vis the dollar has varied considerably in the past several years) in addition to personal expenses including up to £24,000 for a second home, presumably in London (but some MPs claim London their first home, which has led to considerable controversy[6]). The salary of an American congressman is $174,000, staff support is significantly higher, and office space is much more generous.

The House of Commons is dominated by the Labour and Conservative parties, and for more than sixty years one of these parties has formed the government. The Liberals—now the Liberal Democrats—have come to play an important role as a third party, gaining as many as sixty-two seats in 2005 and fifty-seven in 2010; however, as noted in chapter 4, their percentage of the vote would give them many more seats if the British had a proportional electoral system for national elections and not just for the Scottish parliament. Four other parties have also been represented in the House of Commons since the mid-1970s, but they are all regional parties and receive only a handful of seats.

The setting of the House of Commons reflects the idea of one party in control of the government and an opposition party that criticizes it and holds it to account. Unlike the semicircular arrangement of continental European parliaments in which the parties sit from left to right based on their ideological perspectives, government and opposition in Britain sit on benches and face each other, thus symbolizing government versus opposition. The front bench of the government side consists of the prime minister and cabinet ministers; the front bench of the opposition consists of the leader of the opposition and the "shadow cabinet," i.e., MPs who will probably assume ministerial positions if and when the opposition wins the next election. The two front benches are only several feet from each other. The seating arrangement reflects the adversarial proceedings during debates and question time, when the prime minister and/or his ministers must respond to sometimes very hostile questions and comments from the opposition MPs as well as more friendly questions from majority party MPs. There is nothing comparable to question time in the American Congress, and the closest the American president comes to a parliamentary question time is probably the presidential news conference, which, however, tends to be a much milder and more respectful affair and may be held infrequently, depending on the president.

Committees, while important, are not as important in the House of Commons as they are in the House of Representatives or Senate of the United States. Select committees are responsible for overseeing the work of departments and agencies. There are twenty-three select committees, the chairmen of which were selected by party whips; however, since June 2010 chairmen are elected by secret ballots of MPs.[7] Until 2006 most bills were considered in ten standing committees, which are now called Public Bill Committees. The members of these committees are not permanent, as in the United States, but rather selected for the consideration of a particular bill. Party allegiance plays a large role in selection, as does expertise in the subject matter, if desired.

Committees in the House of Commons do not typically alter or amend the bills promoted by the government. Indeed, more than 90 percent of the bills considered are passed by the committees in the form the government wants. This stands in sharp contrast to American committees and is the result of strong party cohesion in the committees and the need of the government party to support its leaders in the cabinet. Dissenting party members may abstain on occasion, but they rarely vote against their own government in the committees or on the final vote in the House of Commons. There are, however, exceptions to the general rule. In the fall of 2005 the House voted against Prime Minister Blair's home security bill. Blair was furious that a number of Labour MPs joined the Opposition in forming a majority against the government, but he did not make the issue a vote of confidence in order to put pressure on the dissident members of his party to support him on this piece of legislation.

The House of Lords. The House of Lords was established as a result of the Magna Charta in 1215. Until recently it was composed of more than six hundred hereditary peers (Lords), about five hundred life peers, and twenty-six high Anglican clergy. Life peerages, i.e., peerages that cannot be passed on to heirs, were not created until 1958, which made it possible for Labour Party prime ministers to appoint life peers and balance somewhat the overwhelming majority of Conservative Party supporters among the hereditary lords. Since lords may not become members of the House of Commons and therefore are excluded from becoming prime minister, a law was passed in 1963 that permitted peers to give up their hereditary peerage during life. This enabled Sir Alec Douglas Home to become prime minister in 1963.

Even though the House of Lords is known as the "upper house" of parliament, it is not an equal legislative branch like the American Senate. While it was long the more powerful house of parliament, it slowly lost its dominance to the House of Commons during the nineteenth century. Since 1911 the lords can only delay legislation passed by the House of Commons, and in 1949 this delay was reduced to twelve months (one month for money bills). The twelve-month delay can become permanent if in the meantime there is a change of government that agrees with the House of Lords. There have also been occasions, though rare, when the rejection of legislation passed by the House of Commons was accepted by the government. A recent example occurred in October 2008, when a large majority of the House of Lords, including many Labour members, rejected a bill that would have allowed government authorities to hold terrorism suspects for forty-two (an increase from twenty-eight) days without being charged. The bill was criticized for being too draconian and unnecessary, since even twenty-eight days of detention without charges is much longer than in other European democracies (the Patriot Act in the United States allows detention of foreigners without charges for seven days and for citizens for forty-eight hours).[8]

During recent decades, the House of Lords has been the subject of considerable controversy, in large part because its legitimacy has been difficult to justify in an increasingly democratic age. In 1999 the composition was changed by a law that abolished the membership of all but ninety-two of the hereditary peers, who are now elected to serve for life; since hereditary peers as such no longer sit in the House of Lords, they may now run for the House of Commons. The somewhat more than five hundred life peers who served before the 1999 reform have been increased in number to about six hundred. The total number of lords, including the twenty-six bishops and archbishops, is now about 740. Since 1999 attendance has increased in spite of the reduction in total membership, with daily attendance now exceeding four hundred.[9]

The changes in 1999 did not end the controversy over the House of Lords. Proposals to reform it or even abolish it have all met with resistance. It might seem that simply making it an elective body would solve the problem, but that raises other questions. For example, should the House of Lords be elected by certain regions, by certain groups, or by the people as a whole? What powers should the House of Lords have if it is an elected body, and what would the effect be on the House of Commons? What effect would election of the House of Lords have on the idea of parliamentary sovereignty, i.e., sovereignty of the House of Commons? Why not make the Lords an appointive body that would be composed of members who had distinguished themselves in certain ways? In the spring of 2007 the House of Commons passed a law that would make the Lords an elective body, but this law was rejected by the Lords which favored an appointive body. About a year after he became prime minister in 2007, Gordon Brown announced that new proposals would be made by his government; however, concrete proposals were not made until March 2010, two months before the parliamentary elections in May, which the Labour Party lost. The new coalition government of Conservatives and Liberal Democrats, formed after the elections in May 2010 pledged to create a wholly or partially elected House of Lords, with details to be worked out by the House of Commons.[10]

Although the House of Lords had few powers at the time of the May 2010 election, some government ministers were members who could answer questions and help in getting legislation passed. Indeed, one of the ministers served as leader of the House of Lords. Party allegiance was less important than in the House of Commons, and as a result the House of Lords could act as a check on the government and its majority in that it could and often did take the time to correct defects in legislation passed by the House of Commons and devote more attention to debating certain bills that passed under time pressures in the House of Commons. In contrast to the House of Commons, committee work was done primarily in the committee of the whole, i.e., the entire House. There were, however, three select committees of importance: the European Union Select Committee, which reviewed drafts of legislation proposed by the EU Council of Ministers; Science and Technology; and Delegated Powers and Regulatory Reform, which reviewed the drafting of legislation by government ministers. While party was important in the assignment of peers to committees, expertise and experience were more important in the work of the Lords than in the more partisan House of Commons.

Germany

Historical Background

While Great Britain has a history of relative stability since the "Bloodless Revolution" of 1689, and the United States has been governed under the same constitution since 1789, France and Germany have gone through numerous fundamental political changes since the late eighteenth century. Indeed, "Germany," like Italy, was more a geographical description than an internationally recognized state until the last decades of the nineteenth century. More than thirty independent states, ranging in size from several city-states and small principalities to Prussia, a major European power, emerged from the Holy Roman Empire after its dissolution in 1806, forming a loose confederation in 1815. The member states, which retained their sovereignty, were associated by language (but with many dialects), culture, history, and economic ties, but it was not until 1867 that all but four southern German states joined in forming a North German Federation under the leadership of Prussia. Prussia had defeated Austria in a brief war in 1866 and, without Austrian participation, had a sizable majority of the total population and most of the territory of the federation. Following the defeat of France by Prussian and other German forces, the south German states and the states in the federation formed in 1871 the Bismarck Reich (empire), also known as the Kaiserreich, Second Reich or Hohenzollern Reich. The Bismarck Reich was also a federation, consisting of twenty-five states, but it was not a democracy. It was a constitutional monarchy, but the monarch, the kaiser, had supreme power in foreign affairs and defense. He also appointed the head of government, the chancellor, who, though dependent on the parliament for the passage of legislation, was accountable not to parliament but to the kaiser. The chancellor was also the head of government in the largest state, Prussia. Thus the German executive, from 1871 to the collapse of the Bismarck Reich in 1918 just before the end of World War I, was very different from the British model. Both countries had hereditary monarchs, but the constitutional monarchy in Britain was largely ceremonial, while the German constitution provided for a ruling monarch in key areas and a head of government dependent on him rather than on majority support in parliament.

With the collapse of the Kaiserreich in the November Revolution and the end of World War I, elections for a constitutional assembly were held in January 1919. The assembly was held in the small city of Weimar, and a new "Weimar Constitution" was adopted in August 1919. The new political system, which was known as the Weimar Republic, was a parliamentary democracy with a chancellor as head of government appointed by the head of state but responsible to the popularly elected chamber, the *Reichstag*. The chancellor was also no longer the prime minister of Prussia. Since the new state was a "republic," the head of state was not a monarch but a popularly elected president of seventeen states, now called *Länder*. They were represented in a second chamber that had sixty-six votes cast by delegations sent to the chamber by the *Land* governments. Prussia had two-fifths of the votes, but the Prussian central government controlled only half of these; the other half were sent by the political parties that were in charge of the Prussian provincial administrations. The power of Prussia was reduced also by the strengthening of the federal government at the expense of the *Länder*, especially in financial matters.

There are a number of similarities between the Weimar Republic and the French Fifth Republic of 1959: a popularly elected president as head of state; a head of government appointed by the head of state but responsible to both the head of state and parliament; a national hero, Field Marshall Paul von Hindenburg, serving as president during nine of the twelve years of the Weimar Republic, while a national hero, General de Gaulle, served as president of France for a little more than the first ten years of the Fifth Republic; and emergency powers for the head of state that were used at crucial periods of domestic crisis in each country. The major differences were the widespread resentment in Germany over the Treaty of Versailles and its many harsh provisions based on the accusation that Germany alone was responsible for World War I, the devastating inflation of the early 1920s that wiped out much of the middle class, the economic depression that began in 1929 that led to widespread unemployment and political radicalism, and the completely polarized multiparty system of the Weimar Republic. This system proved unable to generate stable majority coalition governments, so that the governments that were formed after 1930 became dependent on the emergency provisions of Article 48 of the Weimar Constitution rather than on majority parliamentary support. This led an exasperated President Hindenburg to appoint Adolf Hitler as chancellor in a coalition government in 1933, thinking that he could use his powers together with other members of the government who were not Nazis to check Hitler. Unfortunately, Hitler was able to outmaneuver his opponents, and Hindenburg died in 1934, allowing Hitler to become a dictator without political checks and balances. Indeed, the Nazi contempt for any semblance of regional or local autonomy and democratic rule was clearly evident in the dissolution of the *Länder* and elected local governments and the establishment of the "Third Reich" as a highly centralized party dictatorship with one supreme leader.

After the Allied victory over Germany and the end of World War II, it soon became clear that major tensions based on fundamental political disagreements were developing between the Soviet Union and the West. The Soviets handed over one-fourth of prewar Germany in the east to Poland in spite of agreements that this territory would be under Polish administration until a peace treaty (the loss of this territory was in effect recognized by the German government under Chancellor Willy Brandt in 1970 as a part of his eastern policy [*Ostpolitik*]). The Soviets were also granted an occupation zone over another quarter of the country in what had been the center of Germany before the War but was now the new East. The Americans, British, and French divided the western half of the country into three occupation zones. Soon it was clear that it was impossible for the Soviets and the three Western powers to agree or cooperate on numerous important issues, disagreements that came to a head when the Soviets in June 1948 cut off Western access to Berlin, which was located in the Soviet

Zone and had also been divided into four occupation zones. Supply by train, road transport, and canal boats was stopped by Soviet troops, but the Western powers began an airlift that proved successful in providing West Berliners with necessities. By May of 1949 it was clear that the Soviet plan to force the West to abandon the city had failed, and the blockade was lifted.

After four years of Allied occupation, the Germans in the three Western zones were allowed to write a constitution for a new political order. What they created was a democratic republic and parliamentary system organized territorially as a federation. By May 1949 the constitution, called "Basic Law" to indicate that it was temporary until German unification, was completed, and the first parliamentary elections were held in September 1949. By the mid-1950s the federation consisted of ten *Länder*, two of which were city states (Hamburg and Bremen). West Berlin, which was often counted as a third city-state, was not legally a part of the Federal Republic. Officially, it remained under the control of the Western Allies, but for all practical purposes it was a part of West Germany.

When Germany was unified in 1990, there were some voices that favored the convening of a convention to write a new constitution for the new Germany, as indeed Article 146 of the Basic Law suggested (but did not require) in the case of unification. Although there were staunch advocates of writing a new constitution, especially in what had been East Germany, there were two major objections to this proposal. First, it was argued that writing a new constitution would take too much time, which would cause a serious and costly delay in the complex integration of the two very different political and economic systems. Second, most constitutional experts felt that the West German Basic Law had been highly successful and provided all of the rights, institutions, and procedures that were necessary and desirable. A number of amendments were made in 1994, but these did not represent major changes.

The Executive after 1949

Head of state. The German head of state is the president, elected for a maximum of two five-year terms by an electoral college (federal assembly) consisting of members of the elected parliamentary chamber (*Bundestag*) and an equal number of delegates from the state (*Land*) parliaments and certain persons appointed by them. Since 1949 ten presidents have served, only two for the maximum of ten years. The current office holder, the former Christian Democratic prime minister of Lower Saxony, Christian Wulff, was elected in June 2010 in the parliamentary assembly in a close race with the SPD's popular candidate from the former East Germany, independent Joachim Gauck. Wulff's predecessor, Horst Köhler, a Christian Democrat elected in 2004 and a former head of the International Monetary Fund, was reelected in May 2009; however, in May 2010 he resigned over some controversial remarks he made about German military involvement abroad and protecting economic interests.

As in other parliamentary systems, the German president is essentially a ceremonial figure, which is reflected in the fact that he or she is not popularly elected. Therefore, unlike the German president in the Weimar Republic or the French president today in the Fifth Republic, the head of state in a typical parliamentary system has limited influence over the head of government, who is nominated by the head of state but elected by and accountable to the popularly elected parliament. The president then appoints the head of government, the chancellor, if he or she receives the requisite majority in the *Bundestag*. The president also appoints federal judges, civil servants, and military officers, but only on the recommendation of the chancellor. He has the right of pardon, and he performs the ceremonial functions typical of heads of state such as receiving foreign ambassadors and addressing the nation at certain times, e.g., at the beginning of a new year, celebrating German unification, or remembering the Holocaust.

Though usually a ceremonial figurehead, the German president has had to make important political decisions, especially on two occasions since 1983. The constitution (Basic Law), in contrast to British practice, does not give the head of government, the chancellor, the power to call for new elections. The reason is that the constitutional founders in 1948–49 wanted to avoid the instability of the Weimar Republic in the 1920s and early 1930s that was reflected in numerous elections and changes of government. In 1982 the government of Social Democrat (SPD) Chancellor

Helmut Schmidt lost a vote of confidence in the *Bundestag*, the parliament, because the coalition partner, the Free Democratic Party (FDP), joined with the Christian Democrats (CDU/CSU) in removing Schmidt from office and replacing him with the leader of the CDU, Helmut Kohl. This was a perfectly legitimate move; however, there was criticism of the change because it was not the result of a popular election. Indeed, the point was made that the FDP had campaigned in the 1980 parliamentary election with the argument that a vote for it was a vote for a coalition with the SPD under the leadership of Chancellor Schmidt. As a result of what appeared to be a lack of legitimacy in the minds of some people, the new Chancellor Kohl called for a vote of confidence, which he lost on purpose by having members of his party abstain. Since no other candidate could obtain a majority of votes in the *Bundestag*, a requirement of the Basic Law for the selection of a chancellor, a new election had to be called. The problem was that the president had to agree that this procedure was an acceptable manipulation of the Basic Law. He did agree, and a constitutional crisis was avoided. But the issue had to be reviewed also by the Federal Constitutional Court. Following approval by the court, an approval that was very uncertain at the time, Chancellor Kohl's party and the FDP together won a majority of the popular vote in the parliamentary election of 1983, and Kohl continued to win elections and govern with the FDP for the next fifteen years, until losing to Gerhard Schröder, the leader of the SPD, in 1998.

Another example of manipulation of the Basic Law to get new elections occurred in 2005. In May of that year, the Chancellor, Gerhard Schröder, called indirectly for new elections by asking for a vote of confidence, which he lost on purpose. Again, no other candidate could garner a majority in the *Bundestag*, so again the issue went to the president, who then decided to call for new elections. The Federal Constitutional Court again approved the manipulation, and new elections were held on September 18, 2005. In this case, as in 1983, the president and the Federal Constitutional Court had to make an important and controversial political and legal decision in order for new elections to occur.

Head of government. As noted above, the chancellor is nominated by the president and confirmed by majority vote in the *Bundestag*, the popularly elected legislative chamber. The person nominated by the president is typically the chancellor candidate of the party with the most votes rather than the leader of the majority party, as in Great Britain, because Germany has a multiparty system in which it is virtually impossible for any one party to receive a majority (the CDU/CSU received a majority in 1953, but it still formed a coalition government with a much smaller conservative party). Because this candidate will have arranged to form a coalition government with another party, there is little doubt that he or she will receive a majority of votes in the *Bundestag*. An exception occurred in 1969, when Willy Brandt, the leader of the second-place SPD, was nominated by the president because the SPD had agreed with the smaller FDP to form a majority coalition government.

In contrast to Great Britain (with rare exceptions), then, but more like other parliamentary systems, German governments are coalition governments. These have usually been combinations of one large party, such as the CDU/CSU or SPD, with one smaller party. However, on two occasions a "grand coalition" of these two large parties was formed: from 1966 to 1969 and from 2005 to 2009. In the first case the only third party then in the *Bundestag*, the FDP, was for a variety of reasons a less desirable partner for either of the large parties; in the second case the only feasible combination that would produce a majority in the now five-party system was that of the two large parties. They agreed to share equally the positions in the cabinet, and each party agreed to accept significant compromises regarding election promises.

In theory a grand coalition government should be able to steam-roll its proposals through parliament and, in the process, pass some needed reforms. Indeed, an important finance reform was passed in 1969 and a significant federalism reform was passed in 2006; however, a grand coalition also means that each party can easily check the other when they disagree. This means that grand coalitions can also lead to political gridlock and frustration in the electorate over a real or perceived inability to work together and get things done. The result of this popular dissatisfaction leads to increased support for the smaller third parties, such as the Greens and FDP, but today in particular the Left Party, which consists of former communists in eastern Germany and some disgruntled union leaders in western Germany (see chapter 6 on political parties). Ideally, a government coalition should consist of two parties (there has never been a three-party coalition, although this was an unlikely possibility in 2005) that are not too different ideologically, such as the CDU/CSU and FDP or the SPD and Greens.

Whether in a "normal" coalition or even a grand coalition, the chancellor is in a strong position to dominate the political agenda. The Basic Law gives him (or her, since the assumption of office by Angela Merkel in November 2005) the authority to set the guidelines in the cabinet (government), even though the German cabinet members, like their British counterparts, are responsible for the actions of their ministries. The idea of collective responsibility is not so strong in Germany as in Britain, but a German cabinet minister is not likely to criticize in public the chancellor or cabinet colleagues. As in Britain or in any other parliamentary system, the chancellor must have disciplined, cohesive majority support in the parliament to carry out his or her agenda. This may be more difficult to obtain in Germany, however, because the government is not supported by a single party with an absolute majority as in Britain. The chancellor may also be checked by the second chamber, the *Bundesrat*, which will be discussed below.

If one of the coalition partners decides that it cannot accept certain policies, it tries to persuade the leadership of the other party to change the policy or at least accept some compromise. If the other party refuses, the party seeking change can threaten to withdraw from the coalition government, which would then lose its majority in the parliament. In most parliamentary democracies, this would lead to efforts by the remaining government party to find a new coalition partner and form a new government with a different majority. If this fails, the remaining government party might try to continue government as a "minority government." A minority government might continue on an ad hoc basis to gather majority votes in parliament for its initiatives with the support of one or more parties not represented in the cabinet (i.e., "changing majorities"), but such a government is usually in a precarious situation. A vote of confidence might be called, and if the government loses, it would have to resign and call for new elections. A British prime minister can call for new elections at any time, not just because he or she has lost a vote of confidence.

In Germany the head of government cannot threaten to call for new elections in case a coalition partner considers leaving the cabinet. The collapse of a coalition could lead the remaining government party to attempt to continue as a minority government, but this has never happened. Nor can the opposition party or parties win a vote of confidence just because the chancellor and his government fail to win a majority. The Basic Law provides for the removal of the chancellor only if in a "constructive vote of confidence" another candidate receives a majority of the vote. In 1972 the chancellor, Willy Brandt, had to face a vote of confidence called for by the opposition Christian Democrats, who thought they had a majority (based on the addition of some dissident members of the government parties who had joined the opposition); however, the motion failed by one vote.

On the other hand, as was noted above, the Social Democrat, Helmut Schmidt, was replaced as chancellor in the fall of 1982 when the smaller government party, the FDP, went into opposition and joined forces with the major opposition party, the Christian Democrats, to remove Schmidt as chancellor in a constructive vote of no confidence by replacing him with Helmut Kohl. In early 1983 the Kohl government decided it needed the legitimacy of an electoral victory, but Kohl, unlike his British counterpart, could not call for new elections. A somewhat similar situation faced Chancellor Gerhard Schröder in 2005, who wanted new elections to give his government renewed legitimacy. In both cases, the governing chancellor lost a vote of confidence on purpose, in order to bring about new elections by default. The president agreed to call for new elections in each case. These decisions were challenged before the Federal Constitutional Court, which ruled in favor of the president on both occasions.

The Legislature

We have seen that France and the United Kingdom, like the United States, have legislatures with two chambers; however, whereas the French National Assembly and the British House of Commons are popularly elected, like the US House of Representatives, the French Senate and the British House of Lords are not popularly elected and have far fewer competences than the US Senate. Germany is more like the United States, even though its second chamber, the *Bundesrat*, is also not a popularly elected body (and therefore, from a German legal perspective, not officially an "upper house" of parliament). It is, rather, a "*Länder* chamber" that serves as a legislative/ executive body that represents the sixteen German states (*Länder*). It has far more powers than the House of Lords or French Senate, but it is not equal to the popularly elected house (*Bundestag*), as the US Senate is to the House of Representatives.

The Federal Parliament or *Bundestag*. The *Bundestag* consists officially of 598 members, half of whom are elected directly in single-member districts (like members of the US House of Representatives, the British House of Commons, and the French National Assembly) and half enter on the basis of the proportion of the vote received by the competing parties (see chapter 4 on elections). This means that the small parties may have few, if any, candidates who are elected directly, because they are rarely able to obtain a plurality (most votes) in any district; however, if the party received at least 5 percent of the national vote, it receives seats in proportion to its vote (thus, in principle, the percentage of seats equals approximately the percentage of vote above 5 percent).

Each *Land*, or state, has a certain number of votes in proportion to its population. The large parties win all or most of the direct seats, the number of which is subtracted from the proportion of seats assigned to the *Land*. If the number of direct seats won is larger than the number of seats the party actually "deserves" based on the party's proportion of the vote in the *Land*, the party may keep the "excess" or "surplus" seats (*Überhangmandate*). In the 2009 election, the CDU/CSU won 218 of the 299 district or direct seats and only twenty-one list seats; however, because it won so many district seats by a small plurality, it ended up with twenty-four surplus seats that were more than it "deserved" based on the proportional vote. None of the other parties received any surplus seats, but the extra seats won by the CDU/CSU brought the total number of seats for the legislative term to 622 (598+24). In the 2005 election, the CDU won three more district seats than its actual share of the proportional vote in Baden-Württemberg, and the SPD won three more district seats than its share of the proportional vote in Brandenburg. Altogether, there were fourteen "excess" seats in 2005, so that the *Bundestag* ended up with 612 rather than 598 members.

Those candidates who are elected directly represent from 160,000 to 250,000 voters in their districts. This is a much larger number than British MPs represent, but it is much smaller than US congressional districts. Of the members who entered the *Bundestag* in 2009, 32.8 percent were women (a considerably higher proportion than in the United States, France, and the UK). In the previous parliament average members had been active party members for seventeen years, and there were few, if any, who did not have some experience with party and public office before being nominated by their *party* organizations. This stands in contrast to some American congressmen, who are practically self-selected with little or no participation in party activities before winning their nomination (often as a result of a largely self-financed primary election). Members enter the *Bundestag* on average in their mid-forties and leave on average at age fifty-three; thus the average length of service is about ten years, considerably less than in the US House of Representatives.

Members who come from various civil service positions, including teachers and professors, have the right to return to their former positions. It is much less likely in Germany than in the United States that former members of parliament will be employed by lobbying firms or the private sector. Some need the transition assistance mentioned above in looking for a new position.[11] About a quarter of the *Bundestag* members have outside employment of some kind, often as attorneys; however, this is most likely to be the case among FDP members and, to a lesser extent, CDU/CSU members. On the other hand, about three-quarters of the members are critical of outside employment by their colleagues.

As in other parliamentary systems, most of the members of the cabinet are also members of the parliament (*Bundestag*). The *Bundestag* does, however, exercise control functions over the government. Like other parliaments in Europe, it does this in committee hearings or investigations, but also via question time, when the chancellor and ministers must appear before the *Bundestag* to answer questions, and when the cabinet listens to and participates in debates in parliament that address the issues of the day. The *Bundestag* is known as a "working parliament," in contrast to the British "talking parliament," in that it is organized into standing committees that review government bills and are led not only by the majority parties but also by representatives from other parties in proportion to their seats. There are also special committees that investigate any number of policy or administrative matters that are considered by some to be inappropriate or unacceptable in some way. In this regard the *Bundestag* is somewhat more similar to the US Congress than either the House of Commons or the French National Assembly.

This is due in part to the organizational structure of the *Bundestag*. The leader is the president, whose functions are similar to a speaker of the house. The president is usually from the largest political party group and is assisted by six vice presidents, who represent all of the parties with seats in the *Bundestag*. They form an executive committee, which meets with a so-called Council of Elders, consisting of leading representatives of the various party groups, to plan the legislative agenda and daily activities. The members of the *Bundestag* are organized into party groups (*Fraktionen*), the leaders of which play key roles in the debates and in maintaining party group cohesion. Members are further divided into working groups, which correspond to standard policy areas and the standing committees. Expertise is important, and government proposals may be challenged to some extent even by the majority parties. Nevertheless, party discipline is strong, and it is not often that party groups do not present a united front.

As of January 1, 2009, members of the *Bundestag* received a monthly taxable income of €7,668, or approximately $10,000 plus (at the rate of 1 Euro=$1.35; the dollar equivalent ranged from $1.55 to $1.25 between 2008 and 2011). In addition they received health insurance; reimbursement for district offices; support for office staff, and travel; and a housing allowance in Berlin. After one year in parliament, they receive pension rights that accrue at 2.5 percent per year up to two-thirds of total salary after twenty-seven years of service. Members of parliament are also paid transition money, which they accumulate at one month's salary per year of service and which is paid out in installments equal to their monthly salaries when they leave office for any reason before retirement. This benefit is unknown in the United States.

The Federal Council (*Länder* Chamber) or *Bundesrat*. Many liberal democratic unitary states, such as Great Britain and France, have second chambers, while others, such as Sweden and Denmark, do not. On the other hand federal states, such as the United States and Germany, typically have second chambers that represent in some manner the regional units (states, provinces, cantons, or *Länder*). While there are many similarities among second chambers, there are also significant differences, even among those in federal systems; however, Germany's *Bundesrat* is unique even among federal systems, because it is a *federal*, not a *Land* organ that represents the *governments* (i.e., cabinets) of the *Länder*. This means it is an executive as well as a legislative body, and it means also that it is not a part of parliament, which is the *Bundestag* alone. Rather, it is a constitutional organ along with the *Bundestag*, the federal government, the federal president, and the Federal Constitutional Court that makes it possible for the *Länder*, via their governments, to participate in the legislative process. Legally, it is not an "upper house" of parliament, although it is often incorrectly described as such. It is a chamber of the *Länder*, but not in the sense that its focus is *Länder* issues; rather, its focus is on federalism and legislative and administrative relations between the federation and the *Länder*. This makes the *Bundesrat* an important part of what the Germans call "participatory" and "administrative" federalism.

The *Bundesrat* is composed of members of, and is appointed by, the *Land* governments (cabinets). Only the cabinet members may vote in the plenary sessions, while civil servants may participate in committee meetings. The number of delegates each *Land* sends to the *Bundesrat* depends on the number of votes it has, which in turn varies roughly according to population. Each *Land* has at least three votes. *Länder* with more than two million inhabitants have four votes, with more than six million, five votes; and with more than seven million, six votes. Thus the four largest *Länder*, North-Rhine Westphalia, Bavaria, Baden-Württemberg, and Lower Saxony, have six votes, while the Saarland and the city states of Hamburg and Bremen have three votes each. The total number of votes is sixty-nine, and each *Land* casts its votes *en bloc* on instructions of the *Land* government. In case the *Land* has a coalition government and the parties in the government do not agree on how to vote, the *Land* delegation will most likely abstain; this has the effect of a negative vote, since only positive votes are counted.

The president of the *Bundesrat* is elected each year on a rotating basis, starting with the largest *Land*, which is North-Rhine Westphalia. The president is either a prime minister of a territorial *Land* or lord mayor of a city-state, and he or she is second only to the federal president in terms of protocol. The president calls and presides at the meetings of the *Bundesrat*, usually every third Friday, for a total of about twelve meetings per year.

The *Bundesrat* has the right to initiate legislation, but most bills come from the federal government (cabinet) or, to a lesser extent, from the *Bundestag*. In the most common case, the government sends its bills to the *Bundesrat*, which then has six weeks to respond. The president of the *Bundesrat* sends the bill directly to the relevant committees, where most of the real work of that chamber takes place. The *Land* minister assigned to the *Bundesrat* is the official representative of the *Land* in the committees with the exception of the committee on foreign relations, in which the *Land* head of government serves as the representative. In fact it is common for the *Land* minister to be represented by a civil servant. Each *Land* has one seat and one vote in the committee, and, though the majority vote in the committee usually suggests how the *Bundesrat* will vote, it should be recalled that the *Länder* have from three to six votes that are cast *en bloc* in the plenary session, which could lead to a different result in that session.

After further consideration in a committee composed of all of the official *Land* representatives, the proposal is brought before a plenary session of the *Bundesrat*. If the bill passes, it is forwarded to the *Bundestag* via the federal government, which provides a statement of its views that accompany the bill. The *Bundestag* considers the bill in committee; if it is then passed by the *Bundestag*, the bill is returned to the *Bundesrat*.

If it is a "simple bill" or "objection bill," i.e., one that does not involve the *Länder* in the bill's administration or finances, and the *Bundesrat* approves, it goes back to the government, which gives it to the federal president for his signature. If the *Bundesrat* does not approve, it can call for a meeting of the Mediation Committee, composed of one member from each *Land* and an equal number of *Bundestag* members, for a total of thirty-two. If the Mediation Committee reaches a compromise and the two chambers accept, the bill goes to the government and the federal president for his signature. If, on the other hand, the *Bundesrat* does not accept the compromise, it has the right of a suspensive veto. If the veto consists of a majority of the *Bundesrat*, i.e., at least thirty-five of the sixty-nine votes, it can be overridden by an absolute majority of the *Bundestag*. But if the veto garners a two-thirds majority in the *Bundesrat*, i.e., forty-six votes, the *Bundestag* can override the veto only by a two-thirds vote. Generally speaking, the opposition forces in the *Bundesrat* do not have a two-thirds majority, so the government and its majority in the *Bundestag* can normally pass the "objection bills."

The process becomes more complicated if the bill is a "consent bill," which was the case in about 50–60 percent of all bills before the Federalism Reform of 2006. These bills involve administrative procedures or finances that concern the *Länder*. If a majority of the *Bundesrat* rejects the bill, which is more likely to occur if the opposition in the *Bundestag* has a majority in the *Bundesrat*, i.e., when there is the German version of "divided government," a meeting of the Mediation Committee can be called. However, if the Committee is unable to reach a compromise, the bill is dead. If a compromise is reached, the bill goes back to each chamber for approval without amendment. While there are some examples of legislative defeat for the government because of a failure to get a bill past the *Bundesrat*, that chamber generally approves bills sent to it or accepts the compromises reached by the Mediation Committee. Nevertheless, the need to compromise in many important cases led to provisions in the Federalism Reform of 2006 that were designed to reduce the proportion of consent bills from 50 to 60 percent to 30 to 40 percent.[12] It is still too early to tell how successful these provisions will be.

Conclusion

In contrast to the American presidential and French semipresidential systems, the British and Germans have the more common parliamentary system. There are, however, some major differences between Britain and Germany. One obvious difference is the selection of the head of state: the monarch in the United Kingdom and the president in Germany. The British monarch is, of course, selected on the basis of heredity, while the German president is elected by an electoral "federal assembly" consisting of the members of the popularly elected *Bundestag* and members of the popularly elected state, or *Land*, parliaments and persons appointed by them.

The British parliamentary system is known as the "Westminster system." According to this model, the prime minister is the leader, i.e., head of government, appointed by the monarch on the basis of his or her leadership of the majority party in the House of Commons. This party not only has an absolute majority in parliament; it is also a strongly cohesive, disciplined party, which means that it usually votes together in favor of the initiatives of the cabinet led by the prime minister. He or she can hire and fire the cabinet ministers, dissolve the House of Commons, and call for new elections.

The principle of "collective responsibility," which means that all of the ministers in the cabinet are bound to support cabinet positions or resign, is reflected in the term "cabinet government." The especially dominant positions of Margaret Thatcher and Tony Blair as prime ministers have led some to describe the British system as going beyond "cabinet government" to "prime ministerial government." On the other hand, Mrs. Thatcher was removed from office by her own parliamentary party and replaced by a much more collegial and congenial John Major, and Tony Blair resigned under pressure in 2007, because he was not as dominant a figure after the election of 2005—or, indeed, after he decided to join the United States in its invasion of Iraq in 2003. We noted that there were a number of mostly informal checks and balances in the British system that place certain constraints on "prime ministerial government"; nevertheless, the

British prime minister is generally in a stronger position than the American president to achieve his or her legislative goals.

The German chancellor is also in a strong position to dominate the political agenda. The Basic Law gives him or her the authority to set the guidelines in the cabinet (government), and the chancellor usually has cohesive majority support in parliament to carry out his or her agenda. This may be more difficult to achieve in Germany than in Britain, however, because there is rarely a single party with an absolute majority of votes in the parliament; rather, as in most parliamentary democracies, a coalition of two or more parties is necessary to form a government with majority support.

The British House of Commons, or parliament, is elected by the people, whereas the House of Lords was until rather recently based on heredity. During the second half of the twentieth century, many "life peers" were added; however, efforts to reform the House of Lords continued until it was sharply reduced in number and hereditary peers were excluded at the end of the century. Disagreement exists even today about the selection of the lords and the role they should play in the legislative process, and it appears that a "final" reform of the "upper" house may take some time.

In Germany the *Bundestag* is the popularly elected legislative chamber that is the counterpart of the House of Commons. The second chamber, the *Bundesrat*, is often referred to as the *Länder* chamber, because it represents the sixteen *Länder* that make up the Federal Republic. More precisely, it represents the *Länder* governments, which, under the leadership of the respective *Land* prime ministers, are able to participate in the federal legislative process. Until a 2006 federalism reform, the sixty-nine *Länder* delegates could exercise an absolute veto of up to about 60 percent of the government's legislative proposals and a suspensive veto over the remaining bills. The reform is designed to reduce the percentage of absolute veto power to about 30–40 percent. In any case the *Bundesrat* is a unique second chamber in federal and parliamentary systems, and, though less powerful than the US Senate, it is one of the most powerful second chambers in the world.

Endnotes

[1] Bill Jones and Philip Norton, eds., *Politics UK*, 7th ed. (Pearson Education, 2010), 405.

[2] Gillian Peele, *Governing the UK*, 4th ed., (Oxford: Blackwell Publishing, 2004).

[3] Ibid., 148–156.

[4] Ibid., 160.

[5] For statistics on women, see http://www.parliament.uk/factsheets and *The Telegraph* (March 18, 2011) http://www.telegraph.cl.uk/news/elections-2010.

[6] *Financial Times* (April 4 and 11, 2009), 7 and 10, respectively.

[7] Ibid. (June 3, 2010), 8.

[8] *New York Times* (October 14, 2008), A9.

[9] Jones and Norton, eds., *Politics UK*, 355–56.

[10] Roland Sturm, "Reform von Wahlsystem, Parlament und Kommunalverfassungen: Die Agenda der konservativ-liberaldemokratischen Koalition in Grossbritannien," *Zeitschrift für Parlamentsfragen* 41, Heft 4, (2010), 743.

[11] For a detailed discussion, see Heinrich Best and Michael Edinger, "Redemanuskript für die Presentation 'Politik als Beruf und Berufung' im Deutschen Bundestag am 15. Dezember 2004" (http://www.sfb580.uni-jena.de/typo3/uploads/media/Redemanuskript.pdf.

[12] For an analysis of the Federalism Reform of 2006, see Arthur B. Gunlicks, "German Federalism Reform: Part One," *German Law Journal*, No. 11 (1 January 2007) (www.germanlawjournal.com/article.php?id=792); see also the special edition of *German Politics* 17, No. 4 (December 2008). For a more complete discussion of federalism and federalism reform in Germany, see Gunlicks, "Legislative Competences, Budgetary Constraints, and Federalism Reform in Germany from Top Down and Bottom Up," in Michael L. Burgess and G. Alan Tarr, eds., *Constitutional Dynamics in Federal Systems: Sub-National Perspectives* (Montreal: McGill-Queen's University Press, forthcoming, 2012).

For Further Reading

Conradt, David P. *The German Polity*. 9th ed. Cengage Learning, 2009.

Hancock, M. Donald, and Henry Krisch. *Politics in Germany*. Washington, DC: CQ Press, 2009.

Jones, Bill, and Philip Norton, eds., *Politics UK*. 7th ed. Pearson Education, 2010.

Norton, Bruce F. *Politics in Britain*. Washington, DC: CQ Press, 2007.

Peele, Gillian. *Governing the UK*. 4th ed. Oxford: Blackwell Publishing, 2004.

Chapter 9

Legal Systems and Courts

Introduction

Two legal systems prevail in liberal democracies: the common law system associated with England and the numerous countries it influenced through colonization, including, of course, the United States, Australia and Canada; and the civil law or code law system found in continental Europe, its former colonies, and Japan. The individual countries within each system have their own practices that make them somewhat different. For example, the United States differs in some respects from England, Australia, and Canada within the common law framework, and the province of Quebec and the state of Louisiana differ in important ways from the civil law systems of continental Europe with which they share basic principles. A third major legal tradition, based on Islamic law, is found in many countries of the Middle East and Asia. A fourth tradition would include various tribal or customary legal systems found primarily in Africa. In some cases there may also be a mixture of Islamic and tribal law or some other combination.

Civil Law and Common Law Systems

Civil law is a system based on codes or statutes passed by legislative bodies. As a result precedent based on case law (*stare decisis*) does not play as important a role as it does in common law countries. Civil law dates back to Roman law and Catholic canon law and is the oldest and most widespread legal system. It is found throughout western and eastern Europe, Latin America, and parts of Asia and Africa. Because of the French colonial heritage in Quebec and the French and Spanish influence in Louisiana, these territories in Canada and the United States also have civil law systems. The application of civil law in continental Europe varies somewhat from one country to another, but the exceptionally rational system introduced by Napoleon in 1804, called the *Code Napoleon*, has served as a model in varying degrees for most European states. The European states with civil law systems that have deviated most from the general principles of civil law were the communist countries from the emergence of the Soviet Union in the early 1920s to the collapse of communism in the late 1980s and early 1990s. The deviation consisted of the insertion of Marxism-Leninism into the system, i.e., the role of the communist party and its ideology that focused on "class justice," and the lack of judicial independence from the communist party, especially in cases involving political personalities and issues.[1]

In contrast to what some observers in common law countries believe, civil law systems also guarantee the presumption of innocence.[2] There are, however, certain differences in court procedure that give rise to this misconception. The most important difference, perhaps, is that the civil law systems are *inquisitorial* rather than *adversarial*, as in common law systems. This means first of all that in criminal cases there is a pretrial investigation by prosecutors that is somewhat analogous to the grand jury in the United States, so that trials are unlikely to be held where evidence of guilt is weak. Secondly, it means that the judge, who is a professional whose career path is separate from that of attorneys and who has a somewhat different educational background, may become actively involved in the trial by asking both the defense and prosecution questions about the case in order to obtain facts that might not otherwise be revealed. Another difference is that juries are typically composed of judges and laypersons, rather than only the latter; their number is usually less than the typical twelve jurors in the United States, and decisions are by special majority rather than unanimous vote.

The common law also has a long history in England, where it developed by custom over the centuries.[3] It is law made essentially by judges who, in the Middle Ages, "rode circuit" to hear cases and make decisions based on precedents (or *stare decisis*) collected from various locations in the realm. Statutes were not the source of the law, then, but rather case law.[4]

In common law systems judges and attorneys have the same educational background, which is focused in large part on the study of case law, rather than on codes passed by legislative bodies. There is no special training for the career of judge. Indeed, judges are appointed from the ranks of successful attorneys, though partisan factors play a role as well. Trials are adversarial rather than inquisitorial, which means the judge acts as a neutral mediator between the defense and the prosecution, the latter of which must prove beyond a reasonable doubt or with a preponderance of the evidence that the defendant is guilty or one party is responsible or liable. A jury of peers (who in fact may not be easy to put together because of presumed bias, including race and social/economic background) decides by a unanimous vote whether the charges against the defendant have been proved.

The Organization of Justice

It is difficult to compare individual states and their legal systems, because even when looking at countries that have in principle one system or another, significant differences can often be found in theory and practice. A good example is the comparison of the United Kingdom and the United States, where concepts of internal sovereignty, the parliamentary versus the presidential system, and the impact of the unitary organization in the UK in contrast to the federal system in the United States result in some significant differences.

The British and American Common Law Systems

Foundations: Although they share the common law tradition, there are some rather fundamental differences between the United Kingdom and the United States. One key difference is that in Britain sovereignty is considered to be located in the Parliament or, more precisely, the elected House of Commons. This is an important reason why the British do not have a written constitution as a single document but rather rely on custom, tradition (thus, common law), and important statutes for their basic rules of the game. Of course it also means that no court can declare a law passed by Parliament to be unconstitutional. What Parliament decides is, by definition, a legal expression of British internal sovereignty, and it overrides the common law. Thus one of the best known differences between the United Kingdom and the United States is that the latter has a written constitution that plays a greater role in government and society than in most other countries. In spite of some egregious flaws (for example, allowing slavery in spite of its general protection of individual liberty) and conflicts over interpretation (one of the causes of the Civil War), the American Constitution has served throughout most of American history as an important agent of unity and national pride. Since an early interpretation (*Marbury v. Madison*, 1803), the US Supreme Court has had the right of judicial review, i.e., the right not only to interpret the constitution and statutory law but also to declare certain legislative and executive acts unconstitutional. While most democracies place internal sovereignty in the people (popular sovereignty), Americans (and most other liberal democracies) also consider their constitution to be the highest law of the land as the legal expression of popular sovereignty. This means that the Supreme Court ensures the integrity of the Constitution on behalf of the sovereign people; but it also means that the Supreme Court can rule a law or action supported by a popular or congressional majority to be in violation of the Constitution.[5]

Another much less important but interesting difference between Britain and the United States is the division in England and Wales between barristers and solicitors. A person goes to a solicitor for legal advice and consultation that does not involve litigation. If a case goes before a court, the solicitor engages a barrister, who is specialized for court appearances. This formal separation of function exists in some other common law countries as well; however, in the United States and in most other liberal democracies, there may be a functional separation within a law firm between trial lawyers and others, but not one based on formal criteria, including educational background.

Because the British had no written constitution, the United Kingdom had no supreme court until 2009, although they had a select group of so-called law lords in the House of Lords who were in effect the highest court in the land. They did not, however, have the right of judicial review in the sense of being able to overturn a law passed by Parliament. Because sovereignty has been located in Parliament since the Glorious Revolution of 1688, no court has been deemed competent to overrule parliamentary acts; however, the theory of parliamentary sovereignty has been under serious challenge in recent years. First, membership in the EU has meant that British laws may be and have been overturned by the European Court of Justice (ECJ) in Luxembourg for nonconformity with the EU treaties that Britain has signed. The result is that British courts can now overturn acts of Parliament that it concludes have violated EU law. Second, the United Kingdom is a signatory of the Council of Europe's Convention for the Protection of Human Rights (CPHR), over which the Court of Human Rights in Strasbourg presides. Since 1966 British citizens can bring cases involving human rights before the Strasbourg Court, and since 2000 British courts can decide whether British law conforms to the Convention; however, the government and Parliament must actually bring the law into conformity with the Convention.

Structure of the American court system. The American Founding Fathers believed strongly in a governmental system of separation of powers and checks and balances, and they had an independent judiciary as a goal from the beginning of their deliberations. Article III of the Constitution established the Supreme Court and other federal courts as separate from the legislative (Article I) and executive (Article II) branches, and their independence was further secured by terms of appointment for life tenure, i.e., during "good behavior." (As we shall see below, life tenure is not found in our other liberal democracies.) In addition, compensation of the federal judges was not to be reduced during the term of office. Checks and balances were to be secured by having all federal judges nominated by the president and confirmed by the Senate. While the court has original jurisdiction in certain cases, Congress has the right to decide the other kinds of cases that fall within the court's jurisdiction; Congress can propose constitutional amendments that might affect previous decisions; and judges can be impeached and removed from office.

Article III did not establish a federal court system, but it does authorize Congress to do so. As a result, the federal court system, which includes courts other than the Supreme Court, was established by the Judiciary Act of 1789. A three-tier structure was created, with district courts at the bottom, circuit courts that serve as courts of appeal from district courts, and, finally, the Supreme Court. The Act set the size of the Supreme Court at six, including the chief justice. Since 1869 there have been nine justices—the chief justice and eight associate justices. At the present time there are ninety-four federal district courts and thirteen federal courts of appeal, or circuit courts. Very few of the approximately 300,000 federal cases first heard by the district courts—usually fewer than one hundred—are heard by the Supreme Court.

Each of the fifty states also has a basically three-tiered system. In most states the high court is also called the supreme court. At the bottom are the trial courts, from which cases may be appealed to the state appellate courts. Appeals from these courts go to the high court. Whether a case is heard first in a federal district trial court or a state trial court depends on the jurisdiction of the court. For example, cases involving the federal government or civil suits under federal laws are first heard in federal district courts. Appeals from trial courts to appellate courts also depend on jurisdiction, for example whether the case raises questions under federal law. This includes cases from state high courts that are appealed to the federal supreme court.

In the American federal system, each level of government has its own statutes for criminal law and civil law. The result is that some acts are crimes—felonies, misdemeanors, and offenses—in some states but not in others, e.g., some forms of gambling. Punishments also vary among the states, e.g., different prison terms for the same offense or a maximum of a life term without parole versus the death penalty. Criminal cases are brought by government prosecutors. Civil law deals with the regulation of conditions and relationships between private individuals or companies. Civil cases are brought by those affected.

Appointments to judgeships, especially at the federal level, have become highly political. Republican presidents generally nominate conservative judges, while Democratic presidents nominate moderate or liberal judges. Whether one is conservative or liberal is based not only on views regarding the role of government in society, religious belief, and other factors normally associated with ideology, but especially on judicial philosophy. This concerns the role of judges in interpreting the Constitution, in particular the extent to which the "original intent" of the Founding Fathers or those who proposed amendments should be the focus of interpretation. Those who take this position are also associated with the idea of "judicial restraint," the belief that courts should accept the decisions of the other branches of government to the extent possible. At the other end of the spectrum are the "judicial activists," those who believe one should look at the meaning of the principles of the Constitution as these have evolved over the decades and consider their proper application today. This view is usually associated with those who argue that judges must promote justice, especially in the areas of equality and personal liberty. In most cases, of course, the dividing line is not so clear, but some examples that show the difficulty of deciding between these basic approaches would include school integration in the 1950s, affirmative action, abortion, or gun control, all of which are questions that the Constitution basically leaves open for interpretation by judges. In any case decisions of the Supreme Court can have an enormous impact on domestic and foreign policies. The fact that federal judges are appointed for life terms makes it even more important from the perspective of the president and Senate to have judges at all levels of the federal court system who are sympathetic to their own value preferences and those of their voters.

The appointment of federal judges is also politically important because of the diversity of American society. In recent decades pressure has grown to appoint women, blacks, and Hispanics to the Supreme Court and other federal courts, while there is a fairly long tradition of having a Jewish seat on the highest federal bench. At the state level, two-thirds of state court judges are elected. This raises questions about the independence of the judges not only from political parties and movements, e.g., pro-life and pro-gun groups, but also from certain interest groups that made campaign contributions.

Structure of the British court system.[6] In contrast to the United States, the British courts and legal system have not been a major focus of attention for students of politics. One author cites three reasons for this. First, judges have not been involved in politics as much as their American counterparts, in part because they were bound to parliamentary decisions as the final word. Therefore, they were not an independent voice in political struggles with parliament and the government of the day. Second, few cases involving politics came before the courts. Third, judges generally remained silent regarding political and even legal issues.[7]

Toward the end of the twentieth century and even more recently, some important changes occurred. As mentioned above, a supreme court was established in the United Kingdom in October 2009. Until then, the highest court was located in the House of Lords. A new supreme court is now the highest court of appeal for civil and criminal cases. In general the court does not have the right to overturn acts of parliament, but it can do so if an act violates EU law as interpreted by the European Court of Justice (ECJ) and which British courts are obligated to uphold. The British supreme court may also refer questions concerning EU law to the ECJ for a ruling before making a final decision about a case.

In the United Kingdom, as in other liberal democracies (but with a longer history in the UK), the "rule of law" is a guiding principle of government. General principles include punishment only for specific violations of the law, equality under the law, and individual rights. Individual rights have been protected by tradition and some statutes in the UK, but they were not guaranteed as in the American Bill of Rights. In 1966 British citizens were allowed to bring cases before the European Court of Human Rights in Strasbourg; however, since the British passed the Human Rights Act, which was based on the Council of Europe's Convention on the Protection of Human Rights (CPHR) and went into effect in 2000, individual rights are guaranteed in writing, and citizens may bring cases under the Convention before British courts. The new powers gained by EU membership and adherence to the CPHR have raised the profile of the British high court and led to tensions with traditionalists, who continue to insist on parliamentary sovereignty.

Even though the United Kingdom is a unitary state, it has a number of decentralized features, including some differences in the legal systems of England and Wales on the one hand and Scotland on the other. The former have classic common law systems with origins in judge-made law, while Scotland has a legal system influenced strongly by civil law and reliance on codes. Northern Ireland has a separate system of laws which is more closely related to the English system.

In England and Wales the court system is divided between civil and criminal courts and organized as a hierarchy. At the lowest level in civil cases are tribunals that were established mostly in the last sixty years but are not officially courts. Rather, they adjudicate disputes between individuals and between individuals and institutions. There are now more than two thousand tribunals that resolve a wide variety and large number of mostly minor disputes. They are led by lawyers and two laypersons rather than judges, and they suggest solutions based on the law that can be appealed to a court above the lowest official court, the county court. There are 218 county courts in England and Wales, and they have jurisdiction over contract, personal injury, bankruptcy, divorce, domestic violence, and other matters. They are also small claims courts that deal with claims below a certain amount. Appeals can be made to the next level of courts, the High Court of Justice.

The High Court of Justice has three divisions. First, the Queen's Bench Division has jurisdiction over civil and criminal matters, including claims that are above the level reserved for the county courts. Three specialized courts are also part of this division: the Commercial Court, the Admiralty Court, and the Administrative Court. The second and third divisions are the Family Division and the Chancery Division, which deals with issues of equity law. Its jurisdiction includes trusts, bankruptcy, and tax questions. The Chancery Division also includes two specialized courts: a Companies Court and a Patents Court.

The next level, the Court of Appeal, is divided into a Civil Division and a Criminal Division. The Court of Appeals hears about a thousand cases a year and is generally the court of final jurisdiction in these cases. Only relatively few cases, as in the United States, are successfully appealed to the very highest court, the House of Lords, or now the supreme court. The twelve law lords, who served in the House of Lords because of their legal backgrounds rather than family origins, formed the highest court for civil cases in the entire realm until the new supreme court was created in late 2009.

The lowest level for criminal cases is the magistrates' courts, before which about 95 percent of all criminal cases are heard. There are four hundred magistrates' courts in England and Wales, and they are headed mostly by part-time lay magistrates or justices of the peace who are not paid a salary. Only about one hundred legally trained professional judges serve as "district judges" at this level. Sentences do not exceed six months, unless the law prescribes more, in which case the issue is brought before the Crown Court at the next higher level. There are no juries at the magistrates' court level. About 1 percent of all cases are appealed to the Crown Court.

There are more than seventy Crown Courts in England and Wales that hear about a thousand cases a year. Only a small number of these are appealed further to a higher court, which would be the Divisional Court of the High Court of Justice or to the Criminal Division of the High Court of Appeal, depending on the reason for the appeal. Only in a few cases are appeals to the House of Lords (now supreme court) accepted. Even after that court has decided a case, it can in rare instances be appealed to the EU's Court of Justice in Luxembourg or the Council of Europe's Court of Human Rights in Strasbourg.

Judges in the UK, like judges in other liberal democracies, are independent decision makers. On the other hand, questions were raised in recent years about the propriety of the lord chancellor's holding the three positions of cabinet minister, speaker of the House of Lords, and head of the judiciary. This obvious violation of separation of powers was justified on the basis of tradition, which, however, was changed by a constitutional reform passed by Parliament in 2005, in part as a result of pressures from the Council of Europe. The reform also removed the law lords from the

House of Lords and placed them instead in the new supreme court. The reform not only removed the lord chancellor as head of the judiciary but also weakened his powers to appoint judges by giving these to a new independent appointments body. Finally, it contained provision formally protecting judicial independence.

As a result of the constitutional reform of 2005, a fifteen-member Judicial Appointments Commission (JAC) was established to nominate candidates for judgeships for courts at all levels. One nominee is sent to the lord chancellor for appointment. If the lord chancellor objects, he can send his reasons to the JAC, which may or may not accept his rejection. The lord chancellor's appointments to tribunals do not need approval by the monarch, but judgeships for higher levels are crown appointments. The prime minister becomes involved only at the highest level, i.e., the Courts of Appeal and the Supreme Court. But the prime minister can forward only the names of the nominees selected by the lord chancellor, which were in fact the choices of the JAC. These procedures make the nomination process in Britain today considerably less political than in the United States.

Nevertheless, there is some controversy in the United Kingdom—but less than in the United States—concerning judicial activism on the bench and in occasional statements made in public. In both countries judges may be inclined to become judicial activists in part because of the nature of common law. There may not be a statute covering the particular case, a statute may not be clear for some reason, or the conditions that a statute covers may have changed; in such cases judges may search for a precedent in another case that is somewhat similar, apply the statute to the extent possible to the situation, or decide the case on other grounds. Judges are now also allowed to consult parliamentary debates to try to ascertain the intent of the law. When judges hand down decisions based on EU law or human rights law, they may also be subject to criticism by legal conservatives. A decision by judges that rules that a British statute involving human rights does not conform to the Human Rights Act of 2000 does not overturn the statute, but it does put considerable pressure on the government of the day to make changes in the legislation.

It is clear from the discussion above that a number of important changes have been made in the British legal system in recent decades. British membership in the EU since 1973 has meant that British law must conform to EU law and rulings of the European Court of Justice. The Human Rights Act that went into effect in 2000 codified rights that might have been respected in large part by tradition and custom but nevertheless brought about new protections found in the Council of Europe's Convention for the Protection of Human Rights. It also made it possible for British citizens to bring cases before British courts rather than having to go before the European Court of Human Rights in Strasbourg. Constitutional reforms in 2005 led to significant changes in the independence of British courts from the executive and legislative branches and to a new system of judicial selection procedures.

The German and French Civil Law Systems

Foundations. Until the beginning of the nineteenth century, "Germany" consisted of hundreds of small states and independent cities that made up the weak Holy Roman Empire. Imperial courts during the Middle Ages served to resolve disputes between the princes, or between them and the emperor; however, these courts could not prevent military conflict between the various units of the confederation as, for example, during the Thirty Years' War of 1618–48. This loose confederation-like empire was dominated by Austria and Prussia after 1648, but it included also a number of midsized states such as Bavaria, Hanover, and Saxony. All of these political units had established legal systems based on Roman law, but the lack of uniformity led to demands for change that were met in part by the uniform laws introduced by the German Confederation of 1815–66. Real legal unification did not take place, however, until after political unification in 1871 with the establishment of the Bismarck or Second Reich. A nationwide penal code was enacted in 1871, the code of criminal procedure and the code of civil procedure in 1877. Work on the civil code was begun in 1874, but it was not until 1900 that the all-German comprehensive civil code went into effect and remains largely in effect to this day. German law has had a major influence on the legal systems of Austria, Switzerland, Hungary, Greece, Japan, Turkey, Brazil, Mexico, and Peru. Former communist states in Eastern Europe have also been influenced by German law.

Although the idea and practice of the rule of law (*Rechtsstaat*) have roots in the various historical German states, modern Germany did not become a conventional democratic state—of which rule of law is a key component—until 1919 with the establishment of the Weimar Republic (which was then overthrown by the Nazis in 1933). The Nazis sorely abused the German legal system, but the current Federal Republic falls within the tradition of European civil or Roman law. In some ways it is even similar to the American system. First, and perhaps most importantly, is the role of the Federal Constitutional Court and its powers of judicial review, which make it more similar to the US Supreme Court than any other high court in the world. Second, is the role of the federal order in decentralizing the court system. Nevertheless, there are significant differences between the German and American legal systems, and these will be noted below.

One difference is the tradition in Germany of distinguishing between judicial review and constitutional review.[8] The latter is associated with constitutional monarchism, especially during the period between 1815 and 1918, when the monarchies at the national and state levels ended. It served as a means of resolving constitutional disputes among the states of the German Empire and between them and the national government. The resolution took place in the chamber of the states, i.e., the *Bundesrat*. After 1918, during the Weimar Republic, constitutional issues involving the states were settled in a specialized constitutional court, especially the high court (*Staatsgerichtshof*).

While the traditional German doctrine was for judges to enforce the law as written and not to challenge its constitutionality, there were some well-known jurists who argued in the nineteenth century in favor of judicial review. During the Weimar Republic, the Bavarian constitution authorized judicial review, and some state (now *Land*) courts accepted judicial review in principle if not in practice. And after World War II several *Land* constitutions authorized judicial review but only in specialized courts.

Thus the concept of judicial review was not unfamiliar to the founding fathers of the current German constitution, the Basic Law, when it was written in 1948–49. While the Western Allies, in particular the Americans, wanted judicial review to be included in the Basic Law, it was not imposed on the Germans.

> The Germans decided on their own to establish a constitutional court, to vest it with authority to nullify laws contrary to the Constitution, and to elevate this authority into an express principle of constitutional governance. While they were familiar with the American system of judicial review and were guided by the American experience in shaping their constitutional democracy, Germans relied mainly on their own tradition of constitutional review.[9]

The issue of judicial review and its application created some controversy among the founding fathers, but the basic outline of the court's jurisdiction and the selection of judges were set in the Basic Law of 1949. Some important additional provisions were debated by the different parties in the years following and incorporated by legislation in the Federal Constitutional Court Act of March 1951.

Before the French Revolution of 1789, there was no French legal system as such. Rather, the numerous regions of France had their own legal systems. After the fall of the Roman Empire in the fifth century, Roman law continued to apply to Romans, while the many tribes had their own laws. The feudal system that followed led to the application of the law of each lord to the subjects in his territory. In southern France Roman law remained an important source; in northern France tribal custom from the Germanic tribes was the main source. Over the centuries gaps in the customary laws were usually filled by studying the law of adjoining regions, especially of expanding Paris. Some laws were applied generally in France, namely, canon law of the Roman Catholic Church, and the king's law, which applied especially to the nobility but as of the seventeenth century was broadened in effect.[10]

In general the laws of France promoted inequality by dividing individuals into the nobility, the clergy, and the broad middle classes, or Third Estate. They were also authoritarian, organized in hierarchical guilds, and concentrated rights and powers in the hands of husbands in the case of married couples. And they favored the landowners, to whom the peasants owed various services.

These laws were mostly abolished after 1789. The Declaration of Human and Civil Rights of 1789 became law, incorporating the principles of equality and freedom of conscience, belief, association and expression, and the presumption of innocence until proven guilty. Canon law and regional laws were repealed, and separation of church and state was introduced. Only law enacted by the state was to be recognized. Nevertheless, much remained to be done when Napoleon came to power in 1799. He enacted the *Code Napoleon* in 1804, which applied civil law to the whole of the country, and he introduced the Council of State (*Conseil d'Etat*), which was to control the legality of government actions.[11] Today there are many codes, but the most important are the civil code (not to be confused with the civil law tradition), penal or criminal code, and the fiscal code. The French system had great influence on many other countries in Europe, e.g., Italy and Spain, and from Spain to Latin America.

The civil matters of the code included a broad range of subjects, becoming the main source for family, contract, tort, and property law. It incorporated main ideas of the Revolution as well as older Roman and customary laws, thus providing for considerable continuity. Other codes followed the *Code Napoleon*, and over the past decades many codes have been enacted to update older ones or to deal with new issues. These codes, like codes in other civil law countries, establish general principles rather than detailed rules for the particular situation, and they largely eliminate the practice of *stare decisis*, or precedent, that is typical of common law countries.

The French, like the Germans, divide their laws between private law and public law. Legislation became the primary source for private law, or judicial law, which consists of civil and criminal law. Public law, on the other hand, is divided between administrative law and constitutional law and has developed under the Council of State that was established by Napoleon.

Structure of the German court system.[12] In the American federal system, the state courts and the federal courts each have their own separate judicial hierarchies, with, for example, lower courts and appellate courts at each level (with the right of appeal from state supreme courts to the national Supreme Court when federal law is involved). In the German federal system there is one hierarchy: the courts of original jurisdiction and the appellate courts are state courts, whereas the federal courts are courts of final jurisdiction only. Civil and criminal procedure and the organization of the courts have been codified in national law, beginning in 1877.

Most courts are state (*Land*) courts. They fall under the jurisdiction of the *Land* ministers of justice, who determine tenure and promotion of judges and provide for proper administration. In some of the states a parliamentary committee has some impact on the careers of judges as well.

The local courts are called *Amtsgerichte*, of which there are just under seven hundred. They are the courts of first instance or original jurisdiction in most civil matters, and the larger courts are divided into different divisions or chambers. Many of the cases brought before these courts involve minor legal controversies and issues involving modest sums of money. Minor criminal cases are also tried at this level, generally with a judge and two laypersons, and they serve as family and juvenile courts. The number of divisions and judges depends on the size of the population served.

At the next level there are about 120 state district or regional courts (*Landgerichte*). These are appellate courts for the local *Amtsgerichte* but courts of first instance for the more serious civil and criminal cases. They are divided into chambers for civil, commercial, criminal, and youth matters. As of 2002 the civil chambers have one judge rather than three; the commercial chamber has one judge as chair and two assisting judges, who are businessmen rather than lawyers; and the criminal chamber and youth chamber have three judges and two laypersons each.

The third level consists of twenty-four higher *Land* (state) courts of appeal (*Oberlandesgerichte*). These courts hear cases appealed to them from the district courts. They are divided into "senates," each with a president and three or five judges. There is also a president of the court. In a few instances involving especially serious crimes, it is the court of first instance. Appeals from this court are made to the Federal Court of Justice.

The Federal Court of Justice (*Bundesgerichtshof*, or BGH) is located in Karlsruhe in the *Land* of Baden-Württemberg. It has twelve civil and five criminal senates and eight senates for specialized legal areas. Each senate consists of four judges and one senate president. They are nominated by the federal minster of justice and a special commission and appointed by the president of Germany. There are also two special Great Senates that consider important changes in the law and legal unity in civil and criminal matters. They are composed of one president and one judge from each of the civil senates and the president and two judges from each of the criminal senates. Finally, there is a combined Great Senate that oversees changes of the law and disunity in the law. The BGH is a very busy court that hears thousands of cases every year.

Like France and other civil law countries, Germany also has a large number of specialized courts, including state and federal labor courts; social welfare courts dealing, for example, with social security and unemployment issues; tax courts; and one federal patent court. The Federal Social Court is in Kassel, Hesse; the Federal Tax Court is in Munich, Bavaria; and the Federal Labor Court is located in Erfurt, Thüringia (from 1945 to unification in 1990 a part of communist East Germany). The best known and most important of the special courts are the administrative courts (*Verwaltungsgerichte*) at the state and federal levels. Administrative courts deal with all areas of public life, including planning law, trade and professional licensing, police, water, school regulations, roads, and the civil service. They are necessary because the other courts, unlike American courts, lack jurisdiction in cases and controversies involving administrative agencies and citizens. The fifty-two administrative courts of first instance consist of three professional judges and two laypersons. Appeals from this level are made to the High Administrative Court in each of the sixteen *Länder*. Cases involving federal law can be appealed to the Federal Administrative Court, which is now again located in Leipzig, its original home until the division of Germany after 1945.

The Federal Constitutional Court (*Bundesverfassungsgericht*) is also located in Karlsruhe. It occupies the same constitutional status as the president, federal government, federal parliament (*Bundestag*), and federal council of the states (*Bundesrat*). It can review and overrule all legislative and executive acts of these bodies that are brought before it on the grounds that they are in violation of the German Basic Law (constitution). It hears cases involving disputes between federal institutions, the federation and the *Länder*, and between the *Länder*. It can also hear "constitutional complaints," i.e., final appeals brought by individuals who argue that they have suffered from some violation of constitutional provisions. Such individual complaints make up a large proportion of the Federal Constitutional Court's caseload. The court has two senates of eight judges each. The first senate hears cases dealing with the fundamental rights of the first twenty articles of the Basic Law, while the second senate deals with cases involving disputes between government agencies and the political process. Judges are appointed for twelve-year nonrenewable terms by a two-thirds vote of the *Bundestag* and *Bundesrat*, and they must retire at sixty-eight.

Whereas the American Supreme Court hears only real cases and controversies, the German Federal Constitutional Court can hear abstract cases as well, that is, cases deriving from a law that has been passed but not yet challenged as having actually denied someone certain constitutional rights. Thus the German court, like the French Constitutional Council, can overrule a law before it has been applied.

Finally, there are fourteen constitutional courts at the state level, which deal with state constitutional issues. Schleswig-Holstein and Mecklenburg-Vorpommern are the only states that do not have a constitutional court; they refer constitutional issues directly to the Federal Constitutional Court. Cases from these *Land* courts arising from both *Land* constitutions and the federal Basic Law can be appealed to the Federal Constitutional Court, which alone among German courts enjoys the right of judicial review similar to the practice in the United States.

Structure of the French court system. In France there are two separate court systems: the civil and criminal court system and the administrative court system. On the other hand, some courts do not belong to either of these systems.[13]

The French version of separation of powers holds that the judicial power is limited to judging crimes and disputes between individuals. It does not deal with judging the acts of the administration. After the French Revolution of 1789, a Council of State (*Conseil d'Etat*) was created to deal with administrative matters, but it had only advisory powers. Later an independent administrative court system became an important part of the French republican idea. In contrast, the United Kingdom and the United States have never created a separate administrative law system.

There are a number of specialized courts in both of the French court systems, but the main courts in each system are called the courts of general jurisdiction. At the local level are the neighborhood courts (*le jurisdictions de proximité*), established in 2002. They hear small civil claims worth up to about $6,000 with no right of appeal. The judges are not career judges but rather lawyers, retired professional judges, or certain kinds of civil servants. The judges serve only one day a week and may practice another profession during their seven-year term of office. The next level consists of the specialist courts (*tribunaux d'instance*). They hear small civil cases worth from about $6,000 to $15,000. They may also hear cases involving disputes about rental of property, with civil partnerships, and other matters of local concern. There are about 475 such courts, with one located in general in each *arrondissement*, roughly equivalent to an American or German county or an English local authority district. Most cases are heard by one professional judge. However, there may also be an attempt to encourage the parties to reach a compromise agreement through a process of conciliation, which may be outside the court and that does not involve a professional judge. Appeals are made to the court of appeals, not to the next level of local court described below.

The busiest courts of first instance are the courts of general jurisdiction (*tribunaux de grande instance* [TGI]). They hear all cases worth more than about $15,000 except for those assigned to certain specialist courts. They handle family law, property law, intellectual property, and inheritance law. Unlike the lower courts, legal representation for the parties is required. At least one TGI is located in each of the ninety-six departments of France, but some more populous departments have more than one, for a total of 181. Each court is headed by a president, with the number of judges based on the size of the court. In the small courts, with five or fewer judges, the judges do not specialize, whereas the larger courts are divided into specialized civil and criminal divisions. Cases are heard by at least three judges and decided by majority vote. In some instances, a single judge may decide a case if the president of the court and the parties agree. A single judge also decides cases involving automobile accidents and family law.

Many specialized courts fall outside this court system, including 191 commercial courts. These courts deal with a wide variety of business matters and go back to the sixteenth century. There are also 271 labor courts that go back to Napoleon, 116 social security courts, and more than 400 farm tenancy tribunals. The latter two were first established in 1946 and 1944, respectively.

For all of the upper levels of the courts discussed above, there are thirty-five second-instance courts of appeal (*Cours d'appel*) that go back to the period following the French Revolution. Each court of appeals is headed by a president. They are divided into civil, criminal, commercial, social, and other specialist divisions, the number of which is determined by demand. Each division has a president, and the judges rotate among divisions to prevent overspecialization. Cases are decided by three to five judges, and the majority decisions are published as decisions of the court; dissenting opinions are not published.

The highest court in the hierarchy is the *Cour de cassation*, whose origins go back to 1790 following the revolution. It is the central court for the entire civil and criminal law system. It is not a third instance that examines the facts of the case like the supreme courts of the United States and the United Kingdom and the German high courts; rather, its main role is to ensure a consistent interpretation of the law. Because there is no doctrine of *stare decisis*, or precedent, in France, other courts are not bound to follow its lead. Many thousands of civil and criminal cases are brought before it, in part because it cannot enforce its previous decisions through precedent.

The *Cour de cassation* is located in Paris and is headed by a first president, who is more an administrator than a judge. It has one criminal division and five civil divisions, including a commercial and financial division, a social division, and three general divisions, each specialized according to certain topics. There are eighty-eight full judges, sixty-five assistant judges, and eight administrative assistant judges. In most cases five judges from one division hear a case, although three judges may hear some cases assigned by the various division presidents. In certain cases a joint bench consisting of thirteen judges from three divisions may hear a case, and in rare instances a joint bench of nineteen judges, three from each of the divisions, presided over by the first president, may be formed. In contrast to the courts of appeal, judges in the six different divisions do not rotate, thus promoting specialization and consistency.

Criminal cases are handled differently in France from the United States, the U.K., and Germany. For serious cases, the process begins with an investigation by a judge (*le juge d'instruction*) of a court of general jurisdiction (TGI) into the charges. The investigating judge does not decide guilt or innocence, which is the task of the trial court, but rather other matters, such as whether to hold the accused. There are three trial courts of general jurisdiction: the *tribunal de police*, the *tribunal correctionnel,* and the *Cour d'assises.* Each court hears the case depending on the nature of the charges. The first two courts share the building, judges, and administration of the local courts, *tribunaux d'instance* (TI) and *tribunaux de grande instance* (TGI), which also hear civil cases. The *tribunal de police* handles minor offenses, and the *tribunal correctionnel* hears major, but not serious, offenses. These include traffic offenses, misuse of checks and credit cards, and use of soft drugs. Cases involving business and financial matters are heard by a specialist division of the TGI.

The third court, the *Cour d'assises*, is for more serious cases and also shares judges with the other courts. Cases are heard by a jury of twelve, three of whom are professional judges. Conviction requires the votes of eight members, five of whom must be among the nine lay jurors. There is one *Cours d'assise* for each of the ninety-six departments in France.

In addition to the *Cours d'assise*, which is a court of general jurisdiction, there are a number of specialist courts. At the lowest level are the neighborhood courts, also mentioned above for dealing with minor civil cases. These courts also handle minor criminal offenses. Specialist courts exist for terrorist cases, organized crime, maritime pollution, and other matters. Youth courts are separate.

Appeals from the *tribunaux de police* and the *tribunaux correctionnels* can be made to the court of appeal (*Cour d'appel*), already discussed above regarding civil cases. Appeals from the *Cours d'assise* are made to the *Cour d'assise d'appel*. Cases are heard by twelve lay jurors and nine professional judges, with the votes of ten lay jurors, an absolute majority, required to convict. Finally, a case from the *Cour d'assise d'appel* can be appealed to the highest court in the hierarchy, the criminal division of the *Cour de cassation*, also discussed above.

Unlike the legal systems of the United States and the United Kingdom, France has an administrative court system completely separate from the civil and criminal court structure. The Council of State (*Conseil d'Etat*) is the highest administrative court and dates back to Napoleon in 1799. At first it had an advisory role only, but over time it became an independent court.

There are thirty-seven administrative courts of first instance spread throughout France. Each court has a president and at least three judges. They are organized in divisions, with thirteen in the largest court in Paris. These are courts of first instance with general jurisdiction; however, in a few instances the Council of State at the national level has original jurisdiction. The administrative courts also have a limited advisory role.

With many thousands of cases reaching the Council of State each year, the waiting list of cases brought before it grew in spite of reforms in the 1950s. In 1989 administrative courts of appeal were created, but delays of more than three years still exist for some cases to come before the Council of State. Today there are eight administrative courts of appeal with two to four divisions and usually five judges for each division. The president of each administrative court is also a member of the Council of State. These courts also have a small advisory role.

The Council of State has more than three hundred members, of which about two-thirds are working for the council at any one time. These are positions occupied mostly by graduates of the elite *Ecole Nationale d'Administration* (ENA). The president of the Council of State is the French prime minister, although this is largely a ceremonial position. The real head is the vice president. The council is organized in five administrative divisions and one division that deals with litigation. Members of the council are members both of the litigation division and one administrative division.

As suggested above, the Council of State has an important advisory as well as a judicial role. It must be consulted before the government (cabinet) acts on numerous issues, including legislative proposals; however, the government is not obliged to follow the advice it receives. The government also seeks the council's advice on certain administrative problems, and the council prepares reports at the prime minister's request or on its own initiative.

The Council of State acts as a court of first (and last) instance only rarely for especially important cases. Most appeals are heard by the administrative courts of appeal. The council also advises the lower administrative courts and administrative courts of appeal on points of law. The nature of the case that comes before the council and the court from which it was appealed determine the number of judges in the council that hear it. This is usually three judges, but it can be as many as seventeen who, for example, might hear an important case involving the election of members of the National Assembly or European Parliament.

None of the courts discussed to this point has jurisdiction over constitutional disputes. This is the task of the Constitutional Council (*Conseil constitutionnel*). It is the French counterpart to the US Supreme Court in its role as a constitutional court and to the German Federal Constitutional Court, although the French court's role is more limited. According to the French version of the separation of powers doctrine, judicial review was not accepted by the French revolutionaries. The constitution was considered the highest law of the land, but ensuring that laws were in conformity with the constitution was left to the parliament to decide. The Fifth Republic constitution of 1958 was designed in part by General de Gaulle and his advisers to limit the legislative powers of the National Assembly. One of the means chosen to do this was the creation of the Constitutional Council, which would ensure that the parliament did not interfere with the competences reserved to the government.

The council has nine regular members, who sit for a single term of nine years, with three memberships renewed every three years. Former presidents of the republic are members for life, although only one has taken this option seriously. The president of the republic, the president of the National Assembly, and the president of the Senate each appoints three regular members of the Constitutional Court. Legal qualifications are not required, but they have become more prominent in recent years. Cases are decided by seven judges, and dissenting opinions are not published.

The council's two main judicial roles are to supervise elections and litigation resulting from elections and to judge the constitutionality of statutes, parliamentary standing orders, and international treaties. It also has an advisory role in the case of emergency powers exercised by the president of the republic under Article 16 of the Constitution. The council has a supervisory role in presidential elections and national referendums, and it serves as a court in resolving disputes concerning the election of parliamentary deputies and senators. In the process it can annul an election or declare a candidate ineligible. The council can review laws passed by parliament based on five provisions of the Constitution. It looks at disputes between the government and parliament, the right of the government to amend certain laws and decrees without parliamentary approval, the constitutionality of laws passed by parliament, international treaties, and legislation passed by the local congress of the Pacific island territory of New Caledonia, which is in the process of gaining independence. The council does not review the constitutionality of decisions passed by referendum, laws amending the Constitution, or acts of parliament that have already been implemented (this does not affect government regulations—not laws—that can be reviewed by administrative courts).

The Impact of European Union Law and the European Convention of Human Rights

European Community law. In 2008 the European Union celebrated its fiftieth anniversary. The 1957 Treaty of Rome that established the European Economic Community (EEC), also known as the Common Market, and the European Atomic Energy Community, or Euratom, went into effect on January 1, 1958. The EEC provided for the free movement of goods, services, labor, and capital, and Euratom provided for joint research regarding the peaceful uses of atomic energy. In 1967 a merger treaty combined the separate institutions of the European Coal and Steel Community (ECSC), which no longer exists as of 2002, with those of the EEC and Euratom to form the European Community (EC). The Maastricht treaty, or the Treaty on European Union (TEU), of 1991 created three "pillars" of the new "European Union" that went into effect in 1993. These consisted of the already existing European Community (EC), a new Common Foreign and Security Policy (CFSP), and Justice and Home Affairs, the areas of which were later divided between the EC and Police and Judicial Cooperation in Criminal Matters (PJC). The Lisbon treaty, which went into effect in December 2009 and brought about many institutional changes that will go into actual effect in the coming years, abandoned the three pillars and rearranged their responsibilities into the EU as a whole. The TEU also set in motion the institutional arrangements for the Economic and Monetary Union (EMU). This created a central bank in Frankfurt, Germany, and began preparations for the common currency, the Euro.

Since 2009, then, the EU as a whole attempts to create a common foreign and defense policy, and it is responsible for judicial cooperation; the common agricultural and fisheries policies; environment; competition, internal and trade issues; and other economic issues. In addition, seventeen EU states are part of the Eurozone and use the Euro. All of these areas are regulated today by EU law, which is based on the various treaties signed by the current twenty-seven members of the EU. As in the United States, treaties are "the supreme law of the land" for the member states, thus overriding even the member state constitutions, and conflicts arising under the treaties and the laws and regulations based on them are resolved by the European Court of Justice (ECJ) in Luxembourg. This, of course, affects the sovereignty of the member states, which are said not to give up but to "share" sovereignty in the EU.

The ECJ was first created in 1952 with the signing of the treaty establishing the European Coal and Steel Community (ECSC). It is composed of twenty-seven justices, one from each of the EU member states. Justices serve six-year terms and half the court is renewed every three years. The president of the court is elected by the justices for a three-year term. There are also nine advocates general that review the cases before the court and provide legal opinions for the justices to consider. The court is divided into chambers of three to five judges, who can refer a case to a "Grand Chamber" of thirteen judges or, more rarely, to the full court. To relieve the workload of the ECJ, a Court of First Instance was created in 1992 and consists of fifteen judges, who also serve six-year terms. Decisions regarding questions of law can be appealed from this court to the ECJ, which receives many thousands of cases each year. In most cases the ECJ issues a "preliminary ruling" in which the high courts of the member states are given advice on a particular case involving European law. The ECJ may also be asked to overturn European legislation or to decide whether a member state has abided by European law. [14]

All three of our European liberal democracies have been involved in important cases before the ECJ. On occasion this has brought the ECJ and the highest courts in these countries into a tense situation. Given the strong Euroskeptic (anti-EU) feelings in large parts of the British population and, in particular, in the Conservative Party, it is not surprising that there has been resistance to ECJ decisions that overturn British law. But even in Germany, which has generally been a major supporter of European unity from the beginning and less nationalistic than either the UK or France, there have been decisions by the Federal Constitutional Court that supported the ECJ only reluctantly at best and, in some cases, in effect challenged the right of the ECJ to overturn German constitutional law. However, in the final analysis the member states have little room to maneuver and do abide by the

ECJ's rulings. From an American perspective, the ECJ has played a role in the development of the EU somewhat similar to the role played by the US Supreme Court, especially under Chief Justice John Marshall in the early nineteenth century, after the Civil War, and at other times in American history when there were important constitutional questions concerning the division of power between the national government and the states.

European Convention law. The Council of Europe, created in 1949 and located in Strasbourg, France, now consists of forty-seven states in and on the periphery of Europe (such as Georgia, Armenia, and Azerbaijan). It was formed to promote democracy, human rights, and the rule of law; it should not be confused with the European Union. For our purposes the most important aspect of the Council of Europe is the Convention for the Protection of Human Rights (CPHR), which is the most important of the more than one hundred conventions that members of the Council of Europe have signed. The CPHR was first signed in 1950 by the members at that time and went into effect in 1953. The Court of Human Rights, located in Strasbourg, the headquarters of the Council of Europe, was created in 1959. The court monitors the protection of the human rights of the eight hundred million people who live in the member states, and its rulings are binding on these states that have signed the convention. Individuals can submit cases directly to the court. If the United States were a member of the Council of Europe and had signed the convention, it would soon find itself in violation of the convention and in trouble with the Court of Human Rights because of the death penalty, which was banned in all member states in 1985; the sentencing of youths as adult offenders; certain prison conditions; and possibly for other reasons as well.

The court consists of a president and one judge from each member state. It is divided into five sections with nine judges each, and it has a grand chamber for more important cases. From 1959 to 2009 more than twelve thousand judgments were issued by the court. Applications for a hearing have increased dramatically, to fifty-seven thousand in 2009. More than half of the approximately 120,000 applications that were pending on January 1, 2010, came from four countries: Russia, Turkey, Ukraine, and Romania, in that order. Only a small number of applications are actually accepted and rulings made; for example, in 2009 there were 1,625 judgments. More than half of the violation judgments delivered in the fifty years from 1959 to 2009 concerned five countries: Turkey, Italy, Russia, France, and Poland, in that order. More than half of the judgments in which the court found a violation concerned the fairness of trials or the length of the proceedings.[15]

It is clear from the statistics above that the Court of Human Rights plays an active role in the legal process of the forty-seven states that are members of the Council of Europe. As we have seen above, in the United Kingdom, which has no written constitution with provisions for the protection of human rights, British membership in the Council of Europe and its acceptance of the Convention for the Protection of Human Rights has had a profound effect on British law and the idea of parliamentary sovereignty.

Conclusion

In spite of many basic similarities, legal systems of liberal democracies are different from one another in a number of ways. The first and most obvious difference is the division between common law and civil law systems. Both systems are based on the principle of the rule of law, with the law having been made by elected legislative bodies or, in some cases in common law countries, by judges relying on precedent that can be changed by legislative bodies. Both systems also rely on independent courts that may in some cases have judges appointed by elected officials but who, nevertheless, are expected to uphold the law without outside influence or bias.

Some other differences that emerge between the two systems are the educational backgrounds and appointments of judges. In both the UK and the United States, at least at the federal level and in about one-third of the states, judges are appointed from the ranks of experienced lawyers; however, especially in the United States, it helps to be politically well connected. In Germany and France, judges are mostly drawn from those who decided during or at the time of the completion of their legal education to become career judges. As such they become civil servants and are subject to the rules and regulations of the *Land* ministers of justice in

Germany or the national minister of justice in France. In the United States, judges are appointed for life at the federal level, whereas terms vary among the states; there are terms of office in those states that have elected judges. In the UK, judges serve for limited terms, and there are age limitations. In France and Germany the terms of judges at the higher levels are limited, and judges at all levels are subject to age limits. Still another difference is that the United States and the UK have *adversarial* court procedures for criminal trials, while Germany and France have *inquisitorial* procedures.

In Germany and France the courts are specialized beyond hearing both civil and criminal cases. In both countries there is, first, a special administrative court system, as well as labor courts, social courts, tax courts, patent courts, and so forth. There is a Federal Constitutional Court in Germany which has the right of judicial review and is similar in many respects to the American Supreme Court; however, it has sixteen judges who are divided evenly into two senates that handle different issues, the judges are appointed by a two-thirds vote of the *Bundestag* and *Bundesrat*, and they serve twelve-year nonrenewable terms with retirement required at sixty-eight.

The Federal Constitutional Court also has the right to hear *abstract* cases, that is, cases brought under laws that raise constitutional questions but which have not been applied and contested. In contrast, the US Supreme Court will hear only actual cases and controversies. In France there is a special Council of State that is the last instance for administrative law cases, and there is a Constitutional Council that reviews bills for their constitutionality and decides controversies concerning elections. It does not deal with cases and controversies once legislation has gone into effect.

Within each legal system there are also differences. Only in the United States are jury trials required in certain cases with twelve jurors, where conviction requires a unanimous vote. In the UK there are many instances in which smaller juries decide by majority decision. In Germany and France jury trials typically involve a combination of professional judges and laypersons who decide by a qualified majority. The United States has a federal system, whereas the United Kingdom is organized as a decentralized unitary state. There is, then, legal unity in England and

Wales, but a somewhat different court system in Scotland. In the United States there is a federal legal system and state legal systems with their own laws and procedures, including a civil law tradition in Louisiana. Another important difference is the tradition of parliamentary sovereignty in the UK, which makes it difficult for many Britons to accept the idea of judicial review. But judicial review has entered the British system indirectly via European Community laws based on the EU treaties the British have signed and due to the passage by the House of Commons in 2000 of the Human Rights Act based on the Council of Europe's Convention on the Protection of Human Rights. Of course the other members of the EU and the Council of Europe have also been affected by the role of the supranational ECJ and Court of Human Rights and, in turn, have had to accept judicial review by these courts. In some ways the ECJ and the Court of Human Rights have functioned like the American Supreme Court by applying EU and Council of Europe Conventions to the various member states and thereby bringing about a high degree of legal unity in Europe that otherwise would not exist.

Endnotes

[1] Cf. Gregory S. Mahler, *Comparative Politics: An Institutional and Cross-National Approach* (Pearson/Prentice Hall, 2008), 135–36.

[2] Indeed, many Europeans were upset by the photographs they saw of Dominique Strauss-Kahn standing before a judge in New York City wearing handcuffs after his arrest on charges of raping a hotel maid on the grounds that this was a violation of the principle of innocence until proven guilty.

[3] Frank A. Schubert, *Introduction to Law and the Legal System*, 9th ed. (Boston and New York: Houghton Mifflin Company, 2008), 10–14.

[4] For a discussion of the liberal versus conservative controversy in the United States over the proper interpretation of common law principles, see James R. Stoner, Jr., *Common-Law Liberty: Rethinking American Constitutionalism* (Lawrence, KS: University Press of Kansas, 2003), Introduction and ch. 1.

[5] Cf. Colin Hay and Anand Menon, eds., *European Politics* (Oxford: Oxford University Press, 2007), 257–58.

[6] The section below is based on Bruce F. Norton, *Politics in Britain* (Washington, DC: CQ Press, 2007), ch. 12.

[7] Ibid., 311.

[8] Donald P. Kommers, *The Constitutional Jurisprudence of the Federal Republic of Germany*, 2nd ed. (Durham: Duke University Press, 1997), 4–5.

[9] Ibid., 7.

[10] Catherine Elliott, Catherine Vernon, and Eric Jeanpierre, *French Legal System*, 2nd ed. (London and New York: Pearson Education Limited, 2006), 1–3.

[11] Ibid., 4–5.

[12] Much of the discussion in this section is based on Nigel G. Foster and Satish Sule, *German Legal System and Law* (Oxford: Oxford University Press, 2002), ch. 3.

[13] Much of the discussion in this section is based on the *French Legal System*, ch. 5.

[14] See http://europa.eu/institutions/inst/justice/index_en.htm

[15] http://www.echr.coe.int/NR/rdonlyres/ACD46A0F-615A-48B9-89D6-8480AFCC29FD/0/ FactsAndFiguresEN2010.pdf

For Further Reading

Carp, Robert A., Ronald Stidham, and Kenneth L. Manning. *Judicial Process in America*. 7th ed. Washington, DC: CQ Press, 2007.

Elliott, Catherine, Eric Jeanpierre, and Catherine Vernon. *French Legal System*. 2nd ed. London and New York: Pearson Education Limited, 2006.

Foster, Nigel, and Satish Sule. *German Legal System and Laws*. 3rd ed. Oxford: Oxford University Press, 2002.

Hanbury, H. G. *English Courts of Law*. 4th ed., London: Oxford University Press, 1967.

Chapter 10

Liberal Democracies and Social Policy

Introduction

In chapter 5 we saw that one can identify three major philosophical traditions that have emerged over the centuries in Europe: the conservative, the Liberal and the socialist. The European conservative tradition had its origins in the Middle Ages, and it was characterized in particular by a feudal-agrarian economic system, with a "corporate" division of the population into groups such as the nobility, clergy, peasantry, craftsmen, and merchants. The Catholic Church was an official or state religion, and the rulers were kings and princes at the higher levels and lesser nobles at the local or small regional level of the feudal manor and village. This tradition was challenged and replaced in varying degrees by the European Liberal tradition of the late eighteenth and nineteenth centuries. (As pointed out in chapter 5, "Liberal" should not be confused with the American term, "liberal."). The major characteristic of this tradition is individualism or individual freedom, which translates into economic freedom (free enterprise or laissez-faire), religious freedom, political freedom (free speech, free press, freedom of assembly), elections and representative government at least for the male property owner, and legal (not social) equality (rule of law). Liberalism provides the philosophical underpinning for the growth and development of capitalism, which, as R. H. Tawney[1] and Max Weber[2] have shown, is also associated with the rise of Protestantism.

With the rapid rise of industrialization and capitalism, especially in the second half of the nineteenth and early twentieth centuries, European societies were challenged by new pressures. For the peasants who flocked to the cities for jobs, there were issues of wages, working hours, housing, health care, job-related injury and disability, education, unemployment, and other matters, such as child labor. There was also the important issue of political rights. The Liberals had considerable success in expanding political rights to include the growing, mostly property-owning new middle classes, but they were skeptical of seeing the working classes and peasants—who were, after all, a majority—secure a degree of influence in political decision making that might threaten middle class interests and, of course, the interests of the remaining beneficiaries of the old conservative tradition. Unions and working-class political parties formed to represent worker interests, and these were generally successful in many European countries in forcing changes in the political system to include them as participants. As a result they were able to bring about or at least influence government policies designed to deal with the many problems associated with the rise of the new, industrialized, capitalistic order. These policies evolved over the decades, and today all industrialized democracies are what we call welfare states, i.e., states that have programs and regulations in place designed to ensure—but do not guarantee—that everyone in the society has a basic level of services and security below which no one should fall. These vary, however, in program coverage, organization, generosity, and costs, and one can place the individual countries into different categories of types of welfare systems.

In doing so, it is clear from a single statistic that the United States is more likely to be strongly influenced by the Liberal tradition, i.e., less government and more individual responsibility in dealing with social welfare issues. That statistic is total government spending at all levels as a proportion of gross national product (GDP): 52 percent in France, a little more than 45 percent in Great Britain, about 43 percent in Germany, and about 37–38 percent in the United States. The discussion below will demonstrate clearly that the United States has, indeed, a limited welfare state by international comparison.

Origins of the Welfare State[3]

While there is rarely if ever a particular time and place when a certain era begins in history, one can look at the French Revolution in 1789 as the beginning of the capitalist era of industrialization in Europe, at first in England and France and then in Germany and the United States. Certain events during the nineteenth century promoted a more rapid transition to an industrial economy, for example various inventions, such as the steam engine in the early nineteenth century, and wars in Europe and the American Civil War. The French Revolution was essentially a Liberal revolution in rejecting monarchy and promoting a representative republic with a parliamentary democracy, expansive individual or human rights, and a separation of church and state. It also promoted the idea of nationalism in place of loyalty to aristocratic rulers and religion as a means of creating unity among the people inhabiting a common space. Nationalism came to be associated especially with Napoleon and his policies of conquest.

In terms of capitalism and welfare, the Liberal economist Adam Smith saw the market as the best means of abolishing class, inequality, and privilege; however, his Liberal followers were divided between those who, like the Manchester Liberals, were staunchly laissez-faire and others who, like J. S. Mill, favored a modicum of state regulation. All agreed that there should be a maximum of free markets and a minimum of state interference. On the other hand, Liberals often favored restrictions on the voting rights of workers and peasants, because they feared that universal male suffrage (female suffrage came only in the twentieth century) would undermine the Liberal order by favoring socialist policies. This fear was shared, of course, by conservative monarchies, for example in Germany and especially in Russia before World War I, which were influenced by Liberals (especially Germany) but had generally retained the conservative political, social, and economic order (especially Russia).

The socialists emerged around the middle of the nineteenth century in response to the deep and far-reaching changes that were being brought about by capitalist industrialization. They created unions, political parties, and other organizations, such as cooperative societies, in an effort to promote and defend worker interests; they were often skeptical of parliamentary democracy because they suspected it was not an institution that would really serve their goals of eliminating class divisions and social inequalities. However, reform socialists, or "social democrats," came to see participation in the political process and parliamentary democracy as a means of achieving many if not all of their goals, whereas revolutionary socialists, in particular those who became communists during and after World War I, believed this could be done only by overthrowing conservative and Liberal regimes and eliminating capitalism or private ownership of the means of production.

Approaches to the Welfare State

With the three philosophical or ideological traditions and the political parties they formed in the late nineteenth and early twentieth centuries, there was intense competition and disagreement over the proper political response to the many challenges presented by industrialization, the rise of the factory-oriented working class, the rapid growth of cities, the decline of rural influence, and the "commodification" of society, i.e., the necessity of the worker to "sell" his labor as if it were a commodity.

In the Middle Ages everyone was supposed to have his or her place in the corporate society and was generally protected from economic ruin by family, church, or the lord of the manor. There was some commodification in the form of cash crops and the production and exchange of goods in the towns. Work performance was not irrelevant in securing welfare from corporate entities, but a majority of the population was not dependent on wage-type income for their survival. Families were usually self-sufficient, and there was reciprocity in service to the lord in return for his paternal care. In the Middle Ages corporate societies emerged in towns among artisans and craftsmen as means of promoting their collective interests and in order to control entry, membership, prices, and production. These guilds or fraternal organizations also defined corporate status by ranking members as journeymen or masters; however, the hierarchy created was not class-based. Later, the conservative corporate model of the welfare state saw this corporate tradition as a means of preserving traditional society in the new industrial and capitalist society: the individual worker would be integrated into society by focusing on the corporate bodies as providers of state welfare benefits. The continental conservatives promoted welfare state measures that encouraged middle-class support for the preservation of occupationally segregated social insurance programs and loyalty to the state and to the conservatives who sponsored them.

The Catholic Church found this approach suitable as well, because it was committed to the traditional family. The result was that conservative social insurance schemes introduced or proposed at the end of the nineteenth century and later excluded nonworking wives and encouraged motherhood. The Catholic principle of "subsidiarity" held that the state should intervene only when the family could no longer help itself.

The European conservative tradition developed a corporatist-statist approach that became prominent first in Germany and Austria, and after World War II in France and Italy. In these states the Liberal obsession with market efficiency was never a major issue, and the focus was on preserving status differentials and rights while opposing class conflicts that divided society. Many of the conservative principles were applied in the first welfare state that was introduced by Bismarck in the 1880s in Germany. Bismarck had passed an Anti-Socialist Law in 1878 (repealed in 1890), which was not only directed against the Social Democratic Party of Germany (SPD) but also had negative effects on the "free," liberal, and Christian labor unions. In part as a kind of compensation to gain the loyalty of the workers, he pushed through parliament health insurance in 1883, accident insurance in 1884, and old-age and disability insurance in 1889. In each case the insured were divided by status groups, e.g., miners, industrial workers, white-collar employees, and civil servants. Bismarck's social reforms promoted welfare state measures that encouraged middle-class support for occupationally segregated social insurance programs. The next major reform developments in Europe did not come until World War II and its aftermath, e.g., the Beveridge Report of 1942 in Great Britain that called for a comprehensive welfare state and led to the launching of the National Health Service in 1946.

The Liberal tradition is strongly associated with industrialization and the free enterprise capitalist system during the nineteenth and early twentieth centuries and the rise of a new middle class. The Liberal response to pressures for social and economic measures to deal with the problems created by industrialization was, of course, pro-market with limited government involvement. Pure laissez-faire never existed in practice, but the state was supposed to have a very limited role except in a crisis. The new middle classes enjoyed historically a relatively privileged position in the market because they could usually meet their demands outside the state or as civil servants protected by the state. They were not as concerned as workers about full employment policies, and they were not in favor of income equalization. In the Anglo-Saxon countries, the welfare state was seen to be especially for the working class and the poor, while private insurance and occupational fringe benefits catered to the middle classes. In the Scandinavian countries, on the other hand, the social democrats were able to incorporate the middle classes by providing them with generous benefits.

Liberal dogma held that the free market was emancipatory, promoting self-reliance and industriousness. All who wanted to work would be employed and thus able to provide their own welfare, while insecurity and poverty were largely the result of lack of effort and thrift. Liberals did not pay much attention to the old, the infirm, the blind or crippled, or others who might be dependent on limited and frequently inadequate family support. Practical considerations led Liberals to accept certain public services, for example, public infrastructure such as roads and public sanitation, and to want healthy and educated soldiers and workers. The Liberal work ethic called for social assistance that was means-tested and limited to the needy so as not to encourage workers to choose welfare over work. Recipients of benefits were stigmatized. Liberals held that charity and insurance should be based on volunteerism, thus private insurance schemes were encouraged. The Liberals opposed conservative stratification in favor of individual freedom, equal opportunity, and healthy competitiveness. The "bottom line of Liberal dogma was that the state had no proper reason for altering the stratification outcomes produced in the marketplace."[4]

At first Liberal social policy was essentially poor relief, but later Liberals came to accept social insurance so long as it was basically voluntarist and based on length of contributions. The social security system established in the United States—which was a profoundly Liberal society with a Liberal constitution—was compulsory, but it did not prevent private pension plans. Liberals also promoted education as a means of self-help, and they came to accept collective wage agreements because they were between unions and management, not government-imposed. The Liberal approaches resulted in a "mix of individual self-responsibility and dualisms: one group at the bottom primarily reliant on stigmatizing relief; one group in the middle predominantly the clients of social insurance; and, finally, one privileged group capable of deriving its main welfare from the market."[5] Esping-Andersen suggests that this is basically the American system and, to a lesser degree, the British.

The labor movements in the socialist tradition pursued the goal of working-class solidarity, but they were forced to include the slum proletariat and the status groups promoted by conservative reforms in order to try to gain parliamentary majorities. Therefore, they sponsored principles of universalism and decommodification of social rights not only for the working class but also for others, including the new middle classes. This "social democratic" approach advocated a welfare state that would promote a high standard of equality. Everyone was to fall under one universal insurance system in which benefits would still depend on earnings. The goal was a welfare state that provided care for and assistance directly to children, the aged, and to those in need. "What characterizes almost all early socialist social policy is the notion of basic, or minimal, social rights: the idea was to install strong entitlements, but at fairly modest benefit levels, and typically limited to the core areas of human need (old-age pensions, accident insurance, unemployment and sickness benefits)."[6] The system was supposed to service not only the needs of families but also to allow women the option of working outside the home. Working women would also help pay for the welfare state, which needed full employment to be sustainable. That financial considerations were important to socialists is seen in the goal of providing benefits that would be only a basic floor beneath which no one would be allowed to fall, and until the 1950s and 1960s social programs of labor parties were generally modest in scope and quality.

Labor parties did not bring about the welfare state by themselves, because they rarely had a parliamentary majority or, if they did, a majority that was secure enough to push through their reforms. As a result, political coalitions were necessary. They gave some support to conservative or Liberal social policy as a compromise and pursued gradualism against the far more extreme ideas of the revolutionary communists. They were strongly focused on workers, but they became more universalistic by including all "little people" in their ideas. In Scandinavia, for example, labor parties were supported by small farmers in return for farm price subsidies. In the United States, on the other hand, the labor-intensive South blocked a truly universalistic social security system and opposed further welfare state developments. In continental Europe agriculture was also labor intensive, and unions and socialists were seen as threats. In the United Kingdom the political significance of farmers had declined before the beginning of the twentieth century, and white-collar strata became more important for political majorities. In Scandinavia alliances of white-collar middle classes and social democrats became common after World War II, in part due to the generous benefits promoted by the socialists.

Typologies of Welfare State Regimes

In comparing welfare states, one must consider a variety of dimensions. One is access to benefits, that is, eligibility rules, restrictions on entitlements, and the duration of benefits. Another dimension is income replacement levels. A third set concerns the range of entitlements. For example, almost all advanced capitalist countries have some form of rights to protection against basic social risks such as unemployment, disability, sickness, and old age; however, these vary considerably in terms of the first two dimensions.

Esping-Andersen shows that welfare states cluster around different models, each with a different private-public mix. The conservative corporatist model is characterized by the degree to which social insurance is differentiated and segmented into distinct occupational and status-based programs that vary in benefits between bottom and top. To identify the degree of conservative "etatism," one can look at the relative privileges accorded civil servants. Liberal principles are reflected especially in the amount of needs testing, the financial responsibility assigned to the individual, and the degree of voluntary private-sector welfare. Socialist principles can be seen in the degree of universalism and the modest differences in levels of benefits. Esping-Andersen notes that all welfare states have a mixed system in practice, but states can still be categorized according to the above criteria.

Esping-Andersen develops scores of de-commodification and an index for different social programs. He places France above average among eighteen industrial democracies in terms of old-age pensions, and Germany, Britain, and the United States below average (with the United States the lowest of the four). Germany is above average in sickness funds, France is average, and Great Britain is below average (the United States scored 0, but apparently the author did not consider Medicare and Medicaid). In terms of unemployment funds, Germany was above average, Britain and the United States slightly above average, and France below average.[7]

In his comparison of welfare states, Esping-Andersen also divides the eighteen industrial states into the three welfare regimes of conservatism, liberalism, and socialism and provides a rank for each category based on a point system ranging between a high of 12 and a low of 0 that is designed to take various factors into consideration. (See table 10.1). He ranks Germany and France as strong on the conservatism dimension, Britain and the United States as low (the U.S. is ranked "0"). Regarding liberalism, he ranks the United States as strong but France, Germany, and Great Britain as medium and Norway and Sweden as low. On the dimension of socialism, the Nordic countries are ranked as strong, Germany and Britain as medium, and France and the United States as low (the United States is again ranked "0").[8] While it is clear from table 10.1 that most countries have mixed welfare states in terms of ideological attributes, the United States is ranked "0" on two dimensions and high on one. A striking feature is the very large difference between the United States and the Scandinavian countries in general and Sweden in particular. The United States comes closest to "pure" Liberalism, Sweden to "pure" socialism.

Table 10.1

The Clustering of Welfare States According to Conservative, Liberal, and Socialist Regime Attributes
(cumulated index scores in parentheses)

	Conservatism		Degree of Liberalism		Socialism	
Strong	Austria	(8)	Australia	(10)	Denmark	(8)
	Belgium	(8)	Canada	(12)	Finland	(6)
	France	(8)	Japan	(10)	Netherlands	6)
	Germany	(8)	Switzerland	(12)	Norway	(8)
	Italy	(8)	*United States*	(12)	Sweden	(8)
Medium	Finland	(6)	Denmark	(6)	Australia	(4)
	Ireland	(4)	*France*	(8)	Belgium	(4)
	Japan	(4)	*Germany*	6)	Canada	(4)
	Netherlands	(4)	Italy	(6)	*Germany*	4)
	Norway	(4)	Netherlands	(8)	New Zealand	(4)
			United Kingdom	(6)	Switzerland	(4)
					United Kingdom	(4)
Low	Australia	(0)	Austria	(4)	Austria	(4)
	Canada	(2)	Belgium	(4)	*France*	(2)
	Denmark	(2)	Finland	(4)	Ireland	(2)
	New Zealand	(2)	Ireland	(2)	Italy	(0)
	Sweden	(0)	New Zealand	(2)	Japan	(2)
	Switzerland	(0)	Norway	(0)	*United States*	(0)
	United Kingdom	(0)	Sweden	(0)		
	United States	(0)				

Source: Gøsta Esping-Andersen, *The Three Worlds of Welfare Capitalism* (Princeton University Press, 1990), p. 74.

The American Difference?

A somewhat different comparative analysis is offered by James W. Russell. In answering the question why the United States is so different from France, Germany, and even Great Britain, he emphasizes the fact that welfare policies in the United States developed out of a very different historical and cultural context. As we saw in chapter 5, laissez-faire capitalism could develop without the influences of feudal traditions, and socialist and especially communist movements played a relatively insignificant role in American society. Also Protestants were more influential than Catholics in early America, and the Puritans and the Protestant work ethic predominated.

According to this ethic, "hard work ensured economic success, which was a sign not just of virtue but also of salvation. Whereas the medieval Augustinian-founded Catholic doctrine saw the poor as a part of the organic community to whom the more economically fortunate were obligated to extend charity, the Calvinists saw the poor as deserving their fate because it was predestined by God." Since the poor were responsible for their own fate, they were undeserving of help. A robust European-style welfare state was unnecessary, and "capitalism was thus able to develop in a more uncompromised fashion in the United States than in Europe."[9] This led in turn to the cultural values of individualism, limited egalitarianism, and a suspicion of the state.

In part because of the strong commitment to individualistic freedom, Americans have been unusually suspicious of state activities to promote social welfare. They abhor having to pay taxes to support state social programs. Despite paying the lowest tax rates in the developed world, they continually complain that they are being overtaxed.[10]

American attitudes about equality were also different from those in Europe. In the United States the focus has been on equality of opportunity, with less concern about outcomes or equality of result. America is seen as a land of opportunity, and those who fail have only themselves to blame. It should be noted, however, that policies of affirmative action and similar measures have been introduced in the United States in recent decades.

They are, however, extremely controversial and under continuing attack as discriminatory against white males.

Before the Great Depression and the New Deal reforms of President Franklin D. Roosevelt, there were no general federal welfare state programs. Some states had programs for the poor, disabled, widows, orphans, the aged, and the unemployed, but federal programs were limited to military pensions that were first granted to Revolutionary War veterans. The Social Security Act of 1935 established programs for unemployment insurance, retirement benefits, and direct assistance to the blind, widows, orphans, and dependent children. It did not, however, include health care. The next expansion came with President Lyndon Johnson's Great Society in the 1960s, including Medicare, Medicaid, and Head Start. The presidency of Ronald Reagan began an era in which the question was not how to design new programs but how to reduce or eliminate existing ones.[11]

Instead of including the United States in the European conservative, Liberal, and socialist traditions, Russell sees the United States in terms of a laissez-faire model and Europe in terms of a state interventionist model.[12] He calls the American model "conservative," apparently because of its purer form of free enterprise and resistance to the welfare state. He notes that the laissez-faire approach stresses the principle that responsibility for welfare lies with individuals and their families, i.e., they should be self-reliant and not dependent on outsiders for their needs. It also resists the idea of becoming a burden on others. This means maximizing private incomes and minimizing taxes and social programs.

The European interventionist model calls on the whole society to assume responsibility for welfare provision. From a European conservative standpoint, which he calls Christian Democratic, this is consistent with traditional aristocratic notions of noblesse oblige, and it follows Catholic dogma concerning obligations to the poor. And, of course, it reflects ideas of socialist statism. After reviewing factors such as providers, eligibility, beneficiaries, comprehensiveness of benefits, and financing, Russell offers a typology that is somewhat different from what we saw in table 10.1.

Table 10.2

Conservative, Liberal, Christian Democratic, and Social Democratic Welfare States

	Conservative	Liberal	Christian Democratic	Social Democratic
Representative Countries	United States	United Kingdom	France, Italy, Germany	Sweden, Finland, Norway
View of Class	Organic Class Harmony	Organic Class Harmony	Organic Class Harmony	Class Struggle
Unit of Society	Family	Individual	Family	Individual
View of Inequality	Inequality as Outcome of Marketplace is Desirable	Extreme Inequality As Outcome of Marketplace is Undesirable	Inequality is Natural	Equality as Goal
Attitude toward Religion	Religious	Secular	Religuous	Secular
Social Benefit	Low Amounts	Medium	Medium	High

Source: James W. Russell, *Double Standard: Social Policy in Europe and the United States* (New York: Rowman Littlefield Publishers, Inc., 2006), p. 61.

In spite of the somewhat different approaches reflected in tables 10.1 and 10.2, there are some strong similarities in their categorizations. In both tables the Scandinavian countries are categorized as Social Democratic and France and Germany as Conservative (in table 10.1) or as Christian Democratic (in table 10.2). The two tables differ in their categorization of the United Kingdom as "Liberal" in table 10.2, whereas it is medium

Liberal and medium Socialist in table 10.1. The greatest difference concerns the United States, which is among the most Liberal countries in Esping-Andersen's table 10.1 but is "conservative" in Russell's table 10.2. This is because of the polar attitudes toward the proper role of the state (government) in Europe and the United States and Russell's definition of conservatism in those terms.

Selected Welfare State Programs in Great Britain, France, Germany, and the United States

The European welfare state has the goal of guaranteeing minimum standards as a right, whereas with the exception of public education, the United States provides aid primarily to the "deserving poor" in society based on means tests. There are means tests in Europe as well, but they are much less important than in the United States. Basic programs of social insurance, e.g., old-age pensions, are similar in advanced industrial democracies, but there are numerous and significant differences in public assistance programs and health-care insurance.

Old-age and disability insurance. All industrial democracies have introduced old-age insurance schemes during the past 120 years. Compulsory contributory old-age insurance laws date back to 1889 in Germany, 1910 in France, 1925 in Great Britain, and 1935 in the United States. These vary, of course, in their requirements concerning eligibility, years of contributions, level of coverage, and conditions, but in each case they serve to ensure that those who have been employed during some or all of their adult life will enjoy some minimum level of security in their old age. It should be noted that old-age insurance programs are not "welfare" in the sense of public assistance; rather, they are insurance schemes for which the recipients have paid monthly "premiums" for a number of years.

All of the countries with old-age insurance schemes are experiencing serious problems that have been developing over the last decades but have been exacerbated by the financial and economic crisis of 2008-09 (that has continued in the areas of employment and the housing market in the United States). These problems are demographic and financial, and they are related. The demographic problem lies in the increasing proportion of older people, which means increasing numbers of people qualifying for old-age benefits and the need for increased revenues to cover their costs; it also lies in the fact that people are living longer and therefore are drawing benefits for longer periods.[13]

The financial crisis lies in the low birth rates in Western industrial countries and the declining proportion of young workers who pay into the old-age insurance system.[14] In the pay-as-you-go system typical of countries with old-age insurance, it is the payments from the working population that cover the costs of the benefits for the elderly insured. The unemployed, whose numbers have increased during the current economic crisis, cannot pay into the system, which further reduces the funds available for retirees; many part-time workers also do not pay. In most countries the payments now being made will no longer cover future benefits unless benefits are reduced, payroll taxes are increased, the eligible retirement age is increased, or general funds from government budgets are tapped. One or more of the above measures has already been taken in the United States, Great Britain, France, and Germany, but whatever has been done will not be sufficient to deal with the basic problem of revenues versus expenditures in the coming years. Old-age pensions, then, are already now and will be in the future a major domestic political issue in the liberal democracies as well as in other societies.

In many countries retirement benefits are also offered by employers. In the United States these are of two kinds: the *defined benefit* programs that offer employees a fixed pension after retirement, and the *defined contribution* program into which employees may choose to contribute a portion of their pay, often with employers matching some or all of the employee contribution (these are primarily the so-called 401K programs). In the United States, the current financial and economic downturn has made it more difficult for employers to continue to offer either kind of plan as a part of negotiated total compensation, and many plans have been discontinued. It has also been revealed in recent years that many defined benefit plans have been underfunded, with companies unable to pay the benefits that had been promised. In those industrial democracies with defined contribution schemes, significant losses have been suffered due to the global recession beginning in late 2007. The impact of these losses was especially serious in the United States and Great Britain, because of the role of private savings in their retirement packages. In the United States in 2005, private retirement savings made up 45.1 percent of total retirement benefits, in the UK 43.8 percent, and in Germany and France only 16.9 percent and 8.6 percent, respectively. The OECD average was 19.5 percent.[15]

As noted above, Bismarck was the first to introduce old-age and disability pensions in Germany in 1889.[16] This was a "corporatist" compulsory insurance program that provided pensions to different groups, e.g., various kinds of workers, white-collar employees, and civil servants (including teachers at all levels) who are covered by a separate program funded from general tax revenues. Payments to noncivil servants are based on the number of years of contributions and past income. Today, as then, employees and employers share the costs, each paying one-half; however, the tax is capped at about twice the medium income. Total payroll taxes are higher (hovering around 19–20 percent total) than in the United States (now 12.4 percent).

Like most pension systems, the German system was and still is based on a pay-as-you-go principle, according to which those paying into the system pay for the pensions of current recipients. In 1957 a reform provided for subsidies from general funds, which at first amounted to about 32 percent and then declined to 15 percent of total public pension expenditures in 1973. However, this figure increased in the following years, and an expansion of recipients due to unification in 1990, an influx of migrants with German heritage from Eastern Europe, and the inclusion of women of retirement age for child rearing led to an increase in the subsidy to almost 34 percent by 2005. This subsidy is now the largest item in the German federal budget, amounting to nearly one-third of the total budget. Usually the years one is unemployed are credited for benefit purposes, as is child care for a three-year period. A private voluntary (Riester) pension plan now exists into which participants can contribute up to 4 percent of their gross salaries and receive government subsidies. Public pension spending represents 11.4 percent of the GDP.

Though full retirement age has been sixty-five (with large proportions of the population retiring early), it is being increased in stages to sixty-seven for those who have contributed for at least five years. One can retire at sixty-three with thirty-five years' contributions. For low-income recipients, social assistance (*Sozialhilfe*), which includes housing and fuel costs, is available. The net replacement rate for those earning one-half of average income is 59.2 percent; for those earning twice the average, it is 44.4 percent.[17]

These expenditures result in higher pensions for Germans than Americans receive. This is reflected in the expectation in Germany that the public pension will provide a relatively high living standard during retirement, whereas Social Security payments in the United States are generally considered to be a foundation to which private savings and insurance schemes, often provided by employers, should be added for a comfortable retirement. Thus the income replacement rates for public pensions in Germany have historically been around 70 percent, for Americans about 50 percent (but considerably less in the United States for higher-income recipients). On the other hand, Germans must pay into the system longer than Americans to receive full benefits.

The United States introduced Old Age and Survivors Insurance (OASI) or "Social Security" in 1935 as part of President Roosevelt's New Deal. Nonworking spouses and children were included in 1939. It is a compulsory pay-as-you-go insurance system that today accounts for 12.4 percent of a worker's income, with one-half being paid by the worker and one-half by the employer. The self-employed pay both portions. There is no credit for child care or when unemployed. In 1956 women were allowed to retire at age sixty-two but with reduced benefits; men could also retire at sixty-two as of 1961. Benefits were increased in the early 1970s, and since 1972 benefits have been raised automatically to cover inflation. The calculations for the inflation index were changed and the payroll tax increased in 1977. In 1981 the Reagan administration proposed significant cuts in Social Security, but opposition led to the creation of a panel of experts to consider changes in the system. This panel, which became known as the Greenspan Commission, issued a final report in

January 1983 which served to overcome differences between Democrats and Republicans in Congress and led to reform legislation in 1983. This law raised payroll tax contributions, increased the age for full benefits from sixty-five to sixty-seven between 2000 and 2022, added newly hired federal employees to the system, and made a portion of the benefits above certain levels subject to the income tax. As a result of this reform, expenditures for benefits have been less than the taxes collected, so that a surplus has existed since the 1980s in the Social Security Trust Fund that the law created; however, this fund, which has received interest from federal bonds purchased by the surplus funds, is projected to peak in 2026, after which benefits will exceed payroll tax revenues. The Trust Fund will be exhausted by 2041, at which time there will be insufficient funds to pay for social security benefits. In other words, the Social Security system will revert to a pure pay-as-you-go system that will mean reduced benefits unless changes are made in the meantime.

In addition to regular Social Security benefits, there is a means-tested SSI (Supplementary Security Income) program for low income recipients. The net income replacement rate for people that earned one-half of the average income is 58 percent, while those who earned twice the average income receive 33 percent. Public pension spending represents 6 percent of GDP.

Great Britain introduced noncontributing old-age insurance in 1908 and compulsory contributing insurance in 1925. In the UK the proportion of retirement income from voluntary private pensions is the highest among OECD countries, and public pensions are projected to provide the lowest benefits relative to individual earnings in the OECD. The impact of the global recession therefore had a significant effect on pension income in the UK.

There are two kinds of public pensions: the basic state pension and the reduced state second pension for low earners. The unemployed are credited for the basic state pension, and child care is credited. The age for full retirement benefits will be raised in future years to sixty-eight. The net replacement rate for those earning one-half of average income is 63.8 percent; for those earning twice the average, it is 22.8 percent. Public pension spending in the UK was 5.7 percent of GDP in 2005.[18]

France had a program of noncontributing old-age assistance beginning in 1905, and a compulsory insurance system was added in 1910. Recipients of benefits over sixty-five years of age rely more on public transfers than in any of the other thirty OECD countries except Hungary: 85.4 percent in France, 73.1 percent in Germany, 49.4 percent in the Great Britain, and 36.1 percent in the United States. Future benefits have been cut 20 percent in France, but low earners will be protected. Recipients receive full pensions after forty years' employment, and the normal pension age is sixty. The "minimum contributory pension" starts at sixty-five. As of 2008 the goal is to provide workers with a full career at low wages a pension equivalent to 85 percent of the net minimum wage. Child care is credited, as are certain years of unemployed status. The net replacement rate is 76.2 percent for people earning one-half the average income, 57.5 percent for those earning twice the average. Public pension spending amounts to 12.4 percent of GDP.[19] In the fall of 2010 a reform was passed after significant street protests and strikes that increased the age eligible for retirement in future years from sixty to sixty-two and retirement with full benefits from sixty-five to sixty-seven. Even though this was a very controversial reform in France, it merely put France in line with other major European countries.

It should be noted that discussions of old age pensions, including the remarks above, often do not distinguish clearly between the legal ages for retirement and the actual average age of retirement. Thus while the legal age for males in Great Britain was sixty-five (sixty-eight after 2020), the actual average age of retirement was 63.2; in Germany it was sixty-five (sixty-seven after 2029) and 61.6; and in France it was sixty (changed to sixty-seven in 2010) and 58.7. Even the much maligned Greeks had an average retirement age (62.4) higher than that of Germany and France![20]

Family support programs. In agricultural societies the farm family is an economic and social unit that combines the labors of its members to the extent possible. Children do chores and contribute to the well-being of the family. In modern industrialized urban societies, children's labor is less economically important, and children become dependent on the family wage earners. Children are expensive to raise, and they make it more difficult for families to take care of grandparents and others who are unable to work. The growing numbers of women who enter the labor force also make child-care services necessary; however, these are not always available at affordable cost. These conditions led a number of European countries to introduce programs to "socialize" the costs of raising children, not only because of apparent needs but also to counter falling birth rates. The premise is that "all adults, including those without children, should share to some extent the costs of raising society's children because society as a whole benefits from having children adequately reared. Children grow up to take over the responsibilities of maintaining the survival of the society. They will also be available to provide needed services to both their own parents and aging adults who did not raise their own children."[21] It is an argument similar in principle to the case for public education, and it is one that not only appeals strongly to the socialist tradition but also to the European conservative (especially Catholic) focus on families. Therefore, these traditions have often joined to introduce various child support services in Europe, including family allowances; one-time cash payments, goods, or services given at birth; aid for adopted and disabled children; and nursery schools and kindergartens.

The counterarguments are basically drawn from the Liberal tradition. Thus American "conservatives," who concentrate on laissez faire economics and the minimal state in general, argue that child raising is the responsibility of the family, not of the general society, and that self-reliance, rather than dependency, should be promoted.

Of course children who have been orphaned, abandoned, or whose parents are in prison or unfit are provided with various services such as foster care or special institutions in all liberal democracies, but beyond that programs become controversial. The reasons are not only a product of the ideologies associated with the three traditions: today in Europe there is great concern about low and declining birth rates, but the populations most likely to take advantage of child support programs and generally have more than two children are recent immigrants. An attempt to discriminate between "natives" and "immigrants" would, of course, invite serious charges of racism and legal challenges.

One good example of a child support program that is found in most Western democracies is maternity and paternity leaves designed to help the working parents of a new child who has joined the family either through birth or adoption. These programs vary between unpaid leaves of absence to paid leaves with considerable salary replacement. Of eighteen Western democracies surveyed in one study, Finland was the most generous with three years of leave and forty-four weeks of pay at 70 percent replacement. Germany was second with three years of leave and fourteen weeks of pay at 100 percent, additional weeks to age two at a flat rate, and a third year unpaid. France had sixteen to twenty-six weeks of leave at 100 percent pay and an extension of leave to age two at a flat rate. Great Britain had twenty-five weeks of leave with six weeks at 90 percent pay, twelve weeks at a low flat rate, and thirteen weeks unpaid. The United States introduced its program at the beginning of the Clinton administration in 1993, which was late in comparison to the other countries. It has the lowest leave period of twelve weeks, and then only for women who work for firms with fifty or more employees. The parent is unpaid during this time, which results in many women not taking advantage of the leave time available. On the other hand, 43 percent of working women in the United States have access to paid maternity leaves as a fringe benefit provided by both private and public employers. Another 40 percent have unpaid leaves. In both cases, however, these have been less than the low of fifteen weeks for the other seventeen democracies in the study.[22]

In addition to maternity/paternity leave programs, children's or family allowances are also found in most industrialized democracies. They were first introduced in France in the 1930s to encourage having children at a time of very low birthrates. Today the French give parents more than $2,000 per year for each of the first two children under seventeen years of age (to age twenty if the children are students) and about $2,500 for each additional child. These payments are not taxable; indeed, generous tax deductions apply to families with children and increase after the first two children. Tuition-free preschools are provided from ages three through six. Day-care facilities are subsidized, and tax deductions are provided parents with children in public and private day care. Means-tested public assistance, including support for housing and medical care, is also available to low-income families. Germany also has family allowances that date back many decades. Each of the first three children receives about $3,000 per year, with larger families receiving more. Day-care and preschool facilities are subsidized, but many families complain that there are too few places available, and the costs are still too high. In line with Catholic social thought, German tax policy encourages women to stay home with their children, although increasing numbers of married women are employed. The United Kingdom has had family allowances in various forms since the end of World War II. Today families with one child receive a weekly benefit amounting to about $1,600 per year for one child until the age of sixteen (until nineteen if a student). Tax credits are provided for additional children except for high earners. Working families receive tax credits for day care, but other child-care expenses are not tax deductible. In contrast to the European continent, most day care is private. Middle- and upper-class parents tend to employ nannies, whereas the public facilities are mostly used by low-income families. As prime minister, Margaret Thatcher tried to contain and even cut back spending on social policy, and she emphasized personal responsibility. Even her successors, including Tony Blair, who did introduce some tax credits for day-care expenses, have been reluctant to follow the continental European example of generous family policies. Some countries also offer cash benefits at birth to parents, but these are not as important as the family allowance programs discussed above. Following the May 2010 parliamentary elections in Great Britain, David Cameron's new Conservative government announced cuts in family subsidies, eliminating them entirely for upper-income citizens as one measure to reduce the budget deficit.

The United States does not have a children's allowance program, but it does offer a $500 tax credit to families for each child and tax benefits to married couples. But this does not help children whose parents are not employed and do not pay taxes.[23]

In the United States, where poverty is at least 50 percent higher than in other industrialized democracies, almost 40 percent of the poor are under eighteen years of age, and nearly 20 percent of children under eighteen live in poverty. The majority of the poor live in female-headed families, who make up over one-half of all poor families. While the United States does not have a children's allowance program, it does have programs that directly or indirectly aid poor children. The most important of these is Temporary Assistance to Needy Families (TANF), a program of cash assistance provided by the states based on federal block grants. This program replaced in 1996 Aid to Families with Dependent Children (AFDC), which was a federal entitlement program that came under severe attack for allegedly creating a system of dependence on federal assistance by the poor, especially by single-parent families. Under TANF the states determine eligibility and offer incentives to encourage marriage and promote employment. Adults receiving TANF must generally begin working within two years, and single parents must work at least thirty hours a week. States may not use federal funds for adults who have received benefits for more than a total of five years in their lifetime or for adults who do not work after receiving two years of assistance. States do have some flexibility in granting exemptions to 20 percent of recipients, but they may also restrict benefits to unwed mothers under eighteen and to children born to TANF recipients.[24]

Another cash-assistance program for the poor in the United States is Supplementary Security Income (SSI) which is administered by the Social Security Administration and is supplemented by some states. SSI is designed to help older citizens and the disabled rather than children. Children are more likely to be helped by the Earned Income Tax Credit (EITC) program, which offers tax credits for low-income working families. EITC is the largest means-tested federal cash assistance program that is supplemented by some states; however, it is only accessible to working families, many of whom do not apply for the credit on tax forms for a number of reasons, especially lack of information.

In-kind benefits are also provided by the US federal government, the most important of which is probably food stamps (now called the Supplemental Nutritional Assistance Program [SNAP]). Most recipients must be either seeking work, working twenty hours a week, or participating in work training. The federal government also administers the Women, Infants, and Children (WIC) program and the school lunch and breakfast program.[25]

As one can see from the above, the United States is quite different from other industrialized democracies in its aid to families and children. A number of programs exist that directly or indirectly help children, but there is no one program such as children's allowances that focuses on all children regardless of family income and is sustained over childhood until the age of 18. Two scholars who have written on comparative social policy have noted that "[t]he United States relies more than any other industrialized country on a means-tested approach to family policy."[26] Given the Liberal (i.e., conservative) opposition to taxes and big government in the United States, it is unlikely that any kind of formal children's or family allowance program could be passed by Congress.

Social policy, including the policies discussed above, has been on the agenda of the European Union since its inception in 1957. It has played a relatively minor role in comparison to competition, agricultural, fisheries, and environmental policies, but concerns about social policy led to the European Charter of the Fundamental Social Rights of Workers in 1989. At that time eleven of the then twelve member states signed the "Social Charter"; British Prime Minister Thatcher refused to sign. For a number of reasons the Social Charter did not lead to much action by the EU, but it did find support in principle in the form of a social chapter in the 1991 Maastricht treaty (Treaty on European Union), a chapter that the British again refused to accept. One concrete measure derived from this chapter was the EU directive in 1996 establishing minimum standards for parental leave policies in the member states. Later the EU focused more on research and exchange of information.[27]

Health-care programs.[28] The first country to introduce health-care insurance was Germany. Chancellor Otto von Bismarck pushed through a number of social reforms in the 1880s, beginning with health-care insurance in 1883. This system called for mandatory enrollment in a pay-as-you go, employer-based insurance scheme paid by payroll taxes. Today insurance is provided by numerous private but nonprofit regional or work-sector sickness funds that negotiate prices with physician groups and hospital associations. Outpatient medical services are based on fee-for-service, but hospital physicians are paid a salary. Hospitals are paid a per diem, which varies by region and illness.

Contributions to the social insurance funds do not depend on risk factors but on wage levels, i.e., currently 8.2 percent of the employee's income up to about $65,000. Employers pay 7.3 percent; however, they pay the total cost for low-income employees. Government subsidies help pay for maternity care, children's health care, pensioners, the unemployed, students, etc. that amount to about 25 percent of the sickness fund revenues. Today about 90 percent of the population is covered by 240 sickness funds, all of which must cover physician services, maternity care, hospitalization, and prescription drugs. Patients pay 10 percent copayments for prescription drugs and a modest charge for each outpatient visit and for the first four weeks of hospital care. Since 1994 long-term care is also covered and paid for by a small additional payroll tax.

Three-fourths of the population are enrolled as mandatory members in the sickness funds, while another 15 percent are enrolled voluntarily. The remaining 9–10 percent have selected the for-profit private option, a full-service health insurance that is confined to the self-employed, civil servants, and to relatively high earners. There is a long questionnaire and physical examination requirement for the private option, but once approved the individual insured's coverage cannot be changed. The private insurance option is more expensive than the contributions to the sickness funds, and the insurance payments to providers are somewhat higher. As a result, a two-tier system exists in which privately insured patients are given precedence in seeing a physician or in the provision of a semiprivate hospital room. The German system came under considerable stress after unification because wages in the former East Germany were and still are generally lower, and there was—and to a lesser extent still is—high unemployment. Nevertheless, everyone enrolled in the sickness funds, including the unemployed, enjoys the same benefits. This has required a number of reforms of the system designed to control costs, and these efforts are continuing. Expenditures for health care amount to about 11 percent of GDP.

France began providing health insurance for low-income workers in 1930. After World War II the coverage was broadened so that virtually all citizens were insured by 1978 through large occupational-based funds.[29] The General National Health Insurance Scheme covers 83 percent of French workers, while other occupation-specific funds cover the remainder of the population, such as public employees, miners and farmers, and the self-employed. More than 92 percent of the population have complementary nonprofit private insurance, which pays all or most of the amount physicians may charge patients above the negotiated government-set price for medical procedures; copayments of 10–40 percent may be required. Private health insurers may not deny coverage due to pre-existing conditions. Solidarity, or a demand for universal coverage of citizens, is an important element of the French insurance system, with the result that the more ill a person becomes, the less he or she pays. This means that for people with serious or chronic illnesses, the insurance system reimburses them for all of their expenses and waives their co-pay charges.

Virtually all physicians participate in the public health scheme, but it is not "socialized medicine" as in the United Kingdom; there is no single-payer system, and patients have a choice of doctors. There are also no waiting lists for elective procedures, in contrast to the UK and Canada. Doctors in France earn much less than their counterparts in the United States, but, having studied medicine tuition-free, they have no medical school debts. They also have low malpractice insurance premiums and relatively low nonmedical personnel payroll costs, e.g., for administrative costs regarding medical billing. A majority of hospitals are private, but the public hospitals have more beds.

Most of the revenue for the sickness funds comes from payroll taxes; however, employees pay less than 1 percent, while employers pay almost 13 percent of the total payroll. In addition, most of a 7.5 percent income tax surcharge goes to the sickness funds. The government provides various subsidies and money for hospital construction. French health-care expenditures are about 11 percent plus of GDP.

Among the thirty countries in the OECD, the British health system probably differs most in structure from the United States. National health insurance was first introduced in 1911 for a limited number of poor citizens, but in 1948 the National Health Service (NHS) was established. It is based on the Beveridge Report of 1942 that called for establishment of a British welfare state, including a public health-care system. The NHS, introduced by the Labour Party after its victory in 1945, provided for a national health-care system that covered the entire population, was government-run and financed by general taxes, rather than by joint employer-employee insurance fees as in Germany and France. The NHS pays directly for health-care services and employs doctors and nurses. It also owns and operates most medical facilities. Copayments have been introduced over the years, and today they cover about 10 percent of total costs. Modest copayments exist for drugs, dental, and optical care. As a public, single-payer, universal care system, it is a much better example of "socialized medicine" than the systems in Germany and France.[30]

In spite of universal care, the system has lower overall costs than in France, Germany or, especially, the United States; expenditures for health care in 2009 were about 9.8 percent, slightly above the OECD average of 9.5 percent.[31] One means of keeping costs lower, however, is through waiting periods for routine, nonemergency elective surgery. About 10 percent of the citizenry have supplemental insurance to cover nonemergency care to avoid waiting lists. Another, less controversial, means of lowering costs is the reliance on primary care physicians—of whom there are proportionately more than in the United States—as gatekeepers. Although 100 percent of the population is covered, about 10 percent have private insurance in addition. As in Germany, they enjoy preferential treatment for their higher payments. In spite of the above, a Gallup poll in March 2003 showed that Britons are much more satisfied than Americans with the availability of affordable health care and somewhat less satisfied with the quality of care.[32]

Health-care policy has been a major focus of discussion in the United States since the 2008 presidential election campaign and, especially, since Barack Obama became president in January 2009. As in the past, for example, in 1993 during the first year of the Clinton administration and in 1948 during the Truman administration, resistance to efforts to introduce some form of national health insurance was too strong, and the basic for-profit private health insurance system prevailed (it should be noted, however, that in addition to Medicare and Medicaid there is a federal health insurance program for federal employees and a military health insurance program for the uniformed services). According to the US Bureau of the Census, about 60 percent of Americans are covered by their employer and another 9 percent have purchased private individual insurance. In most cases employees contribute from 15 to 30 percent of the costs of employer-provided health insurance. Health insurance costs have been rising rapidly in recent years, and some firms have dropped their coverage or raised employee contributions.

A serious problem with health insurance in the United States has been the fact that a large proportion of the population, estimated to be as high as forty-seven million, or about 15 percent of the population, have no insurance. Some argue that while some of these people may be poor, others simply refuse to purchase insurance, for example because they are young and healthy or because one can always go to the emergency room of a hospital for free treatment if one has no insurance, since hospitals (including the mostly privately owned hospitals) must by law serve everyone who seeks emergency care. But medical care other than emergency care is not provided, which means that many illnesses, injuries and ailments are not treated; it also means that the costs of emergency care must be borne by those with insurance via higher hospital charges or, in the case of public hospitals, by taxpayers.

In spite of the large number of uninsured and underinsured people, medical costs are higher in the United States than in any other country, namely, 17.4 percent of GDP. The average cost per capita in the United States is more than double the average expenditure per capita in the thirty OECD countries and 20 percent more than Luxembourg, the next highest spending country. The countries with the next highest costs are Switzerland (ca. 12 percent), France (11.8 percent) and Germany (11.6 percent). As already noted, the UK spends about 9.8 percent of GDP on health care.[33] The high expenditures in the United States do not mean, however, that the quality of care is also the highest. Comparative statistics show that while the United States ranks very high in some areas, it ranks below several other countries in other areas. For example, the United States is below average in the proportion of hospital beds. It is among the countries with low wait times for elective surgery, but it has higher wait times for seeing a primary-care physician. It is slightly below average in life expectancy and above average in the rate of death from natural causes.[34] In comparison to the UK, France, and Germany, it is below average in infant mortality figures and life expectancy at birth.[35]

The American system has been severely criticized over the past decades because of the lack of universal coverage, the fee-for-service principle, coverage that is based on insurance payment level, restrictions based on preexisting conditions, limited or no coverage for certain illnesses or procedures, the unaffordable costs for many people, the paperwork resulting from multiple insurers, and other reasons . On the other hand, for those who can afford the best insurance or have good plans offered by their employer, private insurance has worked relatively well.

For certain categories of poor people who have low incomes and do not receive insurance as a job benefit or could never afford private insurance, the Medicaid program was enacted in 1965 as a part of Lyndon Johnson's "Great Society." Medicaid is a means-tested social welfare program, in contrast to Medicare, which is a social insurance *entitlement* program (like Social Security) basically for everyone over sixty-five. The determination of who qualifies for Medicaid is made by the states within certain general federal guidelines. Those eligible are certain categories of low-income individuals, including children, pregnant women, parents of eligible children, and people with disabilities. States pay between 20 and 50 percent of Medicaid costs based on their levels of poverty, and they administer the program with some federal supervision. Some basic dental services are included. States may combine the State Children's Health Insurance Program (SCHIPS) with the Medicaid Program.

In 2008 Medicaid provided health coverage and services to approximately forty-nine million low-income children, pregnant women, elderly persons, and disabled individuals. Nationwide, about 40 percent of the poor were enrolled, and almost half of these were children. Medicaid costs amount to an average of 17 to 22 percent of state budgets, depending on how they are calculated, and they are becoming an increasing burden on the states.

Like Medicaid, Medicare was adopted in 1965. However, Medicare is designed as an insurance program, rather than a social welfare program. Virtually everyone who is sixty-five and qualifies for Social Security is covered. It is administered by the Centers for Medicare and Medicaid Services (CMA), an agency of the Department of Health and Human Services. Costs of the program are covered by a 2.9 percent tax that is added to Social Security contributions paid in equal shares (1.45 percent) by employers and employees. Costs have risen dramatically in recent years, both absolutely and as a proportion of the federal budget, and without reform the Medicare hospital insurance trust fund will become insolvent by 2019. Costs have risen as a result of increases in health-care services, but as with Social Security, demographic changes are also putting a severe squeeze on funding. The proportion of the population over sixty-five is increasing as people live longer and as the birth rate declines; of course the fact that older people have much greater health-care needs aggravates the problem.

The last significant health-care reform introduced in the United States was the Medicare prescription drug benefit program, which provides prescription drugs at subsidized prices with modest or no copayments. While it has reduced costs dramatically for many participants, it has been controversial because of its high costs to the federal government and because of the so-called "donut hole." The plan provides for three drug payment stages: a first stage that requires a copayment until total payments reach $2,830; a second "coverage gap stage," i.e., the "donut hole," that requires the patient to pay the full cost of all drugs until total costs reach $4,550; and a third stage that kicks in and pays most of the costs for the rest of the year (2010 figures).

Harold Wilensky, who has written extensively for forty years about health care in liberal democracies, argues that among the nineteen democracies he has studied, the United States is "odd-man-out in its health-care spending, organization, and results." He notes that

> [i]n the past hundred years, with the exception of the U.S., the currently rich democracies have all converged in the broad outlines

> of health care. They all developed central control of budgets with financing from compulsory individual and employer contributions and/or government revenues. All have permitted the insured to supplement government services with additional care, privately purchased. All, including the United States, have rationed health care [in the U.S., by access to treatment based on insurance coverage]. All have experienced a growth in doctor density and the ratio of specialists to primary-care personnel. All evidence a trend toward public funding. Our deviance consists of no national health insurance, a huge private sector, a very high ratio of specialists to primary-care physicians and nurses, and a uniquely expensive (non)system with a poor cost-benefit ratio ... [N]o rich democracy has funded national health insurance without relying on mass taxes, especially payroll and consumption taxes.[36]

Like Gøsta Esping-Anderson and James Russell in earlier sections of this chapter, Wilensky places his nineteen democratic countries in a table and develops his own typology of economic and health-care systems, a highly condensed version of which is offered below.

Wilensky's typology is based on the degree of "corporatism" in the countries he has studied. "Corporatist" refers in this case to "more-or-less central bargaining among labor, management, government, professions, and political parties." A similar term is "consensual democracies." "Least corporatist" describes the "most fragmented and decentralized political economies." While this differs from the typologies offered by Esping-Anderson and James Russell, it also contains the element of the role of government in society. Thus "corporatist" is closer to the conservative Catholic and socialist tradition and "least corporatist" to the free market Liberal tradition of Europe. It is interesting, however, to note that the United Kingdom, in spite of its ranking in the "least corporatist" category, has probably the most "socialist" health care system.

Table 10.3 shows that the United States spends far less in government funds for health care than other democracies. Although the 45 percent expenditure for Medicare, Medicaid, SCIPS, federal employees, and a military health insurance program for the uniformed services is certainly not a small amount, it is a modest proportion in comparison to public expenditures in other democracies, where the average is about 73 percent. Wilensky suggests that only if about 65 percent or more of health-care costs are covered by public programs can the high costs of the basically private insurance system in the United States be seriously reduced.

Table 10.3

Types of Political Economy, Public Share of Health Spending, and Government Share of Public Spending

Type of Political Economy	Public Share of Total Healthcare Spending (%), average 2000-2005	Government Health Spending per capita, average 2000-2005
Left Corporatist		
Sweden	84	$2,490
Left Catholic Corporatist		
Netherlands	65	$2,093
Catholic Corporatist		
Germany	77	$2,341
Corporatist w/o Labor		
France	80	$2,340
Least Corporatist		
United States	45	$2,429
United Kingdom	87	$2,043

Source: Harold Wilensky (2009) "U.S. Health Care and Real Health in Comparative Perspective: Lessons from Abroad," *The Forum*, Vol. 7: Iss.2, p. 3.

Following the failed efforts to reform the health insurance system during the first year of the Clinton administration in 1993, discussion of reform measures continued. During the primary election campaigns and debates of 2008, it became a key issue, particularly among the Democratic candidates seeking the party's nomination. With the election of Barack Obama, health-care insurance reform was a major focus of domestic policy in 2009. The Obama administration's Affordable Health Care Act was passed in March 2010, in spite of bitter opposition by the Republicans in the House of Representatives and Senate. In spite of their majority in both houses, the Democrats had a particularly difficult time passing their bill in the Senate due to Senate rules requiring sixty votes (rather than fifty-one) to pass legislation blocked by a minority filibuster. After passage, the bill continued to be rejected by the Republicans, who vowed to repeal it at the first opportunity and in the meantime to block federal funds for its implementation.

In addition, several states under Republican control challenged a key provision of the Democratic bill that would require individuals to purchase insurance or pay a fine and took their cases to several federal district courts. This provision was enacted in order to increase the pool of insured, thus making it possible for private insurance companies to offer policies without preexisting conditions and also to reduce the costs of emergency room care for the uninsured that are absorbed by hospitals and, ultimately, passed on to those with insurance. The Republican challenge in the federal courts was made on the grounds that there is no constitutional basis for requiring someone to purchase insurance, whereas the Obama administration and Democrats argued that the interstate commerce clause and the necessary and proper clause allowed such a federal requirement. The challenges were decided differently by the federal judges that heard them, and their decisions were appealed to the federal courts of appeal and ultimately to the Supreme Court. By the fall of 2011, three federal district courts had decided in favor and two against the law, while one court of appeal had ruled in favor and one against; another court of appeals ruled that the states challenging the law lacked standing. Thus, until the Supreme Court renders its decision, the fate of the key provision concerning mandatory purchase of insurance will remain unresolved.

The Affordable Health Care Act would reduce significantly the number of uninsured Americans by requiring everyone to purchase insurance or by adding to Medicaid those who cannot afford private insurance. (Critics note that Medicaid is already under great financial stress, and they express concern over costs). Adding many millions of people to Medicaid would, of course, change the figures for the United States in table 10.3 above by increasing the public share of health spending. On the other hand, that share would still be lower than that of the other industrialized democracies in the table. It should also be noted that health-care insurance would still not be universal, since, in spite of the dramatic reduction in the number of uninsured, many millions would remain without health insurance.

The European Union has only a minor role in health-care policy, since this is an area reserved to the member states. On the other hand, informal health policy mechanisms do sometimes affect public health matters. For example, health ministers meet on occasions in the Council of Ministers to discuss public health issues, and in 2003 the European Commission helped to create the European Center for Disease Prevention and Control. The European Commission also can influence various policies, for example, working conditions, purchasing arrangements, and equality of treatment of consumers. In 1993 it issued a directive creating common standards for medical and nursing degrees in the member states. The European Court of Justice (ECJ) then decided that there must be mutual recognition of medical and nursing degrees in the EU states. In 1993 the EU Council of Ministers issued a directive limiting the working time of medical professionals to forty-eight hours per week. This had a significant impact on the working time of hospital interns and residents, who traditionally work long hours with naps in between, which the court said had to be counted as work time.[37]

Conclusions

Western European societies and party systems in particular have been influenced by three major philosophical traditions that emerged chronologically during the past several centuries: a conservative tradition with deep roots in the corporatist feudal, Catholic Middle Ages; a Liberal tradition that challenged the aristocratic dominance and role of the state and church in society during the eighteenth and nineteenth centuries, pushing in their place for individual political, religious, and economic liberty in politics; and a collectivist socialist tradition that sought economic equality through various policies initiated by government action in the nineteenth and twentieth centuries. These three traditions have not been without relevance in the United States, but the conservative tradition was on the wane in Europe at the time of the American founding and never had an opportunity to take deep root, while the Liberal tradition found an eager acceptance among American elites. This acceptance was clearly reflected in the Declaration of Independence and the Constitution of 1789 (although blacks and Indians were not included). During the nineteenth century conditions were not as favorable as in Europe for the development of a powerful socialist tradition, due in part to the relatively easy acquisition of private property; economic opportunities, including the open frontier, not as available in class-conscious Europe; and ethnic and racial tensions that reduced the political solidarity among the urban and rural poor that a strong socialist movement would have required.

One major result that emerged from the differences between Europe and the United States was the development of the party systems in the two continents, as described in chapter 5. These party systems reacted differently to the rise of industrial capitalism and worker movements in the nineteenth century. The working-class movements were much stronger in Europe, and the conservative, Liberal, and socialist parties each developed their own particular responses. Ironically, it was the conservative Otto von Bismarck in Germany who first introduced the welfare state in the 1880s, including old-age pensions, disability insurance, and health-care insurance. He did so, however, in order to preserve the basic social order and to win the loyalty of the workers to the state (the working-class Social Democratic Party was outlawed from 1878 to 1890). Later, in Germany as well as in other European states, both Liberal and socialist traditions were added in varying degrees to create relatively generous welfare states in all European countries. Each state, however, has a certain mixture of traditions, with one or the other dominating the mix. As was made clear, the Liberal tradition dominates the more limited welfare system in the United States, which is not surprising, given American historical developments. This means that the American welfare state is less generous and, therefore, less costly to taxpayers; it is based more on need and means tests, and recipients are more stigmatized than in Europe.

Rather than describing the entire gamut of welfare state activities in Europe and the United States, which is far beyond the scope of this book, we have looked briefly at three examples of common welfare state programs: old-age pensions, family allowances, and health-care policies.

We have seen that there are many similarities in old-age pension schemes. The United States was the last to introduce social security, but, as with its counterparts, provisions have become more generous over time. All of the pension schemes are basically pay-as-you-go systems, which means that current workers pay for the benefits of current recipients. They all seek to provide the older population with a minimal standard of living, although the length of time employed and the amounts paid into the system are generally factored into the retirement benefits. There are, however, also many differences among liberal democracies, including the generosity of payments, the requirements for receiving them, the ages of eligibility, and so forth. In Great Britain, France, and Germany, years of unemployment and some years of child care are counted for benefit purposes, which is not the case in the United States. All four of our liberal democracies provide supplementary payments to those whose benefits are especially low.

Family support programs are an example of significant differences among liberal democracies, with the Liberal philosophical tradition in the United States exerting an especially strong influence on American public policy. Our three European liberal democracies have concluded that raising a child is not only a family but also a societal responsibility. The American—and to a lesser extent, British—Liberal tradition, in contrast, holds that children are the sole responsibility of their family except, of course, in those cases where parents or families are unable or unwilling to care for the children. In addition there is concern in Europe for the low birthrate and demographic imbalances this is bringing about.

A major component of family support systems in Europe is maternity and, more recently, paternal leave policies designed to assist working parents. All four of our liberal democracies have family leave policies, but the policy in the United States is far less generous. First, the American policy was not introduced until 1993, during the first year of the Clinton administration, decades after their introduction in Europe; second, the American program is far less generous in terms of leave time, size of firms required to participate, and salary or wages paid during leave. On the other hand, many American women—though a minority—receive maternity leave benefits through their employer. The fact that under the public program and in some of the private programs no salary or wages are paid during leave discourages many women from taking advantage of leave time.

Children's allowances are also paid by most European democracies. The United States does not offer a children's allowance program, but it does provide a $500 tax credit for each child. A high percentage of the poor in the United States are children, and nearly 20 percent of all children under eighteen live in poverty. The Temporary Assistance to Needy Families (TANF) program administered by the states provides cash assistance to poor families, a majority of which are headed by single mothers; however, mothers are required to work at least thirty hours within two years, and they may not receive benefits for more than a lifetime total of five years. Some exemptions apply in some states. Some assistance goes to poor children through Supplementary Security Income (SSI), and even more children are helped by the Earned Income Credit (EIC) program. This is a means-tested federal cash assistance program supplemented by some states, but only working families may apply, some of whom fail to do so because of lack of information. Finally, there are the food stamp and school lunch and breakfast programs that benefit children indirectly and directly.

With respect to health care, the United States is the only industrialized country that has no form of national health insurance. Different forms of insurance for most citizens or at least coverage for the poor were first introduced in Germany in 1883, in the United Kingdom in 1911, and in France in 1930. The United Kingdom introduced a socialized medicine system covering the entire population in 1948, and the French also broadened their system after 1945. In the United States, Medicare coverage for the elderly and Medicaid insurance for the poor were introduced in 1965, and a prescription drug plan was passed in 2003. Health-care reform was a major focus of domestic policy in 2009, and the Obama administration's Affordable Health Care Act was passed in March 2010, in spite of bitter opposition by the Republicans. The reform act has been rejected by the Republicans not only in Washington but also in numerous Republican-controlled states, which have challenged the act in the federal courts. In 2011 the different decisions of these courts were being appealed to higher courts for resolution.

Two scholars who have written about public policy in industrialized democracies have suggested that there are a number of obstacles that make it difficult to pass a major health-care reform bill in the United States.

> Many citizens are skeptical of government intervention. Interest groups are able to mount private and public lobbying campaigns on behalf of their preferred policy positions so that reformers find it difficult to see their vision rise to the top of the systemic agenda unchallenged. The federal system dictates that policy can be made (and blocked) at multiple levels of government. The presidential system of executive-legislative relations permits not only the possibility of divided government but also the daily reality of a decentralized legislative process in which multiple poles of power exist in both houses of Congress.[38]

The authors note that President Clinton and President Bush had partisan majorities in both houses of congress when they tried to push through health-care reforms, yet the Clinton proposals never even made it to the floor for a vote, and the Bush prescription drug plan passed only with Democratic support. To what extent and even whether the health reform act passed by the Obama administration in 2010 without Republican support will survive remains to be seen.

Endnotes

[1] R.H.Tawney, *Religion and the Rise of Capitalism* (New York: Harcourt, Brace and Company, 1926).

[2] Max Weber, *The Protestant Ethic and the Spirit of Capitalism* (New York: Scribner, 1958).

[3] Much of the discussion in this section is based on Gøsta Esping-Anderson, *The Three Worlds of Welfare Capitalism* (Princeton: Princeton University Press, 1990).

[4] Ibid., 62.

[5] Ibid., 65.

[6] Ibid., 46.

[7] Ibid., 49–50.

[8] Ibid., 74.

[9] James W. Russell, *Double Standard: Social Policy in Europe and the United States* (New York: Rowman & Littlefield Publishers, Inc., 2006), 48–49.

[10] Ibid., 50.

[11] Ibid., 52.

[12] Ibid., 55.

[13] Indeed, the amount of time spent in retirement in Western industrialized democracies beginning with the normal pension age increased an average of 5.6 years between 1958 and 1999 for both men and women. The expected retirement duration at normal pension age was seventeen years for men and twenty-three years for women in 1999. OECD, *Pensions at a Glance, 2009: Retirement-Income Systems in OECD Countries.*

[14] In 1950 an average of seven people were working for every recipient. At the present time, it is about four, and by 2050 it will be about 1.9; however, in some countries, e.g., Germany, the ratio is already close to 1.9. See Ibid.

[15] OECD, Pensions and the crisis: How should retirement-income systems respond to financial and economic pressures? (http://www.oecd.org/dataoecd/10/26/43060101.pdf).

[16] For a discussion of the German and American old-age pension systems, see Stephen J. Silvia, "Public Pension Reform in Germany and the United States," *AICGS Policy Report 30: Health Care and Pension Reform* (Washington, DC: American Institute for Contemporary German Studies, 2007).

[17] OECD, Pensions and the crisis.

[18] Ibid.

[19] Ibid.

[20] See *Frankfurter Allgemeine Zeitung* (26. August 2010), 10.

[21] Russell, *Double Standard*, 105.

[22] Ibid., Table 11.1, p. 108; for a description of current family policies in Germany, France, and the United Kingdom, see Jessica R. Adolino and Charles H. Blake, *Comparing Public Policies: Issues and Choices in Industrialized Countries*, 2nd ed. (Washington, DC: CQ Press, 2011), ch. 8.

[23] Clarke E. Cochran *et. al*, *American Public Policy: An Introduction*, 9th ed. (Boston: Wadsworth Cengage Learning, 2009), 251.

[24] Ibid., 220, 238–39.

[25] Ibid., 240–42.

[26] Adolino and Blake, *Comparing Public Policies*, 288.

[27] Ibid., 313–15.

[28] For a brief overview of health-care systems in Germany, France, and Great Britain, and in the United State, see Ibid., ch. 8.

[29] For a brief description of the French health-care system, see Healthcare Economist.com/2008/04/14/health-care-around-the-world-france.

[30] For a very brief description of the British system, see http://healthcare-economist.com/2008/04/23/health-care-around-the-world-great-britain/.

[31] OECD data reported in *Frankfurter Allgemeine Zeitung*, (6 July 2011), 11.

[32] http://www.gallup.com/poll/8056/Healthcare-System-Ratings-US-Great-Britain-Canada.aspx

[33] OECD data, see note 31 above.

[34] Congressional Research Service Report for Congress, "U.S. Health Care Spending: Comparison with Other OECD Countries," September 17, 2007, 50–59. (http://assets.opencrs.com/rpts/RL34175_20070917.pdf.)

[35] Adolina and Blake, *Comparing Public Policies*, 275.

[36] Harold L. Wilensky (2009) "U.S. Health Care and Real Health in Comparative Perspective: Lessons from Abroad," *The Forum*: vol. 7: no. 2, Article 7, 1. (http://www.bepress.com/forum/vol7/iss2/art7).

[37] Adolino and Blake, *Comparing Public Policies*, 271–72.

[38] Ibid., 248–49.

About the Author:

Arthur B. Gunlicks retired in 2005 from the University of Richmond, Virginia, where he was a professor of political science for thirty-seven years, served three terms as chair of the department, and served one term as dean of graduate studies and associate dean of faculty. During this time he taught numerous courses in the field of comparative politics, with a concentration on Europe. His research interests focused on Germany, in particular federalism and local government, political parties, and comparative party and campaign finance. He is the sole author of two books, *Local Government in the German Federal System*, Duke University Press, 1986, and *The Länder and German federalism*, Manchester University Press, 2003; he is also the contributing editor of six books on local government, comparative party and campaign finance, and German public policy and federalism. He is the author of several dozen book chapters and articles in professional journals. Since retirement he has been actively engaged in teaching, organizing, and scheduling classes for two organizations that provide learning opportunities primarily for retired persons. He lives in Richmond and is a proud and very engaged grandfather of three grandchildren.

Index

C

D

E

F

G

H

I

J

K

L

M

N

O

P

T

U

V

W

Y

Z